ALSO BY GREG GRANDIN

The Last Colonial Massacre:
Latin America in the Cold War

The Blood of Guatemala:
A History of Race and Nation

Empire's
Workshop

Empire's Workshop

LATIN AMERICA, THE UNITED STATES, AND
THE RISE OF THE NEW IMPERIALISM

Greg Grandin

METROPOLITAN BOOKS
HENRY HOLT AND COMPANY
NEW YORK

METROPOLITAN BOOKS
HENRY HOLT AND COMPANY, LLC
PUBLISHERS SINCE 1866
175 FIFTH AVENUE
NEW YORK, NEW YORK 10010
WWW.HENRYHOLT.COM

METROPOLITAN BOOKS® AND ⋒® ARE REGISTERED TRADEMARKS
OF HENRY HOLT AND COMPANY, LLC.

DISTRIBUTED IN CANADA BY H. B. FENN AND COMPANY LTD.

LIBRARY OF CONGRESS CATALOGING-IN-PUBLICATION DATA

Grandin, Greg, date.
    Empire's workshop: Latin America, the United States, and the rise of the new imperialism / Greg Grandin.
      p. cm.
    Includes index.
    ISBN-13: 978-0-8050-7738-4
    ISBN-10: 0-8050-7738-3
    1. Latin America—Relations—United States. 2. United States—Relations—Latin America. 3. Americans—Latin America—History. 4. United States—Foreign relations—2001—Philosophy. 5. Imperialism. I. Title.

F1418.G66 2006
325'.320973—dc22
      2005056125

HENRY HOLT BOOKS ARE AVAILABLE FOR SPECIAL PROMOTIONS AND PREMIUMS.
FOR DETAILS CONTACT: DIRECTOR, SPECIAL MARKETS.

FIRST EDITION 2006

DESIGNED BY MERYL SUSSMAN LEVAVI

PRINTED IN THE UNITED STATES OF AMERICA

1 3 5 7 9 10 8 6 4 2

For Manu

I kept my workshop of filthy creation: my eyeballs were starting from their sockets in attending to the details of my employment. The dissecting room and the slaughter-house furnished many of my materials; and often did my human nature turn with loathing from my occupation, whilst, still urged on by an eagerness which perpetually increased, I brought my work near to a conclusion.

MARY SHELLY, *Frankenstein*

Contents

Empire's
Workshop

The Camel Not in the Koran

THE ARGENTINE WRITER Jorge Luis Borges once remarked that the lack of camels in the Koran proves its Middle Eastern provenance: only a native author, he explained, could have so taken the animal for granted as not to mention it. Perhaps a similar familiarity explains the absence of Latin America in recent discussions about the United States and its empire. Though Latin America has played an indispensable role in the rise of the United States to global power, it elicits little curiosity from its neighbor to the north. "Latin America doesn't matter," Richard Nixon advised a young Donald Rumsfeld, who was casting about for career opportunities. "Long as we've been in it, people don't give one damn about Latin America."[1] Likewise today. In their search for historical precedents for our current imperial moment, intellectuals invoke postwar reconstructions of Germany and Japan, ancient Rome and nineteenth-century Britain but consistently ignore the one place where the United States has projected its influence for more than two centuries. "People don't give one shit" about the place, Nixon said.[2]

Were it not for Borges's insight, this studied indifference to Latin America would seem ironic, for the region has long served as a workshop of empire, the place where the United States elaborated tactics of extraterritorial administration and acquired its conception of itself as an empire like no other before it. The Western Hemisphere was to be the staging ground for a new "empire for liberty," a phrase used by Thomas Jefferson specifically in reference to Spanish Florida and Cuba. Unlike European empires, ours was supposed to entail a concert of equal, sovereign democratic American republics, with shared interests and values, led but not dominated by the United States—a conception of empire that remains Washington's guiding vision.

The same direction of influence is evident in any number of examples. The United States's engagement with the developing world after World War II, for instance, is often viewed as an extension of its postwar policies in Europe and Japan, yet that view has it exactly backwards. Washington's first attempts, in fact, to restructure another country's economy took place in the developing world—in Mexico in the years after the American Civil War and in Cuba following the Spanish-American War. "We should do for Europe on a large scale," remarked the U.S. ambassador to England in 1914, "essentially what we did for Cuba on a small scale and thereby usher in a new era of human history." Likewise, most discussions of George W. Bush's foreign policy focus on the supposed innovation of a small group of neoconservative intellectuals in asserting the right to unilateral preemptive military action both to defend national security and to advance American ideals. But neither the neocons' dire view of a crisis-ridden world that justifies the use of unilateral and brutal American military power nor their utopian vision of the same world made whole and happy by that power is new. Both have been fully in operation in Washington's approach to Latin America for over a century. The history of the United States in Latin America is cluttered with "preemptive" interventions that even the most stalwart champions of U.S. hegemony have trouble defending.

From the mid-nineteenth to the early twentieth century, the U.S. military sharpened its fighting skills and developed its modern-day organizational structure largely in constant conflict with Latin America—in its drive west when it occupied Mexico in the mid-nineteenth century and took more than half of that country's national territory. And in its push south: by 1930, Washington had sent gunboats into Latin American ports over six thousand times, invaded Cuba, Mexico (again), Guatemala, and Honduras, fought protracted guerrilla wars in the Dominican Republic, Nicaragua, and Haiti, annexed Puerto Rico, and taken a piece of Colombia to create both the Panamanian nation and the Panama Canal. For their part, American corporations and financial houses came to dominate the economies of Mexico, the Caribbean, and Central America, as well as large parts of South America, apprenticing themselves in overseas expansion before they headed elsewhere, to Asia, Africa, and Europe.

Yet Latin America did more than serve as a staging ground for the United States's early push toward empire. The region provided a school where foreign policy officials and intellectuals could learn to apply what political scientists like to call "soft power"—that is, the spread of America's authority through nonmilitary means, through commerce, cultural exchange, and multilateral cooperation.[3]

At first, the United States proved a reluctant student. It took decades of mounting Latin American anti-imperialist resistance, including armed resistance, to force Washington to abandon its militarism. But abandon it it finally did, at least for a short time. In the early 1930s, Franklin D. Roosevelt promised that henceforth the United States would be a "good neighbor," that it would recognize the absolute sovereignty of individual nations, renounce its right to engage in unilateral interventions, and make concessions to economic nationalists. Rather than weaken U.S. influence in the Western

Hemisphere, this newfound moderation in fact institutionalized Washington's authority, drawing Latin American republics tighter into its political, economic, and cultural orbit through a series of multilateral treaties and regional organizations. The Good Neighbor policy was the model for the European and Asian alliance system, providing a blueprint for America's "empire by invitation," as one historian famously described Washington's rise to unprecedented heights of world power.[4]

But even as Washington was working out the contours of its kinder, gentler empire in postwar Western Europe and Japan, back in the birthplace of American soft power it was rearming. Latin America once again became a school where the United States studied how to execute imperial violence through proxies. After World War II, in the name of containing Communism, the United States, mostly through the actions of local allies, executed or encouraged coups in, among other places, Guatemala, Brazil, Chile, Uruguay, and Argentina and patronized a brutal mercenary war in Nicaragua. Latin America became a laboratory for counterinsurgency, as military officials and covert operators applied insights learned in the region to Southeast Asia, Africa, and the Middle East. By the end of the Cold War, Latin American security forces trained, funded, equipped, and incited by Washington had executed a reign of bloody terror—hundreds of thousands killed, an equal number tortured, millions driven into exile—from which the region has yet to fully recover.

This reign of terror has had consequences more far-reaching than the damage done to Latin America itself, for it was this rehabilitation of hard power that directly influenced America's latest episode of imperial overreach in the wake of 9/11.

It is often noted in passing that a number of the current administration's officials, advisers, and hangers-on are veterans of Ronald Reagan's Central American policy in the 1980s, which included the patronage of anti-Communist governments in El Salvador and

Guatemala and anti-Communist insurgents in Nicaragua. The list includes Elliott Abrams, Bush's current deputy national security adviser in charge of promoting democracy throughout the world; John Negroponte, former U.N. ambassador, envoy to Iraq, and now intelligence czar; Otto Reich, secretary of state for the Western Hemisphere during Bush's first term; and Robert Kagan, an ardent advocate of U.S. global hegemony. John Poindexter, convicted of lying to Congress, conspiracy, and destroying evidence in the Iran-Contra scandal during his tenure as Reagan's national security adviser, was appointed by Rumsfeld to oversee the Pentagon's stillborn Total Information Awareness program. John Bolton, ambassador to the United Nations and an arch-unilateralist, served as Reagan's point man in the Justice Department to stonewall investigations into Iran-Contra.[5]

Yet the links between the current Bush administration's revolution in foreign policy and Reagan's hard line in Central America are even more profound than the simple recycling of personnel. It was Central America, and Latin America more broadly, where an insurgent New Right first coalesced, as conservative activists used the region to respond to the crisis of the 1970s, a crisis provoked not only by America's defeat in Vietnam but by a deep economic recession and a culture of skeptical antimilitarism and political dissent that spread in the war's wake. Indeed, Reagan's Central American wars can best be understood as a dress rehearsal for what is going on now in the Middle East. It was in these wars where the coalition made up of neoconservatives, Christian evangelicals, free marketers, and nationalists that today stands behind George W. Bush's expansive foreign policy first came together. There they had near free rein to bring the full power of the United States against a much weaker enemy in order to exorcise the ghost of Vietnam—and, in so doing, begin the transformation of America's foreign policy and domestic culture.

A critical element of that transformation entailed shifting the rationale of American diplomacy away from containment to rollback, from one primarily justified in terms of national defense to one charged with advancing what Bush likes to call a "global democratic revolution." The domestic fight over how to respond to revolutionary nationalism in Central America allowed conservative ideologues to remoralize both American diplomacy and capitalism, to counteract the cynicism that had seeped into both popular culture and the political establishment regarding the deployment of U.S. power in the world. Thus they pushed the Republican Party away from its foreign policy pragmatism to the idealism that now defines the "war on terror" as a world crusade of free-market nation building.

At the same time, the conflicts in Nicaragua, El Salvador, and Guatemala allowed New Right militarists to find ways to bypass the restrictions enacted by Congress and the courts in the wake of Vietnam that limited the executive branch's ability to fight wars, conduct covert operations, and carry out domestic surveillance of political activists. The Reagan White House perfected new techniques to manipulate the media, Congress, and public opinion while at the same time reempowering domestic law enforcement agencies to monitor and harass political dissidents. These techniques, as we shall see, prefigured initiatives now found in the PR campaign to build support for the war in Iraq and in the Patriot Act, reinvigorating the national security state in ways that resonate to this day. The Central American wars also provided the New Christian Right its first extensive experience in foreign affairs, as the White House mobilized evangelical activists in order to neutralize domestic opponents of a belligerent foreign policy. It was here where New Right Christian theologians first joined with secular nationalists to elaborate an ethical justification for a rejuvenated militarism.

In other words, it was in Central America where the Republican Party first combined the three elements that give today's imperialism its moral force: punitive idealism, free-market absolutism, and right-wing Christian mobilization. The first justified a belligerent diplomacy not just for the sake of national security but to advance "freedom." The second sanctified property rights and the unencumbered free market as the moral core of the freedom it was America's duty to export. The third backed up these ideals with social power, as the Republican Party learned how to channel the passions of its evangelical base into the international arena.

To focus, therefore, exclusively on neoconservative intellectuals, as much of the commentary attempting to identify the origins of the new imperialism does, deflects attention away from the long history of American expansion. The intellectual architects of the Bush Doctrine are but part of a larger resurgence of nationalist militarism, serving as the ideologues of an American revanchism fired by a lethal combination of humiliation in Vietnam and vindication in the Cold War, of which Central America was the tragic endgame.

After an opening chapter that makes the case for Latin America's role in the formation of the U.S. empire, the rest of this book explores the importance of the region to the consolidation of what could be called a new, revolutionary imperialism. Taken each on their own, the ideas, tactics, politics, and economics that have driven Bush's global policy are not original. An interventionist military posture, belief that America has a special role to play in world history, cynical realpolitik, vengeful nationalism, and free-market capitalism have all driven U.S. diplomacy in one form or another for nearly two centuries. But what is new is how potent these elements have become and how tightly they are bound to the ambitions of America's domestic ruling conservative coalition—a coalition that despite its power and influence paints itself as persecuted, at odds not just with much of the world but with modern life itself.[6] The book goes on to explore the intellectual reorientation of American diplomacy in the wake of Vietnam and the increasing willingness of militarists to champion human rights, nation building, and democratic reform. The third chapter considers how the rehabilitation of unconventional warfare doctrine in El Salvador and

Nicaragua by militarists in and around the Reagan White House laid the groundwork for today's offensive military posture. Here, the human costs of this resurgence of militarism will be addressed. In the many tributes that followed Reagan's death, pundits enjoyed repeating Margaret Thatcher's comment that Reagan won the Cold War "without firing a shot." The crescendo of carnage that overwhelmed Central America in the 1980s not only gives the lie to such a legacy but highlights the inescapable violence of empire. The fourth chapter turns to the imperial home front, examining how the Reagan administration first confronted and then began to solve the domestic crisis of authority generated by Vietnam and Watergate. It also argues that Reagan's Central American policy served as a crucible that forged the coalition that today stands behind George W. Bush. Chapter 5 is concerned with the economics of empire, how the financial contraction of the 1970s provided an opportunity for the avatars of free-market orthodoxy—the true core of the Bush Doctrine—to join with other constituencies of the ascendant New Right, inaugurating first in Chile and then throughout Latin America a new, brutally competitive global economy.

The last chapter tallies the score of the new imperialism in Latin America. Celebrated by Bill Clinton, and now Bush, as a model of what the United States hopes to accomplish in the rest of the world, Latin America continues to be gripped by unrelenting poverty and periodic political instability, as the promise of living under a benevolent American imperium has failed to materialize. As a result, new political movements and antagonists have emerged to contest the terms of United States–promoted corporate globalization, calling for increased regional integration to offset the power of the United States and more social spending to alleviate Latin American inequality. With little to offer the region in terms of development except the increasingly hollow promises of free trade, Washington is responding to these and similar challenges by once again militarizing hemispheric relations, with all dissent now set in the crosshairs of the "global war on terror."

The history of Latin America, a region that long bore the brunt of the kind of righteous violence enshrined in the Bush Doctrine, has much to say about Washington's current drive toward global hegemony, particularly on how its ideologues have come to believe that American power itself is without limits. More ominously, though, it points to where we may wind up if we continue down this path.

CHAPTER ONE

How Latin America Saved the United States from Itself

FOR OVER TWO CENTURIES, Latin America has been caught in
the crosswinds of empire, buffeted by the United States's revolutionary ambition and battered by its counterrevolutionary cruelty. Take the case of the Ford Motor Company. In the late 1920s,
Henry Ford, on the advice of Secretary of Commerce Herbert
Hoover, set out to build a rubber plantation on the banks of the Tapa-
jós River in the Amazon rain forest in order to break the high-priced
British latex monopoly.[1] Combining fancy and expedience, the project represented more than an effort to bring rubber production under
Ford's direct control. "We would revolutionize the world," said National City Bank president Frank Vanderlip in 1918 of the global
aspirations of early-twentieth-century, pre-Depression American industrialists, financiers, and politicians. Fordlandia, as Ford's jungle
adventure came to be called, was an effort to do just that.[2]

Ford planted rubber trees on a plantation three times the size of
Rhode Island, equipped with state-of-the-art processing facilities

intended to replicate the kind of mechanized industrial production he had pioneered in Detroit. The town that arose on the property soon housed four thousand workers, making it the third-largest city in the Amazon. But unlike those other rough-and-tumble settlements, this one sported concrete sidewalks, fire hydrants, a fully equipped hospital, modest bungalows for workers, larger homes for administrators, grass lawns, and white picket fences. "Shades of Tarzan!" ran a caption under a photograph of smiling plantation worker kids in a promotional brochure. "You'd never guess these bright, happy, healthy school children lived in a jungle city that didn't even exist a few years ago."[3] Churches, a golf course, a movie house, swimming pools, and weekly square dances simulated the customs and conventions of an American factory town, especially Ford's own Highland Park and River Rouge complexes. Just as Ford paid five dollars a day to American workers to create a disciplined working class with middle-class values and consumption habits, Fordlandia hoped to attract a steady labor force with a decent wage, free education, and health care.

The enterprise was doomed from the start. Swindled by a Brazilian con artist, Ford paid much more than the start-up land was worth. The terrain was hilly, which made it impossible to deploy the kind of large-scale mechanization Ford had envisioned. Its sandy soil leached out nutrients, a problem made worse by seasonal heavy rain. Chronic labor shortages and conflicts crippled production, while good pay and health care couldn't compete with the allure of industrializing cities like Rio or São Paulo. Rubber tappers, accustomed to having more control over their lives and work routines, protested the rigidity of the plantation's rules, the segregation of tasks according to race, and the abuse of administrators, who ranked Brazilians on a spectrum ranging from "savagery" to "tameness," much as they would livestock.[4] They also balked at attempts to regulate their social life, diet, and drinking habits. Riots frequently broke out, with workers destroying the time clocks and whistles used to organize the workday. Managers responded with mass firings, which led to more clashes.

Ford had a reputation as a pioneer of applied industrial science, yet for the first five years of Fordlandia's operation he employed not one expert with experience in either tropical agriculture or rubber planting. Plantation managers refused to cultivate disease-resistant clones or to follow the advice of Brazilian botanists who warned that rubber trees needed to be scattered at safe distances throughout the jungle in order to prevent the spread of South American leaf blight. Mimicking the regimentation Ford imposed on his River Rouge factory floor, they instead stubbornly planted trees in tight, well-ordered rows. By 1934, *Microcuclus ulei* had spread from tree to tree, laying waste to the fledgling plantation. But Ford refused to give up. From his office in Detroit, he ordered the whole operation, dance hall and all, moved downriver. This effort, alas, failed too. After seventeen years, an investment of twenty million dollars, and the planting of more than three million trees, hardly any Fordlandia latex found its way into a Ford tire. In 1945, Henry Ford II sold the property to the Brazilian government for $250,000, abandoning the town and its manicured lawns—along with his father's dream of leading a peaceful cultural revolution in Latin America—to the jungle.

Fast-forward three decades: Ford Motor Company had not, of course, deserted Latin America. Far from it, as its factories rolled out cars and trucks for sale throughout the continent. But America's corporate and political leaders were no longer sponsoring revolution but counterrevolution.

Latin American reformers, democrats, and nationalists, along with working-class and peasant allies, had begun to take seriously the twin promises of democracy and development held out by the United States since the 1930s, pressing for both an extension of political rights and a more equitable distribution of national wealth. But their efforts were repeatedly thwarted by their respective nations' ruling classes, made up of military officers, Catholic conservatives, and economic elites. Politics became polarized throughout the continent, as one side increasingly saw revolution as the only way to give birth to a new world and the other embraced terror as the only way to abort it. Washington, by this time more concerned with confronting the Soviet Union than advancing democracy in Latin America, threw in with the forces of order, sponsoring coups, championing death-squad states, and embracing dictators.

Neither did American business stay neutral. In the mid-1960s, executives from thirty-seven corporations organized themselves into the Business Group for Latin America, made up of delegates from Ford, U.S. Steel, DuPont, Standard Oil, Anaconda Copper, International Telephone and Telegraph, United Fruit, and Chase Manhattan Bank. David Rockefeller, whose family had extensive holdings in Latin America going back to the nineteenth century, coordinated the group's activities and served as its liaison with the White House.[5] The idea was both to influence Washington's hemispheric policy and to apply direct pressure at the source, funding the campaigns of friendly Latin American politicians, helping allies hold down prices, and providing financial guidance to cooperative regimes. When lobbying proved insufficient, members of the group, either individually or in concert, worked with the CIA to foment coups, as they did in Brazil in 1964 and Chile in 1973.[6]

Some went further. A number of multinational corporations, including Ford, Coca-Cola, Del Monte, and Mercedes-Benz have been accused in recent years of working closely with Latin American death squads—responsible for hundreds of thousands of killings throughout the hemisphere in the 1970s and 1980s—to counter labor organizing.[7] In Argentina, Ford provided the squads with a fleet of greenish gray Falcons they used in their kidnapping and established on the premises of its manufacturing plant outside Buenos Aires a detention center where union activists were held.[8] Henry Ford's vision may have died in the jungle, but the discipline of his work rules remained: the Ford factory fired kidnapped workers, at least those lucky enough to have survived, because of absenteeism.

As a parable of empire, Fordlandia captures well the experience of the United States in Latin America. The quixotic faith that led Ford to try to remake the Amazon in an American image—a truly utopian endeavor considering that he never set foot in Brazil— reflects a broader belief that the United States offers a universal, and universally acknowledged, model for the rest of humanity. In turn, Ford Motor Company's subsequent support of death-squad regimes demonstrates how that kind of evangelicalism easily gives way to brute coercion.

This chapter follows the long history of the United States in Latin America, swinging as it has between reform and reaction. It makes the case for the region's unacknowledged importance to the development of America's truly exceptional empire, unlike any that have come (and gone) before it. For over a century, Latin Americans resisted, often violently, both the United States's self-assigned mission to reform humanity, of the sort that drove Ford to the Amazon, and the militarism that such a mission inevitably generated. In doing so, they forced the United States, often against the worst impulses of its leaders, to develop more pragmatic and flexible imperial strategies, strategies that proved indispensable in its postwar rise to global superpower.

DREAMERS IN ISRAEL

Even before the United States was its own nation, the land now called Latin America was for Anglo settlers a dreamscape and theater of ambition. Spain conquered much of the Americas nearly a century before English Pilgrims and Puritans set foot on what they would name New England. For seventeenth-century Protestant Nonconformists, the Spanish Crown's rule over large masses of natives represented the most pernicious of what they had left behind, Catholic in its superstitions, languid in its aristocratic pretensions. It was a goad to those who believed that the New World—America— did indeed represent a chance to realize God's will on earth. Latin America also entailed that other quality all useful utopias need, a seeming bountifulness in which dreams could run unchecked. For would-be reformers, the reported guilelessness of its people, the openness of its landscape, the vulnerability of its economy made Latin America appear malleable as clay.

This combination of perceived corruption that demands reform and imagined innocence that begs for guidance was irresistible to successive generations of Christians, capitalists, and politicians. In the late seventeenth century, long before Henry Ford tried to erect a New Detroit in the Amazon, the Puritans Cotton Mather and Samuel Sewall imagined a New Jerusalem rising in Mexico. With New England barely a few score years old, Reverend Mather got busy learning Spanish to help Spain's subjects "open their eyes that they be converted from the shadows to the light, from the power of Satan to that of God" and worked with Sewall, better known as a judge during the Salem witch trials, to realize the dreams of the "dreamers in Israel" in Mexico. "I rather think that *Americana Mexicana* will be the New Jerusalem," predicted Sewall.[9]

Soon after the American Revolution, merchants began to make inroads in the Spanish colonies of the south, vying with steadily increasing success against British traders. By the early 1800s the United States was shipping nearly $7,000,000 worth of goods to Latin American harbors, with Cuba standing behind only Great Britain and France as the United States's largest commercial partner. Sea captains and merchant marines gained experience on the profitable trade route between New Orleans and Havana, before pushing beyond the Caribbean to the rest of Latin America and then China and India.[10]

Investment followed trade. Throughout the nineteenth century but especially after the economic contractions and corporate mergers of the 1890s, many of America's largest international corporations got their start in Latin America, as capitalists poured billions into the region, first in mining, railroads, and sugar, then in electricity, oil, and agriculture. The W. R. Grace shipping company came to dominate Peruvian sugar production. Before investing in diamond mines in the Congo, the Guggenheims set up a branch of their American Smelting and Refining Company in Mexico. Access to Chilean ore allowed Charles Schwab in the first decades of the twentieth century to bypass U.S. Steel's domestic monopoly to turn his Bethlehem Steel Company into the world's largest independent producer. Similarly, the upstart Rockefellers leveraged their power in Latin America to weaken the grip J. P. Morgan and Company had on Wall Street finance. After the War of 1898 opened up the Caribbean to U.S. corporate interests, it was the Rockefeller-controlled Chase National Bank that financed most of the region's agricultural, mineral, and oil production.[11] By the early 1900s, Mexico attracted more than a quarter of total American foreign investment, rendering the border meaningless to U.S. financial houses.[12] Boston and New York banks capitalized the construction of rail lines that opened up the countryside for investment in agriculture, mining, ranching, and oil drilling. American interests took control of mines and smelters in Chihuahua, Durango, San Luis Potosí, Aguascalientes, Michoacán, Zacatecas, Puebla, and Guerrero. Standard Oil geologists fanned out from the American West to the Mexican desert and then down into the Amazon jungle in search of petroleum reserves.[13] By 1911, Americans owned most of Mexico's oil industry, which had become the world's third-largest petroleum supplier, and had established operations in Venezuela, Bolivia, Peru, and Brazil.

By the late nineteenth century, the dynamism of American capitalism and a growing sense of racial superiority had fortified the missionary impulse on display since the time of Mather and Sewall. The "world is to be Christianized and civilized," wrote the Reverend

Josiah Strong in his 1885 best seller, *Our Country*, "and what is the process of civilizing but the creation of more and higher wants. Commerce follows the missionary."[14] A disciple of American expansion, Strong was a counselor to a number of early U.S. empire builders, including Alfred Thayer Mahan and Theodore Roosevelt. He shared with them an unapologetic belief in white ascendancy drawn from social Darwinism, which applied the concept of the "survival of the fittest" to international affairs. God bequeathed the Americas to the "Anglo Saxon race," claimed Strong, to train for "the final competition of races." Strong believed God's gift to be a work in progress, to be realized by what many of his contemporaries understood to be America's "manifest destiny." Following the vision of his Puritan forebears, the first step in the fulfillment of this destiny would be Latin America: whites would "move down upon Mexico," he ordained, "down upon Central and South America, out upon the islands of the sea, over upon Africa and beyond" to "people the world with better and finer material." And they did move down. Evangelical fundamentalists went into Mexico, Central America, the Andes, the Amazon River basin, and the jungles of Paraguay, ministering mostly to the continent's indigenous populations and translating the Bible into native languages. They understood their mission as both extending American power and bringing the world closer to the Second Coming of Christ—two goals that Christian missionaries generally believed to be mutually dependent.

The captains of American industry and finance saw their role in no less grandiose terms. Latin America was a school where business elites honed their sense of self-confidence and historical purpose. With a rock-ribbed faith in American-style capitalism and all the cultural trappings that go with it, corporate leaders sponsored religious and civic organizations, such as the Young Men's Christian Association, which preached the virtues believed to be most conducive to successful free enterprise: individualism, competitiveness, innovation, self-discipline, respect for private property, and, as a reward for such commendable behavior, consumerism. The Rockefeller family, for example, extended its influence in Latin America by creating the secular Rockefeller Foundation to provide countries with critical medical assistance and by patronizing evangelical groups such as the Panama Congress on Christian Work in Latin America, the Commission on Indians in Latin America, and the Committee on Cooperation in Latin America.[15] Corporations also advanced their interests and their values through U.S. company towns, which by the early twentieth century had spread throughout the Caribbean, Mexico, and Central and South America. They were to produce not just sugar, bananas, or ore but, as in Ford's Amazon endeavor, self-disciplined American-style workers. "It takes just four years," calculated one Phelps Dodge engineer, "to complete the Americanization of the Mexican."[16]

All through the nineteenth and early twentieth centuries, mercenaries and militarists, men impatient with the slow unfolding of manifest destiny, took it upon themselves to expand the perimeters of empire. In 1855, the Tennessean William Walker raised an army and launched an invasion of Nicaragua from the port of New Orleans. After an easy victory over local troops, the "gray-eyed man of destiny" declared himself president and reestablished slavery, an institution Nicaraguans had abolished three decades earlier. Quickly recognized by the United States as Nicaragua's legitimate head of state, Walker ruled the country as a quasi-proconsul for a few years before being deposed and, after a failed bid to retake power, executed by Central American troops. A half-century later, the banana tycoon Samuel Zemurray bankrolled the Louisianans Lee Christmas and Guy "Machine Gun" Molony to overthrow the Honduran government and replace it with one that would grant Zemurray's Cuyamel Fruit Company generous land and tax concessions.[17]

Walker, Christmas, and Molony were unofficial advance men for America's growing reach, financed by corporate interests to pull the Caribbean and Central America tighter into the U.S. orbit. But as the 1800s wore on, the federal government increasingly took over the work of imperial expansion.

By the mid-nineteenth century, the United States had incorporated nearly half of Mexico into its territory. It had sent warships into Latin American ports a staggering 5,980 times between 1869 and 1897 to protect American commercial interests and, increasingly, to flex its muscles to Europe.[18] In 1893, the United States quietly backed both a revolution in Hawaii instigated by American sugar barons that eventually led to the annexation of those islands and, with more bluster, a counterrevolution in Brazil, when, at the behest of Standard Oil's William Rockefeller, Washington sent man-o'-wars steaming into Rio de Janeiro's harbor to defeat rebels believed to be hostile to U.S. economic interests. In 1898, the United States took Puerto Rico and the Philippines as colonies and Cuba as a protectorate and established a series of coaling stations and naval bases throughout the Caribbean. In 1903, Theodore Roosevelt teamed up with J. P. Morgan to shave the province of Panama off Colombia, turning the new nation into an important global transit route and, as the eventual home of Southcom headquarters, the forecastle of America's hemispheric might.[19]

Over the course of the next thirty years, U.S. troops invaded Caribbean countries at least thirty-four times, occupied Honduras, Mexico, Guatemala, and Costa Rica for short periods, and remained in Haiti, Cuba, Nicaragua, Panama, and the Dominican Republic for longer stays. Military campaigns in the Caribbean and Central America during these decades not only gave shape to the command and bureaucratic structure of America's modern army (what eventually became known as the Joint Chiefs of Staff, for example, was put into place soon after the 1898 Spanish-American War) but allowed soldiers to test their prowess, to sharpen their senses and skills for larger battles to come in Europe and Asia.[20]

Troops understood their time in the Caribbean, Central America, and the Philippines as an extension of their experience with political violence at home. Many of them either had firsthand experience in the wars against Native Americans or hailed from parts of the United States where Jim Crow held sway. As their successors would do in Vietnam and Iraq, troops described their rebel opponents as "Indians" and hostile territory as "Indian country."[21] And just as violent video games today serve both to quicken reflexes and anesthetize against the effects of violence, shooting practice in state fairs and fun parks made killing somewhat enjoyable for soldiers. It was "more fun than a turkey shoot," exclaimed a marine, recalling how he shot Filipino rebels as they swam across a river in retreat.[22] Lieutenant Faustin Wirkus (a Kurtz-like character who during his nineteen years in Haiti claimed to be the reincarnation of an earlier Haitian ruler and had himself crowned "king" of Vodou societies in the district of La Gonave) recalled how killing Haitian rebels was like playing "hit the nigger and get a cigar" games at amusement parks back home. In one battle that took place in front of a "chalk-like cliff," Wirkus said, black heads that "appeared over the top or around the side of a boulder" were "as clearly outlined as a bull's eye on a painted target."[23]

American soldiers in these so-called small wars learned to project their aggression onto their victims. Marine major Julian Smith testified that the "racial psychology" of "the poorer classes of Nicaraguans" made them "densely ignorant" and "little interested in principles." According to Smith, "A state of war to them is a normal condition." Along the same lines, Colonel Robert Denig observed in his diary, "Life to them is cheap, murder in itself is nothing."[24] When asked if he ever witnessed American brutality in Haiti, General Ivan Miller replied that "you have to remember that what we consider brutality among people in the United States is different from what they considered brutality."[25] (Similar opinions relating the exceptional regard Americans have for human life, even as they were taking it, became commonplace in subsequent wars, such as when the commander of U.S. forces in Vietnam, General William

Westmoreland, famously reported that "Orientals don't value life" the way Westerners did or when National Guard lieutenant Andrew Johansen last year in Iraq said that Iraqis don't "know the values of human life Americans have. If they shoot somebody, I don't think they would have remorse.")[26] Such attitudes led easily to cruelty. "I want no prisoners. I wish you to kill and burn, the more you kill and the more you burn the better you will please me," are the orders General Jacob Smith gave to his troops in the Philippines. And so they did, in what a British witness described not as a war but as "murderous butchery."

Starting in the late 1920s, Nicaragua offered the marines their most effective proving ground, becoming, according to a *New York Times* reporter who accompanied the expedition, the "first practical laboratory for the development of post-war aviation in coordination with ground troops."[27] For six years, U.S. troops fought the "bandit" rebel Augusto César Sandino in a war that allowed them to practice tactics that would become standard elements in twentieth-century air warfare. These included extended reconnaissance flights, ground-to-air communication signaling, use of aircraft to evacuate wounded in combat, propaganda leaflet drops, and long-distance aerial troop rotations and supply missions. They even field-tested a strange-looking contraption with wings, a forward propeller, and a horizontal rotor—a helicopter prototype called an autogiro. "Never before have planes participated in guerrilla warfare," wrote the *Times* journalist, but in Nicaragua "they have proved themselves a most deadly weapon against hidden enemies," helping to overcome mountainous terrain described by one First World War veteran as worse than anything he had seen in France. According to their own accounts, the marines, along with their Nicaraguan National Guard protégés, burned crops, razed peasant huts, bombed and strafed populations, and injured or killed perhaps thousands of Nicaraguans.[28] Scooping the Nazi Luftwaffe, the first dive-bombing campaign in military history was conducted in Nicaragua, when five two-seater de Havilland biplanes swooped down to disperse insurgents just on the verge of routing U.S. ground forces.[29]

By the late 1920s, then, the United States had apprenticed itself as a fledgling empire in Latin America, investing capital, establishing control over crucial raw materials and transit routes, gaining military expertise, and rehearsing many of the ideas that to this day justify American power in the world. But the experience in Latin America, both during this initial "drive toward hegemony" and then during the Good Neighbor policy of the 1930s and 1940s, also pushed U.S. leaders to develop a coherently sophisticated imperial project, one better suited for a world in which rising nationalism was making formal colonialism of the kind European nations practiced unworkable.

The Porcupine Problem

By the end of the nineteenth century, the idea of "expansion" enjoyed broad support across the political spectrum, ranging from financial and manufacturing elites to nationalists, agrarian populists, labor leaders, and secular and Christian reformers. There emerged a "convergence of economic practice within intellectual analysis and emotional involvement," as historian William Appleman Williams puts it, "that create[d] a very powerful and dangerous propensity to define the essentials of American welfare in terms of activities outside the United States."[30] Militarists such as Alfred Thayer Mahan, midwestern Republicans like Senators Albert Beveridge and Robert Taft, industrialists in the National Association of Manufacturers, financiers like Frank Vanderlip, and anticolonialist populists such as William Jennings Bryan may have all been driven by different motivations—social peace, national glory, foreign markets, democratic reform—but they increasingly came to share a vision of the world in which progress and prosperity at home were dependent on the expansion of America's economic and, by extension, military power abroad.

But if expansion enjoyed broad support, the idea of direct colonialism did not. A nativist racism, unlike the imperialist variant expressed by Joseph Strong, led many in the United States to refuse the responsibilities of presiding over large populations of nonwhite peoples. William Jennings Bryan's declaration that the "Filipinos cannot be citizens without endangering our civilization" reflected this sentiment, but it also signaled a wish to protect America's working class from the competition of cheap labor.[31] Republicans like Beveridge and Taft promoted first a mighty navy and then a commanding air force as a way of protecting American shores and projecting American power but fought against the expansion of the army, which, they felt, would inevitably lead to overseas wars and increasing involvement in the messy waters of international politics. Sequential invasions and military occupations did indeed prove costly—particularly in the Philippines, where a bloody insurgency killed 4,000 American soldiers and 200,000 Filipinos—turning the public and many political leaders, including eventually Theodore Roosevelt and Woodrow Wilson, against formal empire. When an aide suggested to Roosevelt that he annex the Dominican Republic to quell political disorder and head off the threat of a German invasion to collect debt, the president replied that he was no more inclined to do so "than a gorged boa constrictor would be to swallow a porcupine wrong-end-to."[32]

Starting with the McKinley administration and carrying forward through the first decades of the twentieth century a consensus developed among American leaders that reconciled competing expansionist and anticolonial traditions. First fully elaborated by Secretary of State John Hay in relation to China, America's "Open Door" diplomacy resolved a number of problems for the young, ascendant empire. Most immediately, a demand for equal and open access to markets provided Washington a wedge to make inroads into areas already under European colonial control. Over the long run, the demand for legal "equality with all competing nations in the conditions of access to the markets" provided the foundation for America's informal empire—finance became a vital instrument of state, allowing Washington to spread its influence while limiting the kind of opposition that direct colonialism inevitably engenders. America's economic ascendancy, it was felt, could both easily compete in an open field against European competitors and shape the economic and political institutions of poor countries to the advantage of U.S. lenders, investors, traders, and manufacturers.

There were two obstacles to the realization of the ideal of the Open Door policy. The first had to do with the inconvenient fact that the United States, following the 1898 Spanish–American War, found itself administrating "new-caught sullen peoples, half devil and half child," not just in Cuba, the Philippines, and Puerto Rico but, for periods of time, in Panama, Nicaragua, Haiti, and the Dominican Republic.[33] Men like Hay hoped that a policy of open markets would prevent war and annexation, yet the drive for markets led to both. In addition to protecting and advancing America's substantial economic and geopolitical interests in the Spanish Caribbean, especially in Cuba, the war of 1898 was propelled by a need to seize the Philippines, also a Spanish colony, and use it as a staging area to project U.S. influence into Asia. That Germany had taken control of Kiaochow, on China's southern coast, in November 1897 prompted fears that European powers, along with Japan, would divide China among themselves and cut the United States out of the spoils. America's political and economic class concluded that Washington had to declare war on Spain not just to quell a rebellion in Cuba and stabilize the Caribbean but to establish a toehold in the Pacific.

The second problem had to do with defining the relationship between private economic interests and the government's geopolitical concerns. Theodore Roosevelt may have had no desire to swallow porcupines, but nineteenth-century "free-market solutions" to let financiers—not to mention thugs like Machine Gun Molony, whom they sometimes contracted—operate as proxies for America's foreign interests proved unstable, as the experience of the New York–based San Domingo Improvement Company in the Dominican Republic demonstrated.

The company, which had purchased the Dominican Republic's foreign debt from European creditors in 1893, was grossly irresponsible and incompetent, floating national bonds in Europe at unsustainable interest rates and printing money that led the Dominican Republic to financial disaster.[34] Dominican nationalist opposition to this predation generated conflict and chaos, forcing Washington, anxious to prevent European, especially German, intervention, to place its Caribbean fleet at the company's command. In early 1905, Roosevelt, deciding that the U.S. military could no longer underwrite the SDIC's speculative escapades, took "virtual control," as the *New York Times* reported, of the Dominican Republic. He seized its customs house and instructed New York banks to refinance its national debts, including those held by SDIC and foreign creditors.

But beyond acting as a financial trustee, the United States set out to reform the country's political, security, and legal system, committing itself to a policy of nation building. Under the aegis of what Roosevelt's secretary of war and presidential successor, William Howard Taft, dubbed "dollar diplomacy," the State Department sought explicitly to extend U.S. interests in Panama, Nicaragua, Honduras, Guatemala, Haiti, China, and elsewhere by brokering and supervising private financial transactions. Washington took it upon itself to arrange for private consortiums either to buy up national debt held by European banks or, in the case of Asia, to invest in railroad development. Notwithstanding an occasional trespass on private profits, as in the Dominican Republic, diplomats continued to understand those national imperatives as the defense of open markets and property rights. But they increasingly saw the need for government intervention to stabilize the broader environment in which free enterprise could flourish.

It was during these first decades of the twentieth century, as the United States developed the rudiments of its exceptional, nonterritorial conception of empire, that the idea that national security, overseas capitalist development, and global democratic reform were indivisible goals began to seep into the sinews of American diplomacy. Taft described his foreign policy as "substituting dollars for bullets," which "appeals alike to idealistic humanitarian sentiments, to the dictates of sound policy and strategy, and to legitimate commercial aims." Yet rather than leading to the promised land of perpetual peace, such a trinity created by the 1920s something akin to perpetual war. Formal annexation may have been off the table, but in the following decades Washington would dispatch marines to invade, occupy, and try to force a host of other Central American and Caribbean nations, quills and all, to conform to the standards of international capitalism.

Your Americanism and Mine

Then, suddenly it seemed, America's overtly imperial moment was over. In 1933, Franklin D. Roosevelt, shortly after his inauguration, under what became known as the Good Neighbor policy, withdrew occupation forces from the Caribbean, abandoned a series of treaties that gave the United States special privileges in a number of Caribbean and Central American countries, and abrogated the Platt Amendment in Cuba's constitution, which granted Washington the right to intervene in that island's politics at will. He also agreed to a precedent-setting policy of absolute nonintervention in Latin American affairs. Washington even began to tolerate a degree of economic independence, allowing, for instance, Bolivia and Mexico to nationalize the holdings of U.S. oil companies. For the first time ever, the U.S. government could reasonably be expected to side with Latin American nations in their tax and labor disputes with North

American corporations. Washington backed loans to Latin America not only for infrastructure development to facilitate the extraction of raw materials and agricultural exports but for potentially competitive industrial production. When no private American steel company would finance the construction of a mill in Brazil, the State Department persuaded the newly established Export-Import Bank to do so.[35] The United States even helped Haiti, as part of its withdrawal plan, to buy back its Banque Nationale, which during the occupation had been taken over by New York's National City Bank. "Your Americanism and mine," FDR said in an address to the Pan-American Union, "must be a structure built of confidence, cemented by a sympathy which recognizes only equality and fraternity."[36]

On the face of it, a radical reversal of decades of U.S. policy had taken place, one that today would be the equivalent of George W. Bush's withdrawing troops from Iraq, repudiating his doctrine of preemptive strikes, signing the International Criminal Court treaty, normalizing relations with Syria and Iran, and permitting third-world nations to have greater control over international capital flows. Roosevelt took office with no reputation as a multilateralist, at least when it came to Latin America. He had previously supported the occupations of Mexico, the Dominican Republic, Panama, and Haiti, referring to the inhabitants of the latter country as "little more than primitive savages."[37] He even once claimed to have personally written Haiti's constitution.

What accounts for FDR's transformation from young imperialist to mature internationalist? First of all, the Great Depression had led to a sudden constriction of American power in the world, as a panic of extraordinary proportions gripped domestic affairs. Financial devastation forced a temporary turn inward, with capitalists and policy planners focusing on rebuilding national production and consumption. Second, even before the Depression, the Mexican Revolution—a violent, cataclysmic upheaval that lasted almost a decade, beginning in 1910, and destroyed massive amounts of U.S.-owned property—was evidence that Latin American economic and political nationalism was a force that had to be reckoned with.

In the years after the Civil War, both the U.S. government and private U.S. interests supplied arms and money to help Mexican economic liberals consolidate power and transform their country into a modern, capitalist nation.[38] New York and Boston financiers bankrolled the construction of roads, rails, and ports, opening up the country's rural hinterlands to development. By the first decade of the twentieth century, more than a billion American dollars had been invested in Mexican oil, agriculture, mining, and ranching, as well as in public utilities like urban electricity, making up more than a quarter of total U.S. foreign investment.[39] To continue to attract capital, the Mexican government cut taxes, allowed high rates of profit repatriation, and repressed labor organizing, while an increasingly militarized state transferred an enormous amount of acreage from subsistence to commodity production for the international market. With untold numbers of peasants dispossessed of their land and industrial expansion insufficient to absorb their labor power, sharp fluctuations of global market prices of basic food goods made droughts and famines that much more lethal. The twentieth century's first, longest, and bloodiest revolution broke out as a result. Millions of people died, and peasant armies flooded U.S.-owned mines and burned U.S.-owned plantations to the ground. From the ashes arose the twentieth century's first third-world developmentalist state. Revolutionary leaders enacted a far-reaching land reform, promulgated, decades before Europe and India put similar charters into place, the world's first social-democratic constitution, and nationalized large portions of the economy, including the holdings of Standard Oil.

American politicians and capitalists reacted at first with expected hostility to Mexico's revolutionary government. After Mexico's nationalization of its oil, the U.S. Treasury Department suspended its purchase of Mexican silver and twenty-two U.S. oil companies organized a boycott, refusing to buy or help refine Mexican petroleum. In response, the new revolutionary government threatened to sell its oil to Germany and Japan, prompting Congressman Hamilton Fish to call for an invasion of the United States's southern neighbor. As reports of "anti-Americanism" increased, particularly around the U.S.-Mexican border, so did calls for U.S. action. "It seems to me that it is about time for the American government to take a little notice and do something to clean things up," a U.S. businessman based in the Mexican state of Durango huffed in a letter to Washington, while government reports predicted that the United States would soon be forced to intervene "in much the same manner as we have done in the smaller and less important republics of Latin America."[40]

But Mexico was not a small and less important republic. It comprised an enormous land mass with a large population and vital natural resources. It also held a disproportionately high percentage of U.S. investment. Wall Street and Washington had to tread carefully. Even before Mexico expropriated the assets of U.S. oil companies, Nelson Rockefeller had returned from a tour of Latin America urging reform in the way U.S. corporations do business in Latin America. After witnessing firsthand widespread poverty and labor unrest in Venezuela, Bolivia, and Mexico he lectured his peers that "we must recognize the social responsibilities of corporations and the corporation must use its ownership of assets to reflect the best interest of the people." "If we don't," Rockefeller, who would play a central role in shaping Washington's postwar Latin American policy, warned, "they will take away our ownership."[41] His fellow capitalists were unconvinced about the need for reform, but they were anxious that ongoing hostile relations with Latin America would benefit European competitors. So they made their peace with Mexico's revolutionary government. For his part, Roosevelt, worried that a conflict with Mexico would derail America's economic recovery and divert attention away from the emerging threat of Japan and Germany, resumed buying Mexican silver and pushed the oil companies to accept the compensation offered by Mexico for their expropriated property.

The Mexican Revolution taught American policy makers that Latin American economic nationalism was a force to be reckoned with. The hit-and-run guerrilla war tactics of Augusto Sandino, who between 1927 and 1933 fought the U.S. Marines in Nicaragua to a draw, further taught them that political nationalism was an equally powerful force and that attempts to counter it with increased militarism would only lead to a deterioration of American influence.

U.S. troops had been in and out of Nicaragua a number of times since the late nineteenth century. In 1926 Calvin Coolidge, who despite his charisma deficit fancied himself a robust expansionist in the Theodore Roosevelt mold, once again dispatched an expedition, this time to quell a budding civil war but also to sequester the kind of revolutionary nationalism that was spreading throughout Mexico. His actions backfired.

Despite overwhelming asymmetrical firepower, including advances in aerial warfare, Nicaragua proved to be the United States's first third-world quagmire. Sandino harassed the Americans not just with attack-and-retreat guerrilla tactics that inflicted a deadly toll but with ideas. As head of a self-styled Defending Army of Nicaraguan National Sovereignty, the rebel leader—who took as his official seal an image of a peasant with a raised machete about to decapitate a captured marine—tapped into widespread Latin American resentment. His brand of patriotism esteemed the dark-skinned, impoverished peasant culture that prevailed throughout Mesoamerica and much of South America, while vilifying not only Yankees but their well-heeled local allies, or, as Sandino called them, *vendepatrias*— country sellers. "Pro-Nicaraguan committees" sprang up throughout Latin America, with Sandino's David-against-Goliath struggle coming to embody a century of aggression and arrogance. Manifestos, grassroots meetings, editorials, and ever larger street protests denounced Washington's war in Nicaragua. Newspapers published regular articles on the crisis and ran photographs provided by Sandino of captured, executed, and mutilated marines, contributing to a sense of U.S. vulnerability.[42] His appeal extended to the United States, where he coordinated his public relations campaign with the activities of the All-American Anti-Imperialist League, sending his brother Socrates on a national speaking tour. In Europe, a Mexican delegate to the 1929 International Congress against Colonialism and Imperialism waved a tattered American flag captured by Sandino's troops to a loud round of cheers and applause. Even London, then in the process of spreading its control over much of the Middle East, took great pleasure in condemning America's actions as "frankly imperialistic."

Tensions came to a head at the Sixth Pan-American Conference, held in Havana in early 1928. By the time of the meeting, pan-Americanism, the idea that the American republics shared common ideals and political interests, was in effect moribund. But it was trotted out every few years in an international forum where Latin American delegates mostly submitted to Washington's directives while silently seething about the latest violation of national sovereignty— in Panama, Cuba, Puerto Rico, Mexico, Venezuela, Honduras, the Dominican Republic, Haiti, take your pick. Proceedings in Havana moved according to script. The closing ceremony was not intended for debate, yet El Salvador raised the issue of Washington's military interventions, opening the floodgates of criticism. The gallery audience applauded each recounting of old and new grievances and hissed at the tepid defense of U.S. policy offered by its envoy.[43] This court rebellion took place in the shadow of Sandino's war, which on the eve of the conference had scored a number of impressive victories. The rebel was not directly mentioned, although one Latin American daily after another read the diplomacy in light of the fighting in Nicaragua. "The high-sounding declarations heard in

Havana do not serve to erase the inexcusable acts committed in Central America," wrote the Buenos Aires *La Nación*. Another compared the United States to the kaiser's Germany. "The Nicaraguan muddle," declared a Uruguayan journal, "is really the death knell of the pan-American ideal."[44]

The Mexican Revolution and the Nicaraguan insurgency were part of and helped catalyze a larger Latin American backlash against U.S. militarism and Washington's dollar diplomacy. That backlash spurred a new thinking among both Republican and Democratic politicians and foreign policy intellectuals that Washington could no longer afford to play catch-up diplomacy and waste its time responding to continual emergencies either caused or inflamed by direct armed interventions.[45] Over thirty military expeditions in but a few decades not only had failed to pacify the Caribbean and Central America but had heated passions even further, leading FDR's Republican predecessor, Herbert Hoover, to begin to talk of being a "good neighbor" to Latin America and to draw down U.S. military ambitions in the region, including in Nicaragua. Adolf Berle, a prominent member of FDR's brain trust, understood this new dispensation as imperialism—he had no problem with the word *empire*, believing that "neither great nor small powers have free choice in the matter."[46] Yet he condemned past U.S. behavior toward Latin America and argued for a "good" empire based on consultation, equity, and respect. "We shall have to be either generous or imperialistic," Berle stated, "and present history is showing that the generous policy is infinitely the more successful."

SAVING THE UNITED STATES FROM ITSELF

By the time Roosevelt won the presidency, momentum had long been building for a change in U.S. policy toward Latin America. Yet FDR's Good Neighbor policy was not initially proclaimed in relation to

Latin America. As president, he first used the phrase broadly, to frame a global doctrine: "In the field of world policy," he said in his inaugural address, "I would dedicate this nation to the policy of the good neighbor—the neighbor who resolutely respects himself and, because he does so, respects the rights of others—the neighbor who respects his obligations and respects the sanctity of his agreements in and with a world of neighbors. . . . We now realize as we have never realized before our interdependence on each other; that we cannot merely take but we must give as well." Elected to deal with the domestic crisis, Roosevelt made no other allusion to foreign policy. But he followed up a few months later with a precocious call to the "nations of the world" to "enter into a solemn and definite pact of non-aggression: that they shall . . . limit and reduce their armaments" and "agree that they will send no armed force of whatsoever nature across their frontiers." Roosevelt's liberal internationalism, however, found little sympathy among the colonialists and militarists who ruled Europe and Asia—his global ambitions were not backed up by global reach.

So he turned to Latin America, using the goodwill engendered by his new policy to gather strength to project New World power back to the Old.

Washington's formal renunciation of the right to intervention opened the way for a decade of unparalleled hemispheric cooperation. It bound the Americas together in a series of political, economic, military, and cultural treaties and led to the creation of an assortment of multilateral institutions, bodies of arbitration, and mechanisms for consultation and joint action in the case of an extra-hemispheric threat. The withdrawal of troops from the Caribbean, the renegotiation of treaties, and the increased tolerance of economic nationalism gave Roosevelt a better claim to legitimacy as he advocated for an end to colonialism and militarism elsewhere. His enormous popularity in Latin America—especially following his 1936 tour of Argentina, Uruguay, and Brazil, where he was greeted by hundreds of thousands of cheering admirers, with even the usually skeptical Argentine press heralding him as a "shepherd of democracy"—further fired his aspirations to world leadership.[47] Increasingly, New Deal diplomats held up the Good Neighbor policy as a "showpiece," as the U.S. ambassador to Germany put it, for diplomatic initiatives in Europe and Asia.[48]

Improved relations with Latin America likewise helped the United States recover from the contractions of the Great Depression. With Asia increasingly off limits and Europe headed for war, Washington looked south for economic relief, both as a market for manufactured goods and a source of raw material. Empowered by the 1934 Trade Agreement Act, which gave FDR fast-track authority to lower targeted tariffs by as much as 50 percent, Washington negotiated trade treaties with fifteen Latin American countries between 1934 and 1942.[49] The U.S. trade deficit with Latin America as a whole fell from $142,000,000 in 1931 to just over $13,000,000 in 1939; it soon after entered into the black, where it remains to this day.

Nelson Rockefeller, who as head of the new Office of Coordinator of Inter-American Affairs was about to take charge of mobilizing the Good Neighbor policy on behalf of the Allied war effort, recognized the importance of Latin America to the revival and eventual extension of U.S. power. "Regardless of whether the outcome of the war is a German or Allied victory," he said in 1940, after his return from yet another tour of South America, "the United States must protect its international position through the use of economic means that are competitively effective against totalitarian techniques." But if an update of Hay's Open Door policy, now directed not against colonialism but fascism and socialism, was to be effective, Rockefeller believed that it would have to be combined with his earlier call for a socially responsible capitalism. "If the United States is to maintain its security and its political and economic hemispheric position," Rockefeller argued, "it must take economic measures at once to secure economic prosperity in Central and South America, and to establish this prosperity in the frame of hemisphere economic cooperation and dependence."[50]

In turn, this economic expansion into Latin America—which after the war entailed not just the extraction of raw materials and the opening of markets for U.S. products but the setting up of manufacturing in foreign countries for local consumption—attracted the support of what political scientists Thomas Ferguson and Joel Rogers describe as an emerging "power bloc of capital-intensive industries, investment banks, and internationally-oriented commercial banks."[51] Firms heavily invested in Latin America, such as Standard Oil, Chase National Bank, Goldman Sachs, and Brown Brothers Harriman, gave their support to what would be the keystones of the New Deal state for the next three decades: "liberalism at home" and "internationalism abroad."

For instance, the U.S. pharmaceutical industry, one of the core export-oriented industries that would go on to become a powerhouse of postwar American capitalist expansion, benefited enormously from the goodwill, stable relations, and commercial treaties with Latin America made possible by Roosevelt's renunciation of militarism. During the 1930s and 1940s, it worked out production and marketing strategies in Latin America that led U.S. corporations to dominate the region. After the war, it put that experience to good use elsewhere: "With the knowledge acquired in cultivating Latin America, more visionary promotion should be conducive to somewhat comparable per capita results in the Eastern Hemisphere," the Department of Commerce's *Digest of International Developments, Drugs and Toiletries* wrote in 1949. "Perhaps the drug-consuming possibilities of Eastern Europe, Africa, the Near and Far East may be developed," hoped the *Digest*, in ways similar to what occurred in Latin America.[52]

Roosevelt also profited from Latin America's tradition of liberal international jurisprudence, which had largely been forged in opposition to U.S. militarism. FDR in fact plagiarized a number of his diplomatic initiatives directly from Latin American jurists. His 1933 peace and nonintervention proposal to the nations of the world was lifted from the Argentine foreign minister Carlos Saavedra Lamas's "Anti-War Treaty on Non-Aggression and Conciliation," drafted a year earlier.[53] Likewise, what became the backbone of the Good Neighbor policy—the policy and principle of nonintervention in both the domestic and the foreign affairs of sovereign nations— represented the central plank in a decades-long struggle by Latin American nations to force Washington to give up the right of intervention, which it finally fully did with much fanfare in 1936. That principle then became the hallmark of New Deal diplomacy, forming the legal core of the United Nations charter, as well as a number of regional alliances, like the Organization of American States.

After the war, Latin Americans continued to reorient international law away from power politics toward multilateral collaboration in pursuit of social welfare and peace.[54] Bringing with them their long experience of pan-American diplomacy and encouraged by their experience of wartime alliance with the United States, twenty-one Latin American representatives—nearly half the total delegates and the largest single regional caucus—gathered in San Francisco in 1945 to found the United Nations. The memoirs of a number of these diplomats convey a hopeful confidence in their ability to create a new global community of peaceful, stable nations.[55] They pressed the United Nations to confront directly the issue of colonial racism and to adopt a human rights policy. Chile and Panama provided draft charters for the Universal Declaration of Human Rights, while Latin American representatives pushed for the inclusion of social and economic rights in the declaration—the right to social security, to work, to an adequate standard of living, to unionize, to rest and leisure time, to food, clothing, housing, health care, and education, and to equality for women. "If political liberalism does not ensure the economic, social, and cultural rights of its citizens," said the

Chilean delegate Hernán Santa Cruz, capturing the broad vision of economic democracy that prevailed at the time of the drafting of the Universal Declaration of Human Rights, "then it cannot achieve an enduring progress. Yet neither can progress be gained by those who suppress liberty under the pretext or illusion of satisfying material needs. Democracy—political as well as social and economic—comprises, in my mind, an inseparable whole."[56]

In short, the 1930s and 1940s marked a turn in the fortune of the American empire, when diverse expressions of what political scientists call "soft power" began to congeal in a coherent system of extraterritorial administration—largely thanks to Latin America. Resistance to U.S. aggression not only revealed the limits of militarism but punctured the puffed-up, self-justifying rhetoric that had been issuing out of Washington since at least the time McKinley had fallen down on his knees to ask the Almighty for permission to take Manila.

Despite its many lapses in practice, the Good Neighbor policy replaced such a holy writ with not only tolerance but pragmatic pluralism. "Your Americanism and mine," was how Roosevelt conceded that there were many paths to progress—a rebuke to the one-size-fits-all "Americanism" that Ford was at that very moment trying to impose by sheer will on the Amazon jungle. With the rest of the world in crisis, negotiated trade treaties during this period not only set the U.S. on the road to economic recovery but fortified a bloc of corporations that provided key support for New Deal reforms and served as the engine of America's remarkable postwar boom. Roosevelt's liquidation of most of the remnants of direct U.S. imperialism (but not all: the Panama Canal zone remained in U.S. hands, as did the Philippines until 1946 and Puerto Rico to this day) was in many ways a final realization of Hay's ideal, allowing the United States to extend its power overseas through the alleviation of important sources of friction. But more than this, in an increasingly troubled and conflictive world, with war clouds gathering in Europe and Asia, it justified Washington's aspiration to global leadership. The Western Hemisphere provided an example of peaceful, cooperative international relations, one that repudiated the stultifying effects of formal colonialism while celebrating the creative promise of equitable capitalist expansion. As World War II wound down, Roosevelt often held up the "illustration of the Republics of this continent" as a model for postwar reconstruction.[57] Latin Americans obliged, using the values and ideas they developed fighting U.S. aggression to create a liberal multilateral order that, in turn, would allow the United States to achieve unprecedented power.

Latin America saved the United States from its own worst instincts. The United States, though, would not return the favor.

The End of the Affair

After World War II there was no region more willing to give up a degree of sovereignty and submit to Washington's leadership than Latin America. The United States repaid its deference with praise. "Here in the Western Hemisphere," said Harry S. Truman during a 1947 state visit to Mexico, "we have already achieved in substantial measure what the world as a whole must achieve. Through what we call our Inter-American System, which has become steadily stronger for half a century, we have learned to work together to solve our problems by friendly cooperation and mutual respect."

For the United States, Latin America may not have been the most politically important or most economically profitable region. But as Truman's comments highlight, the hemispheric alliance system provided a working blueprint—a model that U.S. diplomatic, intellectual, and military leaders followed to extend channels of authority and corporations used to establish chains of production, finance, and markets elsewhere, in Western Europe, East Asia, the Middle East, and Africa.[58] It was a flexible system of extraterritorial administration, one that allowed the United States, in the name of fighting Communism and promoting development, to structure the internal political and economic relations of allied countries in ways that allowed it to accrue more and more power and to exercise effective control over the supply of oil, ore, minerals, and other primary resources—all free from the burden of formal colonialism.

The inter-American alliance system also allowed Washington to undercut the authority of the new United Nations, helping to create what one historian has described as a "closed hemisphere" in an evermore "Open World."[59] Even as Harry Truman's envoys were working with delegates from around the world to create the structure and define the purpose of the United Nations, the United States was negotiating a mutual defense treaty with Latin America, empowering signatory nations to act collectively against outside aggression. Critics charged that the new military pact, formalized in Rio de Janeiro in 1947, would once again open the door to U.S. military intervention. Furthermore, by providing a precedent for the creation of a regional organization bound by its own set of rules and procedures outside of U.N. oversight, the Rio Pact, as the treaty was called, paved the way for both sides in the emerging Cold War to formalize their respective spheres of influence. NATO, for example, as well as the Southeast Asia Treaty Organization, were modeled directly on the Rio Pact.

Yet the goodwill that underwrote this "Inter-American System" quickly began to evaporate as Latin American reformers and nationalists pushed harder to make good on the promise of democracy and development offered by the Allied victory in World War II. While the system itself would remain in place, Washington, faced with mounting challenges to its authority, relied on increasing doses of hard power to enforce its dictates.

Starting in 1944, reform swept the continent, revitalizing old democracies in Chile and Colombia, among other places, and creating new ones in countries such as Guatemala, Peru, Argentina, and

Venezuela. Within two years, every Latin American country save Paraguay, El Salvador, Honduras, Nicaragua, and the Dominican Republic was operating under constitutional rule. Broad coalitions ranging from political liberals to Communists toppled dictators throughout the continent, while new reform governments extended the franchise, legalized unions, expanded public education, provided health care, and implemented social security programs.[60] The United States at first backed this process of democratization. But in 1947 Washington began to send signals that its preference for democrats over autocrats was now contingent on political stability.[61] Support for dictators like the Dominican Republic's Rafael Trujillo or Nicaragua's Anastasio Somoza (who after the marines withdrew executed Sandino and seized power) was no longer understood as the unwanted consequence of the principle of nonintervention. Rather, as a backstop against subversion, such support was now understood to be the centerpiece of U.S. policy toward Latin America.

One reason for this turnaround was, of course, the Cold War. Washington found that it greatly preferred anti-Communist dictatorships to the possibility that democratic openness might allow the Soviets to gain a foothold on the continent. Because of a "growing awareness of Soviet Russia's aggressive policy," wrote the State Department's Division of the American Republics, the United States now "swung back toward a policy of general cooperation [with dictators] that gives only secondary importance to the degree of democracy manifested by [Latin America's] respective governments."[62] Another reason was to protect investment, as democracy led to a wave of strikes calling for more humane standards of living, better wages, health care, social security, and land and labor reform. Threatened by escalating labor unrest, U.S. corporations demanded protection from Washington and stepped up their patronage of local conservative movements. For their part, Latin America's landed class, Catholic Church, and military took advantage of the United States's new Cold War policy to launch a continental counterrevolution, overturning newly democratic governments and forcing those constitutional regimes that survived to the right. By 1952, when Fulgencio Batista took power in a military coup in Cuba, nearly every democracy that had come into being in the postwar period was upended.

Moreover, by the early 1950s, Washington found that it was increasingly difficult merely to support dictators from the sidelines. The frustration of postwar democracy combined with increased political repression to radicalize a generation of young nationalists, who began to identify the United States not as a model but as an obstacle to reform. In the face of such growing opposition to its hemispheric authority, the United States began to take the lead in efforts to "arrest the development of irresponsibility and extreme nationalism," as Thomas Mann, Eisenhower's assistant secretary of state for inter-American affairs, wrote in 1952.[63] The first "arrest," as it were, carried out directly by the United States came two years later.

NOT HEARTS AND MINDS
BUT STOMACHS AND LIVERS

The CIA was established in 1947—the same year Washington served notice that its support for Latin American democracy was conditional on the maintenance of order—and began to develop contacts among military officers, religious leaders, and politicians it identified as bulwarks of stability. Yet it was not until 1954 that it would execute its first full-scale covert operation in Latin America, overthrowing Guatemalan president Jacobo Arbenz and installing a more pliant successor. Arbenz, as CIA analysts and most historians today admit, was trying to implement a New Deal–style economic program to modernize and humanize Guatemala's brutal plantation economy. His only crime was to expropriate, with full compensation, uncultivated United

Fruit Company land and legalize the Communist Party—both unacceptable acts from Washington's early-1950s vantage point.

Operation PBSUCCESS, as the CIA called its Guatemalan campaign, was the agency's most comprehensive covert action to date, much more ambitious than its operations in postwar Italy and France or in Iran the year before. Unlike the ouster of the Iranian prime minister, Mohammad Mossadeq, which took a mere couple of weeks, Arbenz's overthrow required nearly a year. In addition to destabilizing Guatemala's economy, isolating the country diplomatically through the OAS, and training a mercenary force in Honduras, the Guatemalan campaign gave CIA operatives the chance to try out new psych-war techniques gleaned from behavioral social sciences.[64] They worked with local agents to plant stories in the Guatemalan and U.S. press, engineer death threats, and conduct a bombing campaign—all designed to generate anxiety and uncertainty. They organized phantom groups, such as the "Organization of Militant Godless," and spread rumors that the government was going to ban Holy Week, exile the archbishop, confiscate bank accounts, expropriate all private property, and force children into reeducation centers. Operatives studied pop sociologies and grifter novels and worked closely with Edward Bernays, a pioneer in public propaganda (and Sigmund Freud's nephew), to apply disinformation tactics.[65] Borrowing from Orson Welles's *War of the Worlds*, they transmitted radio shows—taped in Florida and beamed in from Nicaragua—that made it seem as if a widespread underground resistance movement were gaining strength; they even managed to stage on-the-air battles.

In the 1950s, the Cold War was often presented as a battle of ideas, yet CIA agents on the ground didn't see it that way. They rejected the advice of their Guatemalan allies that the campaign include an educational component, instead insisting on a strategy intended to inspire fear more than virtue. Propaganda designed to "attack the theoretical foundations of the enemy" was misplaced, one field operative wrote; psychological efforts should be directed at the "heart, the stomach and the liver (fear)."[66] "We are not running a popularity contest but an uprising," rejoined one agent to Guatemalan concerns that the campaign was too negative. U.S. planes flew low over the capital, dropping propaganda material, which for a region that hadn't seen aerial warfare since the marine campaign against Sandino sent a message beyond what was printed on the flyers. "I suppose it doesn't really matter what the leaflets say," said Tracy Barnes, who led the operation.[67]

The "most effective leaflet drops during the operations," concluded a CIA postmortem of the coup, "were those followed by a successful military blow."[68] Such blows were delivered by CIA assets in country, who bombed roads, bridges, military installations, and property owned by government supporters. The agency distributed sabotage manuals that provided illustrated, step-by-step instructions on how to make pipe bombs, time bombs, remote fuses, chemical, nitroglycerine, and dynamite bombs, even explosives hidden in pens, books, and rocks. A how-to guide exhorted Guatemalans to take up violence in the name of liberty, noting that "sabotage, like all things in life, is good or bad depending on whether its objective is good or bad."[69]

Such a "terror program" worked. Arbenz fell not because psych ops had won the hearts and minds of the population but because the military refused to defend him, fearing Washington's wrath if it repelled the mercenaries.[70]

At least some American leaders were fully aware that the Guatemalan intervention marked a watershed in inter-American relations, and they did their best to limit its damage. Assistant Secretary of State Mann, for example, admitted in a private memo that CIA efforts to oust Arbenz represented Washington's first full-scale "violation of the Non-intervention Agreement," the "first of its kind since the establishment of the Good Neighbor Policy." Yet he hoped to hold on to the idea of the Good Neighbor policy, even as the United States corrupted its language and institutions. He therefore gave instructions that each step in the coup "should be justified on technical grounds" to allow the United States to claim plausibly that it was acting within the letter, if not the spirit, of Roosevelt's nonintervention pledge.[71]

But on the heels of Guatemala came Cuba in 1959, a revolution that the CIA found itself powerless to reverse—even though it modeled its 1961 Bay of Pigs invasion, which sought to topple Castro, on its earlier successful Guatemalan operation. Cuban revolutionaries learned well from the Guatemalan experience. Ernesto "Che" Guevara in fact was in Guatemala in 1954, having concluded his famous motorcycle tour of South America to work as a young, socially conscious doctor. He witnessed firsthand the effects of U.S. intervention, taking refuge in the Argentine embassy, where he would meet a number of other future Latin American revolutionaries. After a time cooling his heels, he won safe passage to Mexico, where he joined Fidel Castro's revolutionary movement in exile. "Cuba will not be Guatemala," he liked to taunt Washington.

Taken together, these two revolutions—one failed because of the United States, the other victorious against the United States—fell like a bomb on Latin America, polarizing politics throughout the hemisphere and inflaming a generation of activists. In Guatemala in the early 1950s, the idea of revolution could still mean working with nationalist, modernizing capitalists to follow the model of development laid out by the United States. In Cuba, five short years after the overthrow of Arbenz, revolution meant fighting tooth and claw against both the nationalist bourgeoisie and its imperialist patron. Following the Cuban Revolution, young leftists in one country after another began to form militant organizations, in some cases, such as in Venezuela, Guatemala, and Colombia, taking the step to organize armed rural insurgencies. Cuba tried to coordinate this revolutionary activity, providing military training and logistical support to would-be rebels. But the real threat of the Cuban Revolution resided in its status as a symbol of revolutionary sovereignty, like Sandino's David to the U.S. Goliath.

COMPLETING THE (COUNTER) REVOLUTION OF THE AMERICAS

John F. Kennedy came to office in early 1961, as this crisis was breaking. But Latin America was just the beginning of his troubles, for the young president inherited a world immensely more uncertain that the one bequeathed to his two predecessors, Harry S. Truman and Dwight D. Eisenhower. Beyond Latin America, in Africa, Asia, and the Middle East, European powers were abandoning their imperial holdings, often after having been forced out by protracted anticolonial insurgencies. They left in their wake vulnerable, impoverished, and war-ravaged societies that many observers feared would be susceptible to the political influence of the Soviet Union. Furthermore, decolonization took place in the shadow of rapid advances in the USSR's nuclear missile technology. The arms race recast the terms of the Cold War, making the United States and the USSR more powerful in absolute terms but weaker in relation to each other. Fear of retaliation prevented each country from using the threat of nuclear weapons to back up diplomatic negotiations, while at the same time making the last resort of diplomacy—conventional warfare—less effective. As a result, the outgoing Eisenhower administration came to hold a more sober assessment of the limits of U.S. power than did its Democratic predecessor, Truman, and soon-to-be successor, Kennedy. Ike distanced himself from the absolutist language of the early Cold War. As a lone atomic power, the United States could easily up the rhetorical heat, as it did in its 1950 National Security Council directive, which denounced the Kremlin's "slave state" as a metastasizing, expansionist evil whose "implacable purpose" was to destroy "freedom" and committed Washington's foreign policy to bring about a "fundamental change in the nature of the Soviet system."[72] The Republican president, in contrast, often reminded the electorate that nuclear war was not only unwinnable but unthinkable.

Kennedy, who campaigned in the 1960 presidential election as a committed militarist, entered the White House promising to establish a new foundation on which to ensure the continuance of American power in such changing times. His inaugural call that America was ready to "pay any price, bear any burden" revived a muscular internationalism that had atrophied. In addition to bringing in Robert McNamara from the Ford Motor Company to rationalize the Department of Defense, Kennedy and his civilian advisers looked to counterinsurgency and covert operations as a way of both breaking the nuclear deadlock and controlling the rise of third-world nationalism. Kennedy ordered the military to create a branch of the Special Forces that could operate with more flexibility in the third world and set up a "Special Group" in the White House, headed by General Maxwell Taylor, to coordinate special-warfare policy at the highest echelons of government—with the result that superpower conflict was detoured outside of Europe, particularly into Southeast Asia.

In Latin America, Kennedy's vaulting idealism led to the Alliance for Progress, an ambitious project that wedded the revolutionary and counterrevolutionary traditions of American diplomacy—as did Theodore Roosevelt and other missionary presidents of an earlier era—this time to especially toxic effect. Announcing the program to a room full of Latin American ambassadors soon after his inauguration, Kennedy sought to steal Castro's insurgent thunder, committing Washington to "completing the revolution of the Americas." He promised billions of dollars in development aid in exchange for enacting land, tax, judicial, and electoral reform aimed at breaking up extreme concentrations of economic and political power, "to build," as the president put it, "a hemisphere where all men can hope for a suitable standard of living and all can live out their lives in dignity and in freedom." "Let us once again transform the American Continent into a vast crucible of revolutionary ideas and efforts," Kennedy roared, "a tribute to the power of the creative energies of free men and women, an example to all the world that liberty and progress walk hand in hand. Let us once again awaken our American revolution until it guides the struggles of people everywhere—not with an imperialism of force or fear but the rule of courage and freedom and hope for the future of man."[73]

But while Kennedy's revolutionary rhetoric encouraged those who sought change, his actions empowered those who opposed it, the most illiberal forces in the hemisphere, men who despised democrats and political liberals as much as they hated card-carrying Communists. His administration committed the United States to strengthening the internal security capabilities of Latin American nations to protect against subversion, turning the region into a counterinsurgent laboratory. Advisers from the State and Defense Departments and the CIA worked to reinforce local intelligence operations, schooling security forces in interrogation and guerrilla warfare techniques, providing technology and equipment, and, when necessary, conducting preemptive coups. It was during this period that national intelligence agencies fortified and, in some cases, created by the United States—Argentina's Secretaria de Inteligencia del Estado, Chile's Dirección Nacional de Inteligencia, Brazil's Sistema Nacional de Informações, El Salvador's Agencia Nacional de Servicios Especiales—began to transform themselves into the command centers of the region's death-squad system, which throughout the 1970s and 1980s executed hundreds of thousands of Latin Americans and tortured tens of thousands more, including those Ford workers mentioned earlier. Millions were driven into exile. Throughout the worst of the repression, Washington nominally continued to support Latin America's "democratic left." But the most passionate defenders of liberalization and democracy were likely to be found in the ranks of Washington's opponents—and singled out for execution by Washington's allies.

⌄

As the story of Fordlandia that opened this chapter suggests, it is but a short step, when design doesn't conform to desire, from fantasy to terror. Kennedy and his advisers set out to remake Latin America with almost as little knowledge of the region as Ford had of the Amazon. The Alliance for Progress was based on the supposed appeal the idea of America held for the world. Kennedy offered money—upward of ten billion dollars—but little of it was forthcoming, except the portion that went to build the network of death-squad paramilitaries. JFK believed he could "awaken the American revolution" in the Americas while at the same time containing its threat by arming those most opposed to even the mildest goals of such a revolution. But of course he couldn't. Faced with a choice between containment and change, Washington, as it did in the late 1940s, chose containment. Lyndon B. Johnson and then Richard M. Nixon kept Kennedy's commitment to counterinsurgent funding. But they tossed out his revolutionary ambitions, as well as the pledge to reform the continent's "ancient institutions that perpetuate privilege."[74] It was under Johnson's watch that the United States began to shift the balance of its Latin American diplomacy away from development toward the interests of private capital. Increasingly, economic reform in Latin America meant not industrialization and socially responsible investment but lower tariffs on U.S. exports and lower tax rates on U.S. profits, a policy that would come to full bloom under Ronald Reagan. It was also under Johnson that Washington began either to organize or patronize a cycle of coups— starting in Brazil in 1964, continuing through Uruguay, Bolivia, and Chile, and ending in Argentina in 1976—that completed not the revolution, as Kennedy promised, but the counterrevolution of South America, turning the region into a garrison continent.

By the 1970s, then, the United States had run the gamut of imperial strategies in Latin America, more than once turning full circle from missionary idealism to hardheaded militarism. To its own good fortune, opposition to American hard power had compelled

Washington to elaborate the institutions and ideas that made possible its diplomatic triumphs in the years after World War II. Most importantly, the Good Neighbor policy generated the model for the postwar alliance system, a system that allowed Washington to delegate responsibility for extraterritorial administration to allies while accruing for itself considerable economic, political, and military leverage. Leadership against the Soviet Union in the Cold War allowed the United States to justify its position of predominance in this system, creating the conditions whereby it could present its particular interests as the world's general interests. This ability formed the core of American soft power.

Held in check by superpower nuclear rivalry, the United States would maintain this system in Europe through the end of the Cold War. But in its own hemisphere, where its power after World War II quickly grew unrivaled, Washington first diluted and then, in all but name, dispensed with the multilateralism that made U.S. ascension possible in the first place, opting for a unilateralism that an odd coalition of idealists, religionists, and militarists today dares to replicate on a global scale.[75] For their part, corporations, starting in the mid-1960s, despite their nominal support for a socially responsible capitalism, increasingly opposed any serious effort by Latin Americans to implement a humane model of economic development, supporting coups, dictators, and even, in some cases, death squads, to quell labor unrest.

Neoimperialist historians like Max Boot and Niall Ferguson now dismiss FDR's Good Neighbor policy as an effort to "dress up" what they say was a failure to embrace America's imperial destiny and to carry through on exporting liberal political institutions to Latin America.[76] They also criticize Roosevelt's nonintervention policy as paving the way for the rise of dictators like Nicaragua's Somoza. For them, the history of the United States in Latin America suggests not the instruction of limits but the imperative of transcending limits. "The only thing more unsavory than U.S. intervention," writes Boot, "is U.S. nonintervention."[77] But repeatedly throughout the twentieth century, tenacious Latin American resistance to imperial militarism taught Washington policy makers that American power did, in fact, have limits. It is a credit to midcentury statesmen that they were able to use this knowledge in a way that propelled the United States to unparalleled heights of global power.

Twice in the last century, Washington looked to Latin America to regroup after setbacks limited its global reach. The first time, as we saw, was in the 1930s, with the felicitous result serving the United States well. The second came in the 1980s. As the foremost challenge to America's self-understanding as a just and humanitarian hegemon, Latin America was bound to be the place where Washington, increasingly influenced by the nationalist backlash caused by defeat in Vietnam, would try not only to rearm the Cold War militarily but to reload it ideologically. It is to this rearmament that we now turn.

CHAPTER TWO

The Most Important Place in the World: Toward a New Imperialism

A MERICA'S VITAL INTERESTS AND our deepest beliefs are now one." So declared George W. Bush in his second inaugural address, capturing in a single phrase the philosophical foundation of his post-9/11 global policy: the claim that the best way to ensure America's security is to spread democracy throughout the world. At the end of the day, after all other rationales for the invasion and occupation of Iraq have been proven false, it is this explanation that Bush inevitably falls back on. "The defense of freedom," he insists, "requires the advance of freedom."

There has been much discussion about what to call this curious mix of realism—an unapologetic assertion that it is Washington's right to use preemptive violence to respond to perceived threats—and idealism, a belief that it is "America's duty," in Bush's words, to extend liberty throughout the world.[1] Some identify this position as "hard Wilsonianism," an embrace of Woodrow Wilson's democratic idealism but a rejection of his faith in international organizations and treaties.[2] Others have dubbed it "democratic realism."[3]

Whatever it is called, most observers view the Bush Doctrine as a sharp break from the liberal internationalism of the Cold War period while admitting that it has deep roots in America's political culture. Both idealism and militarism, after all, enjoy venerable pedigrees within the annals of U.S. diplomacy. What is new, at least for the modern American state, is how intimately the two impulses have been bound together, for not since the days of Teddy Roosevelt has the United States so openly championed martial virtue and violence as the best way to spread universal rights. And it certainly is new for the modern Republican Party, dominated as it was until recently by pragmatists and realists, internationalists like Henry Kissinger, who believed that the central task of his diplomatic career was to dampen the messianic zeal that marked the early Cold War period, zeal that marched the United States straight into the muck of Vietnam. Just a few decades ago, Republicans were presided over by a president, Richard Nixon, with a deeply jaundiced view of the ability of poor, undeveloped countries to govern themselves democratically, to say nothing of his low opinion of America's domestic civic institutions. Yet today the party is led by men and women eager to use American military power to spread liberty to the "darkest corners of our world."

Commentators have had difficulty accounting for this turnaround. Pundits correctly identify a rhetorical shift taking place during Ronald Reagan's presidency, reflecting his efforts to restore America's pride and purpose after the melancholy 1970s. They note Reagan's championing of Soviet and Eastern European dissidents. Others focus on the rise of the neoconservatives and their recasting of the Cold War as a struggle between the forces of good and evil, exemplified by Paul Wolfowitz's celebrated role in convincing Reagan to force Ferdinand Marcos in the Philippines to step down and make way for free elections, a remarkable about-face for an administration that had long embraced the dictator. Yet they consistently ignore the one place where Republicans turned themselves into hard Wilsonians. It was in Central America where faith in American righteousness to justify a renewed militarism easily morphed into the kind of idealism that now motivates the neoconservatives.

Doing It Their Way

The first part of Richard M. Nixon's 1958 vice presidential tour of Latin America was mostly uneventful, although Peru offered a hint of what was to come when students stoned Nixon during his visit to the national university. His handlers were nervous about Venezuela, the scheduled last stop on the tour. Just a few months earlier, popular protests had put to an end a ten-year Washington-backed dictatorship, which had given lucrative contracts to American mining and oil interests. And Eisenhower's granting of asylum to a number of the old regime's most hated officials, including the head of the murderous National Security Police, did nothing to ease tensions between Washington and the new democratic government. But buoyed by pro-American rallies that took place in a number of cities, the vice president insisted that the trip continue as planned.

Stepping out of his DC–6 onto the tarmac, Nixon, along with his wife, Pat, was confronted with an angry crowd that had assembled on the balcony of the terminal, screaming "Go home," "Get out, dog," and "We won't forget Guatemala"—a reference to the U.S.-orchestrated overthrow of that country's democratically elected president four years earlier.[4] Members of Nixon's entourage had to pass under the balcony to get to their motorcade and when they did a torrent of spit fell on them that some of the stricken at first thought was rain. On the highway out of the airport, hostile drivers tried to sideswipe the vice president's limousine. Upon entering Caracas's narrow city streets, the motorcade was surrounded by a mob and attacked with sticks, rocks, and steel pipes. Nixon was eventually rescued, but not before his Secret Service detachment drew their guns and not before Eisenhower readied the armed forces to evacuate his vice president if need be. An embassy official later surveyed the limousine and remarked that "it was hard to believe that that black Cadillac with diplomatic license plates 63–CD had borne the Vice President of the United States. The rear windows were shattered, sputum was all over it and the windshield was just a white smear as the driver had tried to remove the spit with the wipers."[5] After holing up at the U.S. ambassador's residence, Nixon left the next day "through a tear gas mist"—the streets had been preemptively gassed to prevent demonstrators from gathering.

The attack on Nixon was in a way the United States's induction into open confrontation with the third world. Washington of course already had a long experience in the Caribbean and Central America. After World War II, it had put down the Huk rebellion in the Philippines, fought a war in Korea, overthrown governments in Iran and Guatemala, and deployed military advisers to South Vietnam. Yet for a country basking in the long afterglow of liberating Western Europe from Nazism and enjoying more than a decade of unprecedented economic growth and cultural influence, Caracas was something different. Nixon's military aide remarked that not even combat in the Korean War had prepared him for the "hate and unrelenting fury that was unleashed on us" in Venezuela.[6] The event was widely covered in the American press, with Nixon, after a short layover in Puerto Rico to give the White House time to prepare for his arrival, receiving a hero's welcome.[7] Pundits and scholars began to ask, specifically now of the third world, a question that continues to puzzle opinion makers to this day: "Why do they hate us?" The United States would go on thinking of America as an anticolonial power, but elsewhere in the world many now condemned U.S. policy as imperialism—informal as opposed to the European variety but imperialism nonetheless.

After the assault on Nixon came the 1959 Cuban Revolution and the 1964 Canal Zone riots in Panama, along with armed left insurgencies throughout South and Central America. "Castro-itis," diagnosed CIA director Allen Dulles, was spreading throughout Latin America. As we saw in the last chapter, John F. Kennedy's response—not just to trouble in the Western Hemisphere but to the broader challenge that nuclear rivalry and decolonization posed—was to resurrect the crusading language of the early Cold War while deflecting it onto the third world. He committed the United States to undertaking counterinsurgency operations wherever necessary and to extending the promise of the American Revolution to the rest of the world, to blazing a third way between colonialism and Communism. Coming late in Kennedy's short tenure, the 1962 Cuban missile crisis—which new documents reveal brought the world much closer to nuclear war than has been previously acknowledged—tempered Kennedy's initial eagerness and revealed the Soviet Union to be not an existential evil but a nation-state with a set of coherent security interests and concerns. But it was too late to prevent the escalation of the war in Vietnam, where Kennedy had staked America's reputation on building a liberal democratic nation. While in its own hemisphere the United States would largely stick to its original counterinsurgency guidelines of working to strengthen the "internal defense" of allied governments, in the years after Kennedy's assassination his successors Lyndon B. Johnson and Nixon would dig themselves further and further into Southeast Asia. The ensuing disaster discredited America throughout the world, disillusioned liberal allies, and united a disparate, internationalist left in condemning U.S. policy. Washington's massive yet fruitless bombing campaigns, napalm, massacres, and assassinations did great damage to its moral authority and raised doubts about its strategic capability.

Détente was Nixon and Kissinger's attempt to respond to this crisis by a return to classic balance-of-power realism. By normalizing relations with the USSR and China—including recognizing the right of each to deal with "internal problems" as they saw fit—Washington was able to play one off the other, forcing both to help the United States extricate itself from Vietnam. A negotiated withdrawal, occurring as soon as possible, was crucial if Washington was to maintain global influence. (In the late 1960s and early 1970s, as the U.S. economy began to feel the effects of increased global competition, many Fortune 500 corporations backed a normalization of global politics in the hopes of opening up the Soviet bloc to U.S. capital—a point that will be taken up in greater detail in chapter 5).

As the architect of détente, Kissinger studiously avoided the moralism that had defined both the early Cold War and Kennedy's short tenure. During his time first as Nixon's national security adviser and then as secretary of state, he worked to replace the inspirational cadences of JFK's inaugural speech with the prose of "business-like cooperation" between Moscow and Washington and closed-door deal making in which each party recognized the authority and legitimacy of the other.[8] In May 1972, Richard Nixon and Leonid Brezhnev signed the first Strategic Arms Limitation Treaty. Later that year, Nixon and Kissinger took important steps to normalize relations with Communist China. Rather than claiming the moral obligation to project its power into the Soviet world, the United States promised to respect the security interests of the USSR and the global division of influence. Domestically, détente was designed to outflank the antiwar left, which was increasingly influencing the national debate. According to journalist James Mann, Kissinger became "preoccupied with the threats to his foreign policy from the political left," from the "forces rising out of the Vietnam antiwar movement and the 1972 Democratic campaign of George McGovern, which sought to cut back on American power and troop deployments overseas."[9] As Kissinger saw it, "refusing to negotiate with the Kremlin would spread the virulence of the anti-Vietnam protest movement into every aspect of American foreign policy, and deeply, perhaps, into our alliances."

In recognition that the United States's "impotent reaction" to being pushed out of Vietnam would not go unnoticed by the rest of the world, Kissinger's détente was designed to allow the superpowers to shore up their authority in their respective spheres of influence.[10] Southeast Asia was lost, but Africa, particularly southern Africa with the end of Portuguese colonialism in 1975, remained contested as both the USSR and the United States worked through allied states and insurgencies to tip that continent's balance of power to their favor. In the heart of the Middle East, American power rested on the four great cornerstones of Iraq, Iran, Saudi Arabia, and Israel, radiating outward, through enormous infusions of economic aid, to Turkey, Egypt, and Pakistan.

Latin America, Cuba aside, belonged wholesale to Washington: "We want to keep it," said Nixon.[11] Through Nixon's one and a half terms, the cycle of South American coups that began during the Johnson administration continued apace, terminating, often with U.S. help, democratic governments in Uruguay, Chile, Ecuador, and Bolivia. As president, Nixon, perhaps because of his 1958 near-death experience, never visited Latin America. But this didn't stop him from appreciating the region's newfound political conversion. "Latin America's had 150 years of trying at it," he observed in late 1971, "and they don't have much going on down there." But unlike in the "black countries" of Africa, its leaders at least knew how to maintain stability. "They at least do it their way," he said. "It is an orderly way which at least works relatively well. They have been able to run the damn place."[12]

Nixon's praise of Latin American dictators, therefore, was not just personal opinion but conveyed the essence of the Nixon Doctrine, which charged the security forces in each country with keeping their own house in order—not unlike Kennedy's promotion of counterinsurgency in the third world but stripped of its ennobling rhetoric about development and democracy. "We must deal realistically with governments in the inter-American system as they are," said the president in 1969.[13] In 1976, Argentina fell to a military junta, bringing the cycle of South American coups to completion. The entire Southern Cone and most of the continent were now ruled by anti-Communist dictatorships. Kissinger, who continued as secretary of state in the Ford administration after Nixon's resignation, gave the Argentine coup his blessing: "We have followed events in Argentina closely, we wish the new government well," he said to its plotters, "we wish it will succeed. We will do what we can to help it succeed."[14] Sounding not too little like Machiavelli—or Tony Soprano—Kissinger advised the junta that "if there are things that have to be done, you should do them quickly."

CHILE AND THE END OF THE NIXON DOCTRINE

Happy with the political direction Latin America was moving in, Nixon was caught off guard when he learned in late 1970 that Chileans had elected the Marxist Salvador Allende president. "That son of a bitch, that son of a bitch," screamed Nixon. When the president noticed his startled ambassador to Chile, he calmed down and said, "Not you, Mr. Ambassador. . . . It's that bastard Allende." He then commenced a seven-minute monologue on how he was going to "smash Allende."[15] He instructed the CIA to "make the economy scream," and over the next three years, Washington spent millions of dollars to destabilize Chile and prod its military to act. It finally did on September 11, 1973, in a coup that brought Augusto Pinochet's seventeen-year-long regime to power.

The overthrow of Allende was a quintessential expression of détente, which sought to eliminate any and all threats to the bipolar world then being designed by the United States and the USSR. Allende's Popular Unity government rejected both Soviet-style suppression of civil liberties and American economic dominance, believing it could steer Chile down a peaceful road to socialism while maintaining political freedoms. Chile's challenge, therefore, was not that it would be turned into another Castro-style dictatorship but that it wouldn't. "I don't think anybody ever fully grasped that Henry [Kissinger] saw Allende as being a far more serious threat than Castro," remarked one NSC staffer. "If Latin America ever became unraveled, it would never happen with a Castro. Allende was a living example of democratic social reform in Latin America. All kinds of cataclysmic events rolled around, but Chile scared him."[16] Another aide recalled that his boss feared that the effects of Allende's election would spill over into Western Europe, particularly into Italy, where the Communist Party had broken with Moscow and was trying to chart a middle path similar to Allende's. "The fear," according to Seymour Hersh in his biography of Kissinger, "was not only that Allende would be voted into office, but that—after his six-year term—the political process would work and he would be voted out of office in the next election. Kissinger saw the notion that Communists could participate in the electoral process and accept the results peacefully as the wrong message to send Italian voters."

But much had changed since 1954, when the CIA could overthrow Guatemalan president Jacobo Arbenz with little scrutiny, even though the agency left more than a few footprints indicating its involvement. Chile was different. Taking place as the United States was losing Vietnam and as the Watergate crisis unfolded, the CIA's 1973 role in Chile was impossible to hide from both an angry Congress and a skeptical press corps. In September 1974, the *New York Times* published a series of articles by Seymour Hersh based partly on classified documents leaked by a member of the House of Representatives detailing the role of the American government and of American business interests, including International Telephone and Telegraph, in Allende's downfall. The series spurred Congress to investigate the matter further.[17] Nixon's own 1974 ouster fed the feeding frenzy, and many of his top aides, including CIA director

Richard Helms, testified that the president personally ordered the overthrow of Allende.[18] In 1975, a Senate committee chaired by Frank Church released the findings of its investigation into the CIA's central role in Allende's downfall.

Chile was just the tip of the iceberg. The Church Committee investigated covert government activities throughout the third world, producing fourteen volumes dense with facts documenting the CIA's ties to the Mafia, involvement in coups, attempts to assassinate foreign leaders throughout the third world, and improper storage of toxic material.[19] At the same time, a committee chaired by Nelson Rockefeller released its report on covert activity within the United States, finding that the agency had infiltrated political organizations, run experiments with behavior-changing drugs on unknowing subjects, and carried out illegal surveillance of political activists. Congressional investigations exposed the FBI's harassment of leaders such as Martin Luther King. The bureau not only kept tabs on individuals it deemed a threat but engaged in illegal covert actions designed to provoke violence that would discredit the civil rights and antiwar movements and divide their memberships.[20]

Vietnam, Watergate, and revelations about abuses conducted in the name of national security contributed to an upheaval in America's political culture. Nixon and Kissinger's cavalier attitude toward ethical concerns became increasingly unviable, as the fallout from the war and the rise of antimilitarist opposition compelled both the Democratic and Republican parties to work to reestablish U.S. diplomacy on a moral foundation. Increasingly, dissidents held the United States and the USSR equally responsible for the Cold War and nuclear proliferation. Rejecting an interpretation of U.S. history as a progressive unfolding of political freedom, they focused instead on the darker side of America's rise to world power, on the connection between racial violence and poverty at home with militarism and economic imperialism abroad—a perspective now confirmed by no less an authority than Congress itself. The Watergate scandal revealed something more damning than the criminal behavior of a president and his top aides. It exposed Nixon's pathological style, providing an archetype of the politician not as moral leader but as paranoid conspirator that could be endlessly recycled through popular culture, in movies, songs, and books. All this knowledge combined to create something more powerful than organized dissent. It formed—even after the end of the Vietnam War and Nixon's resignation led to the dispersal of the peace movement—a permanent antimilitarist opposition, never a majority but, until recently, heavy enough to provide a counterweight to the kind of soaring rhetoric that justified the early Cold War.

In the mid-1970s it seemed that this opposition would, as Kissinger feared, gain political power. In 1974, seventy-four Democrats—the largest freshman class since 1948—joined an already Democratic-majority Congress determined to strengthen its oversight of the executive branch and rein in the intelligence community.[21]

The Ninety-third Congress (1973–75) was perhaps the most anti-imperial legislature in United States history, passing a series of measures that, for many of its members, were designed to repudiate American militarism. The 1973 War Powers Act gave Congress the power to review, and reverse, executive decisions to send troops abroad. For the first time ever, the intelligence system was placed under the supervision of Congress: the 1974 Hughes-Ryan Amendment required that the CIA inform up to eight congressional committees of its covert operations; two years later, the Senate, followed by the House, created a permanent committee to monitor intelligence activity. In 1975, Congress upgraded the already existing Freedom of Information Act with a powerful enforcement mechanism and abolished the Un-American Activities Committee, which had been operating under a new name, the Internal Security Committee. In 1976, the Clark Amendment banned Washington from supporting anti-Communist rebels in Angola, while Attorney General Edward Levi issued new guidelines that ruled out domestic covert operations. In 1976, Gerald Ford signed Executive Order 11905, prohibiting peacetime assassinations of foreign leaders. Between 1974 and 1976, Congress cut military aid to Turkey and placed limits on assistance to South Korea, Chile, and Indonesia. During this period, Congress also gave itself the power to review and veto proposed major arms sales and shuttered the Office of Public Safety, a government agency implicated in torture and other human rights abuses in the third world.

Before Jimmy Carter made "human rights" the centerpiece of his diplomatic policy, young reformist congressional Democrats such as Tom Harkin of Iowa, Ed Koch of New York, and Donald Fraser of Minnesota attempted to transform the Cold War liberal moralism of Truman and Kennedy into an ethical concern for the immediate suffering caused by Washington's national security policies. Latin America, where the United States had the greatest influence and the Soviet Union the least, was the natural venue to try out efforts to make human rights a foreign policy concern. They focused on dictatorships in Uruguay, Brazil, Argentina, and Chile and on the civil wars of Central America, which were then just beginning to gain the attention of the U.S. press.[22] In 1976, during Gerald Ford's administration, the reformists scored their first major victory when Koch pushed through an amendment that ended aid to Uruguay. In retaliation, Pinochet's secret police hatched a plan to assassinate the New York congressman—not an idle threat considering that in that same year Chilean agents executed the Allende official Orlando Letelier, along with his assistant, Ronni Moffitt, with a car bomb in Washington's Dupont Circle.[23]

Despite this unprecedented run of cuts, prohibitions, abolitions, and inquiries, Kissinger's assessment of the strength of American antimilitarism was greatly overstated. There remained in Congress more than a few conservative and moderate Democrats, not to mention Republicans, willing to extend the executive branch slack when it came to national security. The Democratic New Deal electoral coalition, which had set domestic and international policy since 1933, was breaking down under the simultaneous pressures exerted by opposition to the war and the rise of social movements demanding racial justice and equal rights for women. The more formidable reaction to the defeat in Vietnam would come from the right.

VIETNAM, DÉTENTE, AND THE NEW RIGHT

As with the New Left, the Vietnam War radicalized the New Right. However, while for the Democratic Party this led to fragmentation of its different constituencies, for the Republicans it furthered consolidation. The diverse groups that made up the conservative coalition pursued many, often contradictory, objectives, yet they came together over the need to restore America's authority in the world and they increasingly understood this authority in military terms.

During the 1970s, a young generation of "civilian militarists," as political scientist Chalmers Johnson describes them, began to exert ever greater influence on foreign policy, first within the White House during the Ford interregnum and then from outside the Carter administration, manning the ramparts of the growing number of think tanks and lobbying groups—the Committee on the Present Danger, the Committee for a Free Congress, the Committee for the Free World, the Committee to Maintain a Prudent Defense Policy— dedicated to defense and foreign policy issues.[24] They were more bellicose than the professional soldiers, not only to prove their mettle but to overcome what they felt was a crippling caution instilled in the ranks of the military by Vietnam. Among this group were many of today's most prominent hawks, including Robert Kagan, Elliott Abrams, and Paul Wolfowitz. Committing themselves to reversing détente, which they derided both for making undue concessions to the Soviet Union and for repudiating America's providential role in world history, they set their sights on its draftsman.

By the time of Nixon's 1974 resignation, Kissinger, untainted by Watergate, had amassed power and prestige, staying on in Gerald Ford's administration as both national security adviser and secretary of state. He fully expected the global diplomatic framework that he helped put in place to continue to mature. Focused as he was on the threat from liberal Democrats, Kissinger was blindsided from the right. Donald Rumsfeld, Ford's secretary of defense, and Dick Cheney, Ford's chief of staff, joined forces to undercut Kissinger's power and derail a new Strategic Arms Limitation Treaty with Russia. Cheney even managed to convince Ford that he should include in the Republican Party platform a "morality plank" proposed by Ronald Reagan in his 1976 challenge for the Republican nomination. The plank was a slap at Kissinger, repudiating his diplomatic philosophy in unmistakable terms. It criticized the "undue concessions" and "secret agreements" that had taken place under détente and called for a global stance motivated not by power politics but by a "belief in the rights of man, the rule of law and guidance by the hand of God." By the time Jimmy Carter entered the White House in 1977, détente had all but dropped out of the political lexicon of the Republican Party.

With détente out of the way, conservatives turned against the antimilitarism that had seeped into the Democratic Party, with Carter's presidency serving as a lightning rod to help advance the New Right agenda. Soon after his inauguration in 1976, Jimmy Carter pardoned draft resisters, declared human rights to be the moral compass of his foreign policy, and announced that America was "now free of that inordinate fear of communism which once led us to embrace any dictator who joined us in that fear." It seemed as if, as Kissinger had feared, the peace movement that had emerged in the wake of Vietnam was setting the national agenda.

But much more than his predecessor, Gerald Ford, Carter had to deal with the fallout of defeat in Southeast Asia. Widespread domestic and international distrust of Washington's motives, demands to cut the defense budget and reform intelligence operations, calls to scale back overseas commitments all combined to limit his foreign policy options. Critics derided his responses to a series of crises, including revolutions in Iran and Nicaragua, hostage taking in the Middle East, the Soviet invasion of Afghanistan, and Marxist insurgencies in Africa and Central America. Chronic inflation and gas shortages contributed to a general feeling that America was in decline. Carter's supposed willingness to, in the words of Jeane Kirkpatrick, "negotiate anything with anyone anywhere" only confirmed to conservatives their critique of détente, which had devolved, as they had warned it would, into acquiescence and appeasement.[25] Conservatives attacked Carter's stated concern for human rights, which they claimed he applied more to allies like South Africa than to foes like Cuba, as a symptom of a larger malady. It was nothing less than a manifestation of a crisis of confidence in the principles and values that made America great.

But while Carter's incoherent presidency allowed militarists to sharpen their knives, a number of his actual policies facilitated the rearming of the Cold War that his successor would execute in full. It was Carter, not Reagan, who began to increase the military budget at the expense of domestic social services. It was Carter who first proposed the creation of a Rapid Deployment Force to be dispatched into trouble spots outside of Europe, designed, according to his NSC adviser Zbigniew Brzezinski, to strike "pre-emptively" against brewing trouble.[26] It was Carter who initiated support for the mujahedeen in Afghanistan six months *prior* to Moscow's 1979 invasion.[27] Such support, Brzezinski recently admitted, was meant to provoke the invasion and drag the USSR into its own Vietnam-style quagmire.[28] It was also Carter who began America's more active military engagement in the Persian Gulf, threatening in his last State of the Union address to defend the region "by any means necessary." And while conservative detractors belittled his human rights diplomacy, America's first born-again Christian president did reinvest foreign policy with a sense of ethical principle—an investment that his successor, Ronald Reagan, successfully exploited.

Reagan's 1980 election gave the first generation of fledgling hawks an opportunity to occupy influential if not publicly prominent roles in his administration. Drawn from think tanks, universities, and the defense industry, they often had no actual expertise in specific regional areas, but all were broadly dedicated to restoring a sense of national purpose, which, in their minds, inevitably meant a restoration of military power. Here began the isolation and purging of regional experts in the CIA and the State Department who might suggest a more nuanced policy. As head of the State Department's policy planning staff, for instance, Wolfowitz replaced nearly all of the staff's twenty-five members with neoconservative allies—familiar names such as Francis Fukuyama, Alan Keyes, and Lewis "Scooter" Libby—many of whom were recruited from his former teaching posts at Cornell and the University of Chicago.[29]

Joining these civilian militarists was a generation of Vietnam vets politicized by their time in Southeast Asia. Many of the New Right's most committed cadres, such as Oliver North, Richard Secord, John Singlaub, and Richard Armitage, had served multiple tours of duty, bringing their firsthand experience of defeat to their work as midlevel analysts and operatives in the shadowy front lines of foreign policy. Armitage, for instance, played a role in the CIA's infamous Phoenix program in Vietnam, which was accused by the same congressional committee that exposed the U.S. role in Chile of executing tens of thousands of South Vietnamese civilians. Armitage served as point man for third-world low-intensity warfare operations during his tenure as Reagan's assistant secretary for international security affairs, developing close relations with Pakistan's Interservices Intelligence Directorate and the jihadists of Afghanistan's anti-Soviet mujahedeen.[30] Others, such as Singlaub, mostly stayed out of government service, instead influencing public policy through the development of a thick international and interlocking network of anti-Communist associates, political pressure groups, and think tanks.

Bound together not by their knowledge of the world but by a devotion to American power, members of this new "strategic class," either from within the government or without, in think tanks and magazines that now had the administration's ear, were committed to reorienting diplomacy, as Chalmers Johnson notes, to "policies in which military preparedness"—and, one might add, a generic belligerent response no matter what the specifics of the crisis— "becomes the highest priority of state."[31] The United States, they insisted, was called to a higher purpose and Washington should pursue a global agenda more certain of its values, one not so eager to truck with Communist regimes. It meant confronting the idea that U.S. strength was in decline—which, paradoxically, often entailed promoting the idea that it was in decline so as to rouse politicians to action. It meant not only blocking efforts to cut defense spending but reversing cuts that had already been made, through the promiscuous support of any and all weapons systems. It meant weakening congressional power and reversing or undercutting legislative reforms designed to monitor the executive branch and intelligence system. And it meant a restoration of the authority, legitimacy, and secrecy of the government in general and the presidency in particular.

Ronald Reagan promised to restore American power in the world, yet the complexities of that world forced a degree of pragmatism and caution on him, and he continued to work within the established international diplomatic framework. He did ratchet up the rhetoric by branding the USSR an "evil empire," musing openly about the inevitability of "Armageddon" and the possibility of a "winnable nuclear war." During a radio broadcast, Reagan quipped— perhaps unaware that he was on the air but perhaps not—that he had "signed legislation that will outlaw Russia forever. We begin bombing in five minutes." Yet he advanced arms-control negotiations beyond anything Kissinger could have hoped to attain.

Reagan even refused to act against Cuba. When his first secretary of state, Alexander Haig, told him at an NSC meeting that "you just give me the word and I'll turn that fucking island into a parking lot," Reagan demurred.[32] In South America, Reagan was lucky to have inherited a largely pacified continent, as nearly every country south of Costa Rica was secure under the thumb of dictators, of the kind lauded by Nixon and encouraged by Kissinger. He had to do little but restore aid and diplomatic relations.

But closer to home, in a number of small Central American countries, a crisis was looming that would help forge the ideas and alliances of the gathering internationalist New Right. Up until the late 1970s, Guatemala, El Salvador, and Nicaragua were ruled, as was most of Latin America, by corrupt, deadly, but pro-American dictatorships. But in 1979, the Nicaraguan regime fell to the leftist Sandinistas, with the State Department worrying that El Salvador and Guatemala, also challenged by armed insurgencies, would soon follow. With little geopolitical importance, few consequential allies, and no significant resources, these countries afforded the White House an opportunity to match its actions with its rhetoric. While Reagan in effect carried on détente everywhere else in all but name, in Central America, all bets were off.

THE MOST IMPORTANT PLACE IN THE WORLD

Just as Paul Wolfowitz, Richard Perle, and think tanks such as the Project for a New American Century laid the groundwork for the 2003 war in Iraq long before George W. Bush took office, conservative rhetoricians outside the political establishment charted the path Ronald Reagan would take in Central America during his predecessor's reign. In a series of articles and manifestos, a group of disaffected hawks challenged Jimmy Carter's Central American policy, which they held responsible for the triumph of Nicaragua's Sandinista revolution. Months before Reagan's November 1980 election, would-be policy makers organized the ad hoc Committee of Santa Fe—one of the many groups formed by conservative activists in the 1970s to deal with foreign policy issues, this one specifically related to Latin America—to produce the document "A New Inter-American Policy for the Eighties."

In the same way that Wolfowitz's 1992 Defense Planning Guidance papers—which envisioned a United States so overwhelmingly powerful that no rival would think to challenge it and justified the right of the United States to respond preemptively to emerging threats—would later be dismissed as too extreme, so was the committee's 1980 manifesto repudiated. Yet a number of its authors took important midlevel posts in Reagan's White House. Roger Fontaine became director of Latin American affairs in the National Security Council. Lewis Tambs, a professor of Latin American history at Arizona State University, was made ambassador to Costa Rica, where he worked with Oliver North to organize the Contras' southern front.[33] And retired Lieutenant General Gordon Sumner served as special assistant to the assistant secretary of state for inter-American affairs.

"A New Inter-American Policy for the Eighties" is a classic example of New Right rhetorical action. It sounds familiar themes of Soviet expansion, American weakness, and looming ideological and moral conflict calculated to raise alarm and steel will. It opens by declaring that "war, not peace, is the norm in international relations." Diplomacy is a zero-sum power game in which the end is not international stasis but the advancement of national interest: "WWIII is almost over," the Soviets are on the march, and America is "everywhere in retreat." The crisis confronting the United States, the manifesto intones, is not just strategic but "metaphysical." The "inability or unwillingness" of America "either to protect or project its basic values and beliefs has led to the present nadir of indecision and impotence and has placed the very existence of the Republic in peril."

The Santa Fe manifesto explicitly presented Latin America—alternately described as "America's Balkans," its "exposed southern flank," and its "soft underbelly"—as the place where the United

States could "salvage" a foreign policy wrecked in Vietnam. Less than a decade earlier, Nixon had hailed Latin America as a paragon of stability. Republican presidential platforms in 1972 and 1976, aside from obligatory condemnations of Castro and calls to retain control of the Panama Canal, barely mentioned Latin America. But the Central American insurgencies once again put the region on the map. Jesse Helms inserted into the 1980 platform a lengthy discussion of Nicaragua, Guatemala, El Salvador, and Honduras. Jeane Kirkpatrick took to calling Central America "the most important place in the world for the United States."[34] "Colossally important," she insisted, to "vital national interests."[35]

Once in office, Reagan came down hard on Central America, in effect letting his administration's most committed militarists set and execute policy. In El Salvador, over the course of a decade, they provided more than a million dollars a day to fund a lethal counterinsurgency campaign. In Nicaragua, they patronized the Contras, a brutal insurgency led by discredited remnants of the deposed dictator's national guard designed to roll back the Sandinista revolution. In Guatemala, they pressed to reestablish military aid to an army that was in the middle of committing genocide, defending the country's born-again president even as he was presiding over the worst slaughter in twentieth-century Latin America. All told, U.S. allies in Central America during Reagan's two terms killed over 300,000 people, tortured hundreds of thousands, and drove millions into exile.

Reagan could afford to execute such a calamitous policy not, pace Kirkpatrick, because of the region's importance but because of its unimportance. The fallout that resulted from a hard line there could be, if not managed, then easily ignored. Unlike the Middle East, Central America had no oil or other crucial resources. Nor did Washington's opponents in the small, desperately poor countries have many consequential friends. Unlike Southeast Asia, the region was in America's backyard—the USSR would not support the

Sandinistas or the rebels in El Salvador and Guatemala to the degree it did its allies in Vietnam. "The eagle that kills the deer in Central America," declaimed national security scholar Robert Tucker, "will not frighten the bear in the Middle East."[36]

Central America's very insignificance, in fact, made it the perfect antidote to Vietnam: "Mr. President," Secretary of State Alexander Haig assured Reagan, "this is one you can win." The region was not high on Reagan's agenda, concerned as he was with pushing through domestic initiatives, as well as tending to other, more pressing problems in Poland, Iran, and Afghanistan, making it a cheap reward to the hawks who helped elect him. "They can't have the Soviet Union or the Middle East or Western Europe. All are too important. So they've given them Central America," remarked a Senate staffer in Jesse Helms's office.[37] "There was just a vacuum," he said, and conservatives rushed to fill it.

Headed by soon-to-be national security adviser Richard Allen and closely monitored by Helms, the transition team that helped staff the Reagan administration purged a number of seasoned Latin American hands from the foreign service.[38] Conservative cadres, either civilian militarists or Vietnam veterans, were installed in the Defense Department, State Department, and various intelligence agencies, functioning as an interagency war party, with radiating spokes connecting to hard-line senior officials such as Allen, Kirkpatrick, Haig, Secretary of Defense Caspar Weinberger, and CIA director William Casey. The hawks included Fred Iklé, Richard Burt, Nestor Sanchez (a CIA careerist who had been the agency's deputy chief in Guatemala during its 1954 coup), Constantine Menges, Alfonso Sapia-Bosch, Robert McFarlane, Vernon Walters (who accompanied Nixon on his ill-fated 1958 Latin American trip), William Clark, Craig Johnstone (a veteran of Operation Phoenix in Vietnam), Major Oliver North, General Wallace Nutting, and Major General Robert Laurence Schweitzer, along with a number of the drafters of the Santa Fe document. Marginalizing area experts in the State Department and operating under the radar screen, these second-tier bureaucrats started to craft a more aggressive posture toward Nicaragua and El Salvador (creating, as we shall see, the transnational organization that would give rise to the Iran-Contra scandal).

A RESURRECTED REALISM

George W. Bush's current embrace of Wilsonian idealism has baffled many observers, seeming as it does to stand at odds to the Republican tradition of diplomatic realpolitik. But the realism that powered America's military resurgence in the 1980s was of a particular variety, deeply ideological and committed to a fulfillment of American purpose in the world. Central America was its proving ground, as a group of conservative defense intellectuals worked hard to restore America's sense of self-confidence in order to justify the carnage taking place there in the name of national defense. Jeane J. Kirkpatrick was the most prominent of this group, and it was she who provided the moral and intellectual framework to rationalize Reagan's Central American policy. In so doing, she merged the realist and idealist traditions of American diplomacy into a powerful synthesis.

Kirkpatrick considered herself a realist when it came to foreign policy, in the tradition of Hans Morgenthau, Dean Acheson, and George Kennan. Though a lifelong Democrat, she found herself repulsed by the self-flagellation that she believed had overcome her party. Attracted as a result to Reagan's bid for the White House, Kirkpatrick met with the candidate early in 1980 and pronounced his "intuitive grasp" of foreign affairs "generally correct and very realistic" and soon accepted his invitation to join his campaign.[39]

As an "action intellectual"—to borrow a phrase coined by Theodore White to describe the academics who abandoned their scholarship to join FDR's New Deal and JFK's New Frontier governments—Kirkpatrick combined practice and theory to rebut the philosophical premises that underwrote post-Vietnam antimilitarism.[40] Appointed by Reagan to the position of ambassador to the United Nations, she served notice that condemnation of Washington, which had come too easy in the past, would now have a cost. Her office compiled and distributed the voting records of each member nation, and when one or another country maligned this or that U.S. policy, she called its envoy into her office and demanded an explanation. In her speeches and writings, she repeatedly pointed out the hypocrisy of condemning Israel while praising Libya, say, or censuring apartheid in South Africa while ignoring human rights violations in Cuba.

But Kirkpatrick did more than just point out double standards. Prior to serving as ambassador to the United Nations, which under her tenure was raised to a cabinet-level position with direct access to the president, she worked as a Georgetown political scientist who mostly researched the arcanum of the presidential nominating process. She had a broad engagement with intellectual history, though, and where groups like the Committee of Santa Fe offered visceral but not very effective reactions to the Vietnam syndrome, Kirkpatrick wrote terse, accessible essays that updated the conservative tradition to the current moment. Drawing on Thomas Hobbes's respect for the centrality of power in human affairs and Edmund Burke's respect for the intractability of tradition to understand the limits of that power, Kirkpatrick not only pointed out what she described as the hypocrisy behind criticisms of countries such as El Salvador and South Africa but actively defended the institutions of those countries as important bulwarks of order and stability.

It was in Latin America where Kirkpatrick's ideas were most fully elaborated and applied. In a series of articles, she used the region to refute what at the time seemed like an emerging consensus on the correct role of America in the world. The U.S. military's defeat by a poorly armed peasant insurgency in Vietnam led many in the Democratic foreign policy establishment to rethink the wisdom of seeing all global conflict through the bifocal lens of superpower conflict. They began to recommend an acceptance of "ideological pluralism"—the belief that not all societies will follow the same road to development. Accordingly, third-world nationalism of the kind that drove the United States out of Southeast Asia was to be dealt with on its own terms and not as a cat's paw for Soviet Communism.[41] Even Carter's hawkish national security adviser, Zbigniew Brzezinski, argued that increased technological and commercial interdependence had made the world less ideological; in this, he foreshadowed much of the techno-optimistic writing on globalization during the Clinton years. Old dogmas concerning the relationship of territory to national interests no longer held, Brzezinski suggested, which meant that the United States could adopt a "more detached attitude toward revolutionary processes."[42]

Kirkpatrick responded point by point to this sanguine philosophy of international relations, while broadly countering it with an old-fashioned conservative insistence on the dark side of human nature. Carter, of course, had either ignored or opposed much of the new liberal internationalism, yet Kirkpartrick successfully linked it to his administration to account for the fall of Nicaragua and Iran, the spread of insurgencies in El Salvador and Guatemala, the ongoing influence of Castro, and the emergence of revolutionary nationalism throughout the Middle East and the Caribbean.

Kirkpatrick provided the Republican administration with the argument it needed to justify continued support for brutal dictatorships.[43] Autocrats, no matter how premodern their hierarchies and antimodern their values, allowed, she said, for a degree of autonomous civil society. By contrast, Marxist-Leninist totalitarians such as the Sandinistas mobilized all aspects of society, which made war, as a means to maintain such mobilization, inevitable. Since political liberalization was more likely to occur under a Somoza than under a Marxist regime like that of the Sandinistas, Kirkpatrick insisted that a foreign policy that forced allies to democratize was not only bad for U.S. security but detrimental for the concerned countries as well: it led in Nicaragua and Iran not to reform but to radical regimes and was threatening to do the same in Bolivia, El Salvador, Guatemala, Brazil, Argentina, Chile, Uruguay, and South Africa. Kirkpatrick's analysis was not original. It recycled not just dubious distinctions between "authoritarian" and "totalitarian" regimes but also well-rehearsed justifications for supporting Latin American dictators dating back to the beginning of the Cold War.[44] Yet it did provide the Reagan administration with a rationale for undoing many of Carter's human rights initiatives.

Kirkpatrick went beyond merely justifying alliances with unseemly allies. In repudiating the "rational humanism" of the liberal internationalists, she gave voice to what may be called the Hobbesian impulse in U.S. foreign policy—an insistence that brute power and not human reason establishes political legitimacy. In a 1980 essay titled "The Hobbes Problem: Order, Authority, and Legitimacy in Central America," she invoked the seventeenth-century philosopher to attack Carter's conditioning of military aid to El Salvador on the implementation of social reforms, including a land reform, and on the reduction of human rights violations.[45] Such requirements, she wrote, were wrongheaded because they ignored the fact that "competition for power," rooted "in the nature of man," is the foundation of all politics. Kirkpatrick advised the incoming Republican administration to abandon Carter's reform program and sanction the Salvadoran military's effort to impose order through repression, even if it meant the use of death squads. Such a course of action was justified, she contended, because Salvador's political culture respected a sovereign who was willing to wield violence—proof of which was that one of the death squads took the name Maximiliano Hernández Martínez, a dictator who in 1932 slaughtered as many as thirty thousand indigenous peasants in the course of a week. Kirkpatrick described Hernández Martínez as a "hero" to Salvadorans and argued that by taking his name the assassins sought to "place themselves in El Salvador's political tradition and communicate their purpose." (Perhaps a similar logic explains why a notoriously corrupt and brutal Contra unit in Nicaragua took the name "Jeane Kirkpatrick Task Force.")[46] Washington needed to think "more realistically" about the course of action it pursued in Latin America, Kirkpatrick argued elsewhere: "The choices are frequently unattractive."

Kirkpatrick also repeatedly attacked what might be called the Kantian impulse in U.S. foreign policy, after Immanuel Kant, the eighteenth-century Enlightenment philosopher who believed that human progress would result in a peacefully ordered world government. Again and again she hammered against the conceit that U.S. power should and could be used to promote universal, internationalist abstract goals such as "human rights," "development," and "fairness." She warned against trying to be the "world's midwife" to democracy. "No idea," she complained, "holds greater sway in the mind of educated Americans than the belief that it is possible to democratize governments, anytime, anywhere, under any circumstances." In classic conservative terms, she cautioned that "thought set free from experience is unlimited by the constraints of experience or of probability. If history is not relevant then the future is free from the past. Theories cut loose from experience are usually blinding optimistic. They begin not from how things are but how they ought to be, and regularly underestimate the complexities and difficulties concerning how you get there from here."

It is important to emphasize that Kirkpatrick was not arguing against morality in foreign policy. Far from it, for she believed that a conviction in the righteousness of U.S. purpose and power was indispensable in the execution of effective diplomacy. But for America's foreign policy establishment, Vietnam shook that conviction. The optimism in which liberal internationalists approached the world, she charged, was but a thin mask to hide the shame they felt over American power. The problem was not idealism as such but Carter's misplaced application of it, which led him and his advisers not only to doubt American motives but to abandon the responsibility of power for the abstractions of history. Carter's White House, Kirkpatrick pointed out, repeatedly explained foreign policy setbacks in impersonal terms such as "forces" or "processes." "What can a U.S. president faced with such complicated, inexorable, impersonal processes do?" Kirkpatrick asked; "The answer, offered again and again by the president and his top officials, was, Not Much."

Setting the stage for today's neocons, she called for a diplomacy that once again valued human action, resolve, and will. If America acted with moral certainty to defend its national interests, the consequence would, by extension, be beneficial for the rest of the world. "Once the intellectual debris has been cleared away," she believed, "it should become possible to construct a Latin American policy that will protect U.S. security interest and make the actual lives of actual people in Latin America somewhat better and somewhat freer."

American diplomacy here, even in the hands of a committed realist such as Kirkpatrick, is an article of faith, expressed in the self-confident writ of policy makers that when America acts in the world, even when it does so expressly to defend its own interests, the consequences of its actions will be in the general interest. It is in such assuredness that the roots of the punitive idealism that drives the new imperialism can be found, roots that began to sprout in Reagan's Central American policy.

When Hobbes Met Kant in Central America

Until the 1980s, it was the Democratic Party, from Woodrow Wilson to John Kennedy, that best represented the Kantian impulse in U.S. diplomacy. Republicans, generally suspicious of big-government initiatives, balked at such lofty rhetoric. "I never believed we should compete with revolutionaries," said Thomas Mann, a Republican who twice served as assistant secretary of state for inter-American affairs, about the insurgent ambitions contained in Kennedy's Alliance for Progress.[47] As for human rights and democracy, Reagan himself criticized Ford for signing the 1975 Helsinki Human Rights Accords and campaigned in 1980 against Carter's human rights diplomacy. And once in office, he restored diplomatic relations with repressive anti-Communist allies, while he and his wife, Nancy, feted dictators such as South Korea's Chun Doo Hwan and the Philippines' Ferdinand Marcos with state dinners where the praise for their rule was as lavish as the food. Reagan's first secretary of state, Alexander Haig, early in the administration, reaffirmed the principle of détente when he dismissed calls for Washington to force democratic reform on other nations. "Clearly," Haig said, "we don't have a right and the Soviet Union or their proxies do not have a right to insist on a political formula in any developing country."[48] True, the New Right had long disparaged Kissinger's ethical bankruptcy. But most in the ascendant Republican foreign policy establishment shared Kirkpatrick's understanding of the role of morality in foreign policy: it was to be used to act with resolve and certainty in the world but not to remake the world.

But once in office, Reagan picked up the torch of idealism traditionally borne by Democrats and embraced human rights and democracy as vital foreign policy concerns. This shift is often credited to the first generation of midlevel neoconservative policy makers, such as Elliott Abrams and Paul Wolfowitz, who shared Kirkpatrick's disdain of liberal internationalism yet felt that hard-headed appeals to the moral legitimacy of national defense would not serve to excuse alliances with death squads and dictators. They pushed for a foreign policy that made an ethical distinction between the USSR and the United States. In 1981, Abrams, as secretary of state for human rights, circulated a memo approved by his boss, Haig, arguing that while a military response to the Soviets remained crucial, the United States also needed an "ideological response."[49] "We will never maintain wide public support for our foreign policy unless we can relate it to American ideals and to the defense of freedom. Our ability to resist the Soviets around the world depends in part on our ability to draw this distinction and to persuade others of it," Abrams wrote. "Our struggle is for political liberty."

Most observers focus on the Soviet Union, Eastern Europe, or Asia when discussing the ramifications of this rhetorical shift. Dissident movements in Russia and its satellites, such as Poland's Solidarność, gave the White House a way to discard a central component of détente and criticize the internal affairs of the Soviets. The exodus of boat people out of Vietnam and the harsh treatment of that country's dissidents allowed Washington to retake some moral high ground lost during the war. And in 1985, acting on advice from Wolfowitz and others, Reagan reluctantly did exactly what Kirkpatrick roasted Carter for doing: he pushed Philippine president Marcos first to reform and then—after Marcos tried to steal an election—out. But it was largely in Central America where Reagan first forcefully embraced human rights and support for democracy as a legitimate objective of American diplomacy.

The turnaround was dramatic. Just before his inauguration, Reagan described to *Time* magazine the approach he planned to take in El Salvador, sounding like he ripped a page straight out of Kirkpatrick's "The Hobbes Problem." "You do not try to fight a civil war and institute reforms at the same time," the president-elect said. "Get rid of the war. Then go forward with the reforms."[50] But once in office, Reagan greatly expanded Carter's "nation building" program and even continued his predecessor's land reform and advocacy on behalf of human rights. Not since Vietnam, according to former Rand Corporation analyst Benjamin Schwarz, had Washington ever "been so deeply and intimately involved in attempting to transform a foreign

society that it had not defeated in war and hence did not control."[51]
Likewise, in Nicaragua, Reagan broke with diplomatic protocol and
insisted that the Sandinistas not only stop arming rebels in El Salvador
and Guatemala but hold free elections, respect human rights, and
protect political pluralism.

In other words, it was in Central America, more than anywhere
else, where nationalists once again cast the Cold War as a moral
struggle between good and evil. In Vietnam, as the war progressed
and American involvement grew both more violent and more
damned, idealism slowly drained out of Washington's public pro-
nouncements. By the war's end, Nixon rarely justified the conflict in
terms of promoting democracy but rather by the need to protect national security and save face. In Central America, the opposite occurred. In the face of mounting evidence of atrocities committed by
U.S. allies, Reagan, in his fights with Congress, consistently raised
the ethical stakes. By the mid-1980s, the Great Communicator was
peppering his Central American speeches with references to the
Great Emancipator. Continued aid to the Nicaraguan Contras,
whom he elevated to the "moral equivalents of America's founding
fathers," would keep faith with the "revolutionary heritage" of the
United States, a heritage that, borrowing from Lincoln, bestowed a
"hope to the world for all future time." "Who among us," he asked
Congress in 1986, "would tell these brave young men and women:
'Your dream is dead; your democratic revolution is over; you will
never live in the free Nicaragua you fought so hard to build?'"

One reason for this lofty oratory was that the Reagan administration faced resistance to its Central American policy from a grassroots movement that, while growing out of the peace demonstrations
of the 1960s and 1970s, had much more of a prominent religious
component than did the mobilization protesting the Vietnam War.
Quakers, Catholics, and liberal Protestants cast opposition to Reagan's wars in Nicaragua and El Salvador in the language of Christian
social justice, organizing rallies, speaking to church groups, holding

candlelight prayer vigils, and providing sanctuary for Central American refugees fleeing violence perpetrated by U.S.-backed regimes. The White House needed something more than cold realism to reply to this challenge.

It was also in Central America and the Caribbean where the conservatives were most successful at inverting rhetoric usually associated with the left. The Committee for Santa Fe, for instance, boldly called for the resuscitation of the Monroe Doctrine, which in 1823 announced to European empires that Latin America fell under Washington's exclusive sphere of influence. Evoking a "New World" under threat by the "Old," the manifesto appealed for Washington to lead a "war of national liberation" in Cuba and to defend El Salvador and Guatemala from "the intrusive imperialism of extracontinental powers." By casting the USSR not only as an imperialist power but as old, reactionary Europe, the authors reclaimed the position of revolutionary vanguard, the agents of progressive historical change. They turned the tables on those who portrayed America's brutal opposition to third-world nationalism as standing on the wrong side of history. Reagan himself even dared assert spiritual kinship with the "real Sandino." A "genuine nationalist" is how he described the anti-American rebel murdered in 1934 by the U.S.-installed head of Nicaraguan security forces. By 1985, even the staid George Shultz, who replaced Haig at State, in a speech to the San Francisco Commonwealth Club hymned that a "democratic revolution" was "sweeping the world."[52]

Another reason for this rhetorical escalation is that during Reagan's tenure speechwriters in the White House and at State had come to influence foreign policy matters to a much greater degree than ever before. Journalist Roy Gutman wrote that Reagan's "speechwriting shop was a repository of true-believers," who worked closely with CIA director Casey and other hard-liners to ratchet up the oratory.[53] Just as David Frum served as a transmitter of ideas gleaned from neoconservative think tanks to shape George

W. Bush's post-9/11 foreign policy, New Right activist speechwriters became the "guardians of Reagan's conservative conscience, and with some reason they felt that they made a difference."[54] Over at State, Robert Kagan has said that as Shultz's "principal speechwriter" he drafted "broad statements of Reagan administration foreign policy, including the fullest official explication of what has been called the 'Reagan Doctrine'"—which committed the United States to not just containing but rolling back Soviet influence, particularly in the third world.[55]

The inclusion of democracy and human rights in Washington's diplomacy was also a result of intramural struggles early in the Reagan presidency, as the hawks sought to wrest foreign policy out of the hands of establishment diplomats. Reagan, as mentioned earlier, pursued a course of moderation in most foreign policy areas. But conservative activists considered Central America theirs, hence their anger when Thomas O. Enders was appointed assistant secretary of state for inter-American affairs, a position responsible for formulating Central American policy.

Enders was no dove. Educated at Exeter, Yale, Harvard, and the Sorbonne, Enders, from a wealthy Republican banking family, had helped direct the infamous aerial bombing of Cambodia from the U.S. embassy in Phnom Penh. "He took charge of administering the Nixon Doctrine," wrote William Shawcross in *Sideshow: Kissinger, Nixon, and the Destruction of Cambodia*, "with a vigor" that others in the embassy "found distasteful."[56]

But Enders was a career diplomat, not a movement conservative, thus suspicious to Jesse Helms and other militarists. Helms, who exerted a good deal of control over foreign policy appointments, held up Enders's confirmation for months until the nominee agreed to staff his office with New Right ideologues.

Upon taking office, Enders confirmed Helms's suspicions by his willingness to consult with Democrats to find a negotiated solution to the crises in Central America. He laid out his plans for El Salvador in a speech to the World Affairs Council in July 1981, where he proposed to continue Jimmy Carter's policy of land distribution, human rights, and elections—the very kind of social reforms that Kirkpatrick and other hawks condemned. Enders also incensed conservative militants when he raised the possibility of negotiating with the rebels and proposed giving Congress the power to review and certify progress on human rights issues and political reform. Like Elliott Abrams, Enders believed that the language of human rights and social justice that had gained ground with the antiwar movement could be harnessed on behalf of U.S. foreign policy.

Enders's strategy worked, winning over enough congressional Democrats with his talk of promoting democracy and human rights to allow Reagan to continue funding the Salvadoran military. And so, over the objections of the militarists, Washington embarked on its most ambitious liberal democratic nation-building program since Vietnam, one that entailed not only spending billions and billions of dollars on military aid to stop a revolution but, theoretically at least, distributing land, transforming the country's legal and fiscal structure, and cultivating a culture of tolerance and respect for human rights.

In Nicaragua, though, concern for democracy and human rights came from an unexpected source—from Enders's opponents, the hawks. During the first year of Reagan's term, Enders worked to find a negotiated settlement with the new Nicaraguan leadership. In his talks with the Sandinistas, he downplayed democracy and didn't push for internal reforms, instead focusing on security issues. "You can do your own thing," Enders told a high-ranking Sandinista official, "but do it within your own borders, or else we are going to hurt you." Mindful of American might, Sandinista leaders cooperated and in August 1981 pledged not to export their revolution, and pledged to keep the country's military small and to limit ties with Cuba and the Soviet Union. In exchange, Enders promised that Washington would restore economic aid and sign a nonaggression pact.

But the war party—led by Helms, Fontaine, Casey, Kirkpatrick, Clark, Iklé, and McFarlane—had other ideas, demanding, in the words of a Helms staffer, that Enders take "harder action."[57] Turning Enders's diplomatic maneuver to their own ends, they insisted on holding the Sandinistas to the same human rights standard to which he was holding the Salvadoran government. In February 1982, in a speech to the OAS, Reagan insisted that the Sandinistas adopt internal reform. Two months later, Washington told Managua that "free elections" would be "essential elements of the political context of future relations between our two countries." Such demands derailed negotiations, with the Sandinistas balking at Enders's sudden stipulation that the United States have a say in Nicaragua's internal affairs. This suited the hawks just fine since they had already convinced Reagan five months earlier, in November 1981, to throw his support behind the Contras.

Hobbes had met Kant in Central America, and the Republicans were well on the way to becoming "revolutionaries."

To get a sense of how far the Republican Party has traveled in its rhetorical embrace of idealism in the realm of diplomacy, one has only to compare the Nixon Doctrine with a speech given by George W. Bush in March 2005 summarizing the objectives of the war on terror. The former was the apotheosis of international realpolitik, ceding to the security forces of other nations the responsibility of keeping order, justified by no rationale other than national security. The means might not be pretty, but, as Nixon said in praise of Latin American dictators, "it is an orderly way which at least works relatively well. They have been able to run the damn place."[58] In contrast, Bush's speech repudiated Washington's long history of cozying up to dictators. "Decades of excusing and accommodating tyranny in pursuit of stability," he said, "have only led to injustice and instability and tragedy."

At first blush, these two presidential doctrines seem to represent opposing positions, the first stripped to naked self-interest, the second redolent of American righteousness. Yet as Jeane Kirkpatrick, consummate realist *and* supporter of the Bush Doctrine, noted decades ago, in the "cool reassuring plans of our founding fathers, informed by history and inspired by a passion for freedom, idealism and realism were closely interwoven." They are, she insisted, "mutually reinforcing principles."[59] It was Kirkpatrick more than any other Republican intellectual who, with Central America as a backdrop, helped bridge the two poles represented by Nixon and Bush, demanding that politicians draw on their faith in American decency and purpose in order to act with certainty and resolve in the world. Such a synthesis paved the way for the Republican Party to embrace democratic nation building and human rights in El Salvador and Nicaragua even as it was not only patronizing brutal executioners and torturers but hailing them as freedom fighters. "The time has come to stop using murder as a tool of policy," Bush warned Middle East regimes in his March 2005 speech. But in Central America in the 1980s, as we shall see in the next chapter, not just murder but mass slaughter became a crucial instrument of U.S. foreign policy.

CHAPTER THREE

Going Primitive:
The Violence of the
New Imperialism

IN THE 2004 VICE PRESIDENTIAL DEBATE, Dick Cheney justified his administration's plan to move forward with elections in Iraq despite escalating violence by evoking the courage of Salvadorans, who in 1984 lined up for hours to vote even as a civil war raged. The "human drive for freedom," Cheney said, "is enormous."[1] But around the same time, the military men charged with securing Iraq were making a different kind of comparison with El Salvador, one less concerned with the reported achievements of nation building than with the success of paramilitary violence in forestalling an insurgent victory. With the United States failing to defeat the rebels on its own, the Pentagon came to debate the "Salvador option," that is, the use of local paramilitary forces, otherwise known as death squads, to do the kind of dirty work that it was either unwilling or unable to do.[2] It turned to men like James Steele, who in the 1980s led the Special Forces mission in El Salvador and worked with Oliver North to run weapons and supplies to the Nicaraguan

Contras, to train a ruthless counterinsurgent force made up of ex-Baathist thugs.[3] The press reported that U.S. and British aid was being diverted to paramilitaries accused of assassinations and torture, including burnings, electric shock, strangulation, sexual violence, and the use of electric drills in victim's kneecaps.[4] "Do you remember the right-wing execution squads in El Salvador?" a former high-level intelligence agent asked journalist Seymour Hersh. "We founded them and we financed them," he said, and the "objective now is to recruit locals in any area we want. And we aren't going to tell Congress about it." Beyond Iraq, into Syria, Iran, wherever, "we're going to be riding with the bad boys," said another military officer.[5]

These two lessons drawn from the recent history of the United States in Central America seem to contradict each other—one celebrates America's role in bringing liberty to a war-wrecked land and another admits that Washington allied with murderers, rapists, and torturers to establish imperial order. Yet such a disjuncture lies at the very heart of the new imperialism, propelled as it is by the kind of punitive idealism that took its modern form in Central America in the 1980s. It was through support of counterinsurgent regimes in El Salvador and Guatemala—two countries faced with powerful guerrilla movements—that the United States relearned, after the disaster of direct involvement in Vietnam, to farm out its imperial violence. This outsourcing, in turn, again allowed U.S. leaders like Cheney to claim that the achievements of the American empire in places like El Salvador stemmed from the universal appeal of its values when in fact "success," as a former RAND Corporation analyst admitted, "was built on a foundation of corpses."[6] In Guatemala, the United States went even further in its approval of violence in order to restore American authority abroad, championing an evangelical zealot, Efraín Ríos Montt, even as he was presiding over a military campaign the United Nations later ruled to be genocidal.

Nicaragua, where the United States backed not a counterinsurgent state but anti-Communist mercenaries, likewise represented a disjuncture between the idealism used to justify U.S. policy and its support for political terrorism. Here, militarists seized on the opportunity provided by the 1979 Sandinista revolution to go on the offensive. They set out, in the words of one strategist, to "take the revolution out of the hands of revolutionaries" and nudge the United States away from a policy of "containment" toward one of "rollback." In so doing, conservative cadres could imagine themselves as liberal revolutionaries engaged in a global democratic crusade even as they trained and then unleashed the most feverishly illiberal thugs imaginable.

The corollary to the idealism embraced by the Republicans in the realm of diplomatic public policy debate was thus political terror. In the dirtiest of Latin America's dirty wars, their faith in America's mission justified atrocities in the name of liberty.

GOING PRIMITIVE

"Real counterinsurgency techniques," says John Waghelstein, the army colonel who led the United States's military advisory team in El Salvador, "are a step toward the primitive"—an apt description of the journey that took place in Central America during the 1980s.[7]

Although equipped with state-of-the-art weaponry, U.S. allies in El Salvador and Guatemala preferred to conduct their killing with artisan expertise. The bodies of their prey regularly appeared on early-morning city streets bearing the marks of unhurried, meticulous cuts, amputations, and burns made while the victim was still breathing. Whatever pathological satisfaction such old-fashioned cruelty provided, it was also calculated to avoid leaving bullets that could be traced to the military.

In the countryside, army detachments conducted massacres in peasant communities with more primal ferocity but with a similar exactitude. In December 1981, the American-trained Atlacatl Battalion began its systematic execution of over 750 civilians in the Salvadoran village of El Mozote, including hundreds of children under the age of twelve. The soldiers were thorough and left only one survivor. At first they stabbed and decapitated their victims, but they turned to machine guns when the hacking grew too tiresome (a decade later, an exhumation team digging through the mass graves found hundreds of bullets with head stamps indicating that the ammunition was manufactured in Lake City, Missouri, for the U.S. government).[8] Between 1981 and 1983 in Guatemala, the army executed roughly 100,000 Mayan peasants unlucky enough to live in a region identified as the seedbed of a leftist insurgency. In some towns, troops murdered children by beating them on rocks or throwing them into rivers as their parents watched. *"Adiós, niño"*—good-bye, child—said one soldier, before pitching an infant to drown. They gutted living victims, amputated genitalia, arms, and legs, committed mass rapes, and burned victims alive. According to a surviving witness of one massacre, soldiers "grabbed pregnant women, cut open their stomachs, and pulled the fetus out."[9] It was not easy to compel conscripts to commit such acts. Guatemala's basic training, therefore, put cadets through a curriculum designed to purge civilization out of them: they were beaten, degraded, made to bathe in sewage and then forbidden to wash the feces off their bodies. Some were required to raise puppies, only to be ordered to kill them and drink their blood. In Nicaragua, the U.S.-backed Contras decapitated, castrated, and otherwise mutilated civilians and foreign aid workers. Some earned a reputation for using spoons to gorge their victims' eyes out. In one raid, Contras cut the breasts of a civilian defender to pieces and ripped the flesh off the bones of another.

Waghelstein oversaw U.S. training of the Salvadoran army in the early 1980s, when the killing was at its apex. But his advice to go "primitive" had less to do with the kind of face-to-face bloodletting that his apprentices were conducting than with an effort to transform

America's military focus. Waghelstein had done two tours of duty in Vietnam, one in the Special Forces and the other in the Airborne Division. Like other midlevel veterans politicized by defeat, he was concerned that his superiors had not absorbed a crucial lesson from that conflict. The army, he complained in the early 1980s, was "still preparing for the wrong war" and was not ready to fight in the way that would be needed to win in the most likely venue of future conflicts: the third world.

For Waghelstein, going primitive meant moving away from a dependency on ever more technologically sophisticated firepower and preparing for nontraditional low-intensity conflict. Soldiers needed to be trained in "psychological operations, civic action, and grass roots, human intelligence work, all of which run counter to the conventional U.S. concept of war." The different branches and services of the military had to overcome their bureaucratic rivalry and learn to work together in a coordinated manner to not only defeat insurgents militarily but integrate rebel supporters, or potential supporters, into local and national political structures, reform those structures so that they would be seen as a legitimate source of authority, and alleviate poverty—in short, carry out a project of democratic nation building. The objective, Waghelstein said, was "total war at the grass-roots level."

This vision of warfare was diametrically opposed to the institutional and ideological restructuring of the armed forces in the wake of defeat in Southeast Asia. The military's leaders, wanting to put what they hoped was the "aberration" of Vietnam behind them, had returned to planning either for nuclear conflict or for traditional warfare on the plains and rolling hills of Central Europe. Elaborating the principles of what would become known as the Weinberger and then the Powell doctrines, the high command reoriented the military in ways that would make it hard for civilian policy makers to use war as an offhand extension of politics. The standing army was made dependent on reserves, ensuring that politicians would think twice before committing troops to large-scale combat or involving them in long, drawn-out nation-building campaigns with no clear exit strategy or markers to gauge progress.[10] By the early 1980s, funding for Special Forces and covert operations had plummeted, with military colleges either dropping or greatly reducing the number of hours dedicated to counterinsurgent training.

Reagan supported the military's drive toward autonomy and professionalism, but he also came to office pledged to reverse America's reported decline. Like John F. Kennedy two decades earlier, the new president outlined a vision of national security in which third-world revolutionary nationalism was understood primarily though the prism of superpower conflict. And just as Kennedy encouraged creative and aggressive counterinsurgent and covert methods to overcome the stalemate reached by the Soviet Union's acquisition of nuclear technology, the Reagan Doctrine revitalized nonconventional warfare in the third world—a revitalization that stood at odds with the high command's attempt to erect a firewall between war and politics.

Leading this revival was a cohort of special-warfare operatives from either the military or the CIA—counterinsurgent luminaries, such as Waghelstein, bound together by the common experience of clandestine, often violent, and usually extralegal operations in Laos, Cambodia, and Vietnam. America's withdrawal from Southeast Asia, along with many of the reforms forced on the executive branch and intelligence agencies during the Ford and Carter presidencies, led to the suppression but not the dismantling of this network. It is estimated that over eight hundred covert operatives found themselves off the CIA payroll by the end of the 1970s. And while counterinsurgent activists used defeat, as well as budget and personnel cuts, to build a sense of urgency and persecution, after Vietnam, aside from clandestine operations in Angola and Mozambique, there were few opportunities to apply their experience. Then came Central America.

Uniting behind Ronald Reagan's presidential campaign, they provided civilian defense intellectuals with important muscle in the struggle to revive the Cold War, particularly in the third world. Theodore Shackley, for example, had served in the CIA in Laos, where he supervised a secret paramilitary army of twenty-five thousand ethnic Meos, and in Vietnam, where he worked with the Phoenix program, which was responsible for the execution of tens of thousands of suspected Vietcong supporters. In early 1981, he published *The Third Option*, a mass-market primer whose title refers to its endorsement of the "use of guerrilla warfare, counterinsurgency techniques, and covert actions" to settle third-world crises—the first two options being direct military engagement, as in Vietnam, or sitting back and doing nothing, which was how conservatives derided Carter's foreign policy.[11]

Once Reagan took office, men like Shackley either filled the second-tier administrative ranks of intelligence and defense agencies or provided their services to the White House as private contractors. In Southeast Asia, General John Singlaub had presided over a "joint unconventional warfare task force" that conducted raids into Cambodia and Laos. Under Reagan, he headed the Special Operations Policy Advisory Group and became a key player in the Contra war. Oliver North, another notorious Iran-Contra figure, served under Singlaub in Vietnam. Richard Armitage, a Phoenix program graduate, was Reagan's assistant secretary for international security affairs, responsible for coordinating covert activities throughout the third world.[12] Shackley himself was discredited due to his involvement in an operation that provided C–4 plastic explosive to Libya, yet he nonetheless played an important extragovernmental role in the supply operation to the Contras. These frontline defense activists joined forces with civilian militarists in the new Republican administration, such as Fred Iklé and Richard Perle, to push the United States to prepare to fight what was now generally referred to as "low-intensity conflict."[13]

Just as ideologues used Central America to invigorate America's moral purpose in the world, strategists looked to the region as the ideal venue to rehabilitate an understanding of war that many, both members of the military establishment and critics of it, hoped Vietnam had consigned to the dustbin of history. And while Waghelstein's call for a return to primitivism did not openly endorse the kind of terror described above, such brutality was a constitutive element of low-intensity warfare, as many of its practitioners would come to admit.

Phrasing the Threat

Low-intensity warfare theorists often argue that the best way to respond to an insurgent threat is to eradicate the "root causes" of instability. And even the most ardent hawk had to admit that El Salvador had its share of root causes: its history was one of almost unbroken military and oligarchic rule, in which a small coterie of landowners held the country's political institutions, workforce, and land in an iron grip, while the vast majority of people lived in wretched poverty. The economy rested on the exportation of a single product, coffee, and the political system was built on corruption, privilege, and cruelty. One U.S. official reported that prior to the 1980s the rich held human life so cheap that a favorite pastime of their sons was to drive through the countryside and shoot peasants for sport.[14] In the 1960s, the social order decomposed as the number of landless peasants skyrocketed and poverty increased. Beginning in 1974, the government responded to demands for political and economic reform by ratcheting up death-squad executions, which climbed to unprecedented levels, claiming as many as eight hundred victims a month by the end of the decade. Government repression united and radicalized the opposition, made up of peasant organizations, unions, social democratic parties, and, most notably, large sectors of the Catholic Church. In 1980, following the assassination of Archbishop Oscar Romero, a leading spokesperson for the poor and persecuted, a number of the most important oppositional organizations decided that they were left with no option other than armed revolution, joining together to form a united insurgent front. Within a year, the Frente Faribundo Martí para la Liberación Nacional, or FMLN, was mounting frontal offensives against the Salvadoran armed forces that threatened to bring the rebels to victory.

But what was not apparent in most analyses of the Salvadoran crisis was Washington's role in generating it.

There was not even a whiff of a rural insurrection when in the early 1960s agents from the State Department, Green Berets, CIA, and USAID organized two paramilitary groups that would become the backbone of that country's death-squad system: the Agencia Nacional de Servicios Especiales, or ANSESAL, an intelligence agency designed to coordinate Salvador's security forces, and Organización Democrática Nacionalista, ORDEN, a rural militia charged with carrying out not only surveillance and infiltration of political organizations but propaganda work as well.[15]

The creation of ANSESAL and ORDEN was part of Kennedy's campaign to respond preemptively to potential Communist subversion in the third world. In the wake of Castro's victory in Cuba, Washington committed itself to preventing similar revolutions elsewhere in Latin America. To that end, the United States set out to professionalize and expand Latin America's security agencies. The goal was to turn lethargic, untrained intelligence units of limited range into a national network capable of gathering, analyzing, and acting on information in a quick and efficient manner. American advisers helped coordinate the work of the competing branches of a country's security forces and supplied intelligence agencies with phones, teletype machines, radios, cars, guns, ammunition, surveillance equipment, explosives, cattle prods, cameras, typewriters, carbon paper, and filing cabinets. They instructed their apprentices in the latest riot control, record keeping, surveillance, and mass-arrest techniques. Such training and fortification directly led to the emergence of a dense, Central America–wide network of death-squad paramilitaries.

In El Salvador and Guatemala, as elsewhere, death squads operated under their own colorful names—an Eye for an Eye, the Secret Anti-Communist Army, the White Hand—yet were essentially appendages of the very intelligence systems that Washington either helped create or fortified. The United States, of course, publicly denied its support of paramilitarism, but in Latin America the first sustained campaign of death-squad-executed "disappearances" of political dissidents occurred in Guatemala in 1966, carried out by a unit created and directly supervised by American security advisers.[16] By that time, the promotion of clandestine terror units was standard fare for counterinsurgent strategists. General William Yarborough, for example, advised the Colombian government in 1962 to set up an irregular unit trained to "execute paramilitary, sabotage and/or terrorist activities against known communist proponents"—as good a description of a death squad as any.[17]

Yarborough is more famous for his role in organizing the Green Berets in Vietnam, where too by the early 1960s extrajudicial executions were becoming a standard feature in counterinsurgency strategy. (Yarborough would also help bring the counterinsurgency home to the United States, when in the late 1960s he coordinated the army's intelligence services with the FBI's infamous COINTEL-PRO program, which targeted civil rights and antiwar activists for harassment.)[18] As in Central America, the point of death squads in Vietnam was not just to eliminate those thought to be working with the enemy but to limit the actions of rebels or potential rebels by keeping them in a state of fear and anxiety. To that end, the U.S. Information Service in Saigon provided thousands of copies of a flyer printed with a ghostly eye. The "terror squads" then deposited the eye on corpses or "on the doors of houses suspected of occasionally harboring Viet Cong agents."[19] The technique was called "phrasing the threat." It started being used at roughly the same time in Guatemala, where it took the form of a "white hand" left on the body of a victim or the door of a potential victim.

In both Vietnam and Central America care was taken to make sure that death squads appeared to be unaffiliated with regular forces. David Galula cautioned in his 1964 classic *Counter-Insurgency Warfare* that "elimination of the agents must be achieved quickly and decisively . . . by an organization that must in no way be confused with the counterinsurgent personnel working to win the support of the population."[20] The point was to allow a plausible degree of deniability. But in Central America in the 1960s, the bodies piled so high that even State Department embassy officials, often kept out of the loop as to what their counterparts in the CIA and Defense were up to, had to admit the links between U.S.-backed intelligence services and death squads. "Several rightist 'anticommunist' organizations which the general public and U.S. observers previously believed responsible for many of the vigilante forays now appear to be largely phantom groups, established and maintained to mask the army's role in vigilantism," admitted one 1967 report issued from the U.S. embassy in Guatemala. "These units are formed by well trained and highly motivated younger military personnel and are believed to operate under the direction of high-ranking military officers."[21]

Throughout the 1960s, Latin America and Southeast Asia functioned as the two primary campuses for counterinsurgents with men such as Yarborough traveling back and forth between the two regions applying insights and fine-tuning tactics. John Longan, for example, the U.S. adviser who set up Guatemala's first death squad, hopscotched from Guatemala and Venezuela to Thailand and back again to Guatemala. In fact, for a time in the early 1960s, the budding civil war in Colombia between the state and breakaway Communist-organized peasant republics was seen as a potentially greater crisis than the one in Vietnam. Not only were the Green Berets working with the Colombian military, the country, according to investigative reporter Gerard Colby, served as a "pre-Vietnam experiment in [Robert] McNamara's 'systems' approach to integrating communications (command and control), rapid air mobility, concentrated firepower, and computer-assisted intelligence for finding and tracking an enemy."[22] In 1964, the U.S.-trained Colombian armed forces enacted a scorched-earth campaign, razing rebellious villages and setting up "strategic hamlets" in order to establish control over the countryside. It was during this operation that napalm was used in combat for the first time.

The support of death squads was part of what counterinsurgents liked to call "counterterror"—a concept hard to define since it so closely mirrored the practices it sought to contest.[23] Field manuals, journal articles, and whole books were dedicated to debating the correct proportion of violence needed to defeat a rural insurgency.[24] In a sense, counterterror was merely an extension of tactics used decades earlier by the United States in the Philippines and, as we saw in the opening chapter, Guatemala, where the CIA set out to induce fear and terror—not win political allegiance.

There was, however, one important difference. Starting in the early to mid-1960s, attempts to create anxiety in a targeted population were increasingly filtered through rational-choice theory—a framework borrowed from economics and political science that understands human behavior both as rational and as conditioned by the imposition of a limited set of options.[25] In terms of guerrilla warfare, this new approach argued that supporters or potential supporters of insurgencies were basically rational actors no matter the stage of their society's development and that the struggle between authority and rebellion was in effect a "contest in the effective management of coercion."[26] "When two forces are contending for the loyalty of, and control over, the civilian population," wrote Franklin Lindsay in a 1962 *Foreign Affairs* essay, "the side which uses violent reprisals most aggressively will dominate most of the people, even though their sympathies may lie in the other direction."[27] Counterinsurgent theorists now advised treating insurgencies like an economic system and working on increasing the cost, through coercion and terror, of supporting oppositional movements. A right balance had to be struck between "hot" violence—that is, retributive violence exacted in anger or with racist animus, often threatening total annihilation of the targeted population—and "cold," precise coercion designed to impress fear and cooperation. "Partial annihilation, intended to convince the target population that one is resolved to go the whole way," argued RAND specialists Nathan Leites and Charles Wolf, needs to be carefully measured: "ferocity and capriciousness" must not be "*so* massive as to make compliance with demands seem as unsafe as non-compliance."[28]

Central America, or at least the fantasy of Central America, figured prominently in these debates. The army's 1966 *Handbook of Counterinsurgency Guidelines* summarized the results of a war game modeled on the fictitious Central American country of "Centralia," a composite of the ethnic and class structure of El Salvador, Guatemala, and Nicaragua. The rules of the game allowed players to use "selective terror" but prohibited "mass-terror." "Genocide," the guidelines stipulated, was "not an alternative."[29]

Back in El Salvador, ANSESAL and ORDEN had been accused of torturing and killing political activists since their creation, yet it was in the late 1960s when they fused to form the nerve center that coordinated the political repression that escalated throughout the 1970s and 1980s. Congressional Democrats during the Carter administration managed to reduce military aid to El Salvador, but by the late 1970s any chance of political compromise or reform had been destroyed. The counterinsurgency had finally conjured up the insurgency that justified the terror in the first place. So by the time Reagan came into office committed to prevent a rebel victory at any cost, the only option was indeed to go primitive.

THE ONLY WAR IN TOWN

"El Salvador is Spanish for Vietnam," read a 1980s bumper sticker popularized by opponents of Reagan's policies in Central America. Military strategists did not disagree, seeing in the country a textbook opportunity to apply low-intensity warfare doctrine. "El Salvador represents an experiment," according to a report by four army colonels, "an attempt to reverse the record of American failure in waging small wars, an effort to defeat an insurgency by providing training and material support without committing American troops to combat." Vietnam, notwithstanding its "catastrophic outcome," supplied "proven techniques for successfully conducting counterinsurgency operations."[30] The problem, in other words, was not the theory but the practice. And El Salvador offered an opportunity to get it right, requiring, wrote U.S. Army War College professor Steven Metz, not a "radical revision of either strategy or doctrine, but simply better application."[31]

Special Forces officers "stood in line to sign up for positions as military advisors in El Salvador," remembered a senior army intelligence analyst, Lieutenant Colonel Victor Rosello. As "the only war in town," it offered an opportunity for "prestigious" and "exciting" duty.[32] It also gave counterinsurgents a chance get their hypotheses right. Not only did Central America's political geography closely map the Vietnam conflict—with Sandinista Nicaragua replicating the threat of North Vietnam and besieged, crisis-ridden El Salvador playing the part of South Vietnam—but the nature of the conflicts themselves, especially in El Salvador, provided a near-perfect model to wage Waghelstein's "total war at the grass-roots" level.

But if El Salvador was Spanish for Vietnam, Washington worked to make sure it was the Vietnam of the early 1960s, before that country's Americanization. To that end, the White House committed to staying once removed from the conflict. Congress placed a strict limit on American engagement in El Salvador in terms of personnel, permitting no more than fifty-five military advisers in country (in reality, the number went as high as 150, along with an equal number of CIA agents). American trainers at the time often complained of this restriction, yet in retrospect many credit it for preventing an escalation of troop strength and for forcing advisers to train Salvadorans to fight their own war. "Nobody has cursed the 55-man limit more than I probably have," said the commander of the military group from 1984 to 1986, Colonel James Steele (who now supervises Iraqi paramilitaries), "but I just have to tell you that doing it with a low U.S. profile is the only way to go. If you don't, you immediately get yourself into trouble, because there is a tendency for Americans to want to do things quickly, to do them efficiently—and the third step in the process is to do it yourself. If you take that third step here, you have lost."[33]

Military strategists also believed that the political component of counterinsurgent warfare had to be implemented more effectively than it had been in Southeast Asia. Theoretically, the Salvadoran military had to be reformed, the government stabilized and made legitimate, and the economy made more equitable and less abusive. "There are many, many wars going on in El Salvador," said Southcom commander General John Galvin, "and we want to be fighting them all."[34]

The most immediate concern, considering the strength of the guerrillas, was to transform the Salvadoran military into a competent counterinsurgent force. Troop strength was increased from a little over five thousand to fifty-three thousand, and the United States began to train cadets, mostly at Fort Benning, Georgia. The idea was to reorient the army's mission away from violent, vengeful defense of the status quo and toward a dispassionate professionalism and to weaken the ironclad hold that ultraconservative and deeply paranoid military elites had on the institution. To do so, Washington hoped to groom a new officer corps that advanced through merit and service. By 1983, the army, fully outfitted with U.S.-supplied weapons and other equipment and supported by a centralized U.S. intelligence and reconnaissance system based in Honduras and Panama, was deploying some small-unit search-and-destroy operations that made headway against the insurgents, forcing the rebels to adopt more traditional hit-and-run guerrilla tactics.

Despite some initial success in small-unit operations, Salvadoran commanders preferred to conduct large-scale sweeps through the countryside—of the kind that resulted in the El Mozote massacre—and to rely on heavy firepower and aerial attacks made possible by U.S.-supplied helicopters and planes. Of course, indiscriminate bombing and strafing made all the talk of "winning hearts and minds" meaningless. Psychological operations often entailed little more than entertainment in the form of mariachi bands, soldiers donning clown outfits to hand out candy and antiguerrilla leaflets, or "skimpily clad dancers between speeches by Salvadoran army officers."[35] The military did try to organize some communities into civil defense units and USAID massively funded Vietnam-style civic action programs, in which the soldiers were to provide education, health care, road building, and food. The idea behind such programs was to militarize the countryside, to use the provision of food and other basic necessities as leverage to substitute the army for the guerrillas as the primary institution in daily life. Such efforts generally failed, stymied by the corruption and violence of the military and ongoing rebel support—in 1988, the FMLN was still fielding upwards of seven thousand rebels backed by a supporting militia of forty thousand.[36]

As the war dragged on, El Salvador became Washington's most ambitious nation-building project since South Vietnam. And much as in that earlier conflict, the United States found few acceptable allies to work with. There were not many civic-minded reformers left alive, and most of those who had survived opted to join the insurgency. For their part, the Salvadoran military and the oligarchy were preternaturally violent. Their solution to the crisis, according to

Reagan's own ambassador, Robert White, was apocalyptic: the country must be "destroyed totally, the economy must be wrecked, unemployment must be massive," and a "cleansing" of some "3 or 4 or 500,000 people" must be carried out.[37] Their interests were represented by the National Republican Alliance (ARENA), a political party that was in effect the public face of the death squads, a "violent fascist party modeled after the Nazis," according to Ambassador White.

Washington therefore worked with a faction of the Christian Democratic Party—a reformist party decimated by the repression—that didn't opt to join the insurgency, backing its leader, José Napoleón Duarte, in the much-publicized 1984 presidential election. Duarte's victory in that election was trumpeted by the White House as evidence that its reform program was working, yet following his inauguration the feebleness of Washington's position quickly became apparent. Any efforts by El Salvador's new president to initiate political or economic reform or to prosecute members of the military for human rights violations were countered by the army with the threat of a coup. The military may have allowed the United States to improve its tactical competence but it resisted efforts to modernize its worldview. "It is precisely the young, aggressive, U.S.-trained officers," according to a report commissioned by the Department of Defense, "who are the most intoxicated by the extreme right's vision and most resentful of America's influence over the conduct of the war, and who commit many of the worst atrocities."[38] Even the mildest political and economic reforms sought by Washington were rejected out of hand as "socialist."[39] For his part, Duarte, overpowered on his right, came to rely on renewed political repression to contain a growing mass movement partially led, ironically, by anti-Communist unions substantially funded by the United States.

Washington further boxed Duarte in with its "free trade" approach to nation building. On the one hand, the Reagan administration directed over two billion dollars between 1979 and 1987 to

nonmilitary projects, providing financial support to reformist political parties, labor unions, and oppositional organizations not aligned
with the guerrillas, to develop infrastructure, reform the judicial system, and cultivate a coalition of responsible business elites capable
of acting as a balance to the reactionary right. Yet despite all the talk
of modernization, the Reagan White House was ideologically dis-
inclined to promote the kind of state-managed development that
could create employment or to break up Salvador's extreme concen-
tration of political and economic power. By 1983, the United States
had all but abandoned its celebrated land reform—by that point
planters and their military allies had already executed hundreds of
individuals who tried to take advantage of its provisions, rendering the
reform dead in all but name.[40] Far from promoting industrialization
and a more equitable distribution of the nation's wealth, the Reagan
administration insisted that Duarte orient the economy toward free
trade while at the same time cutting back on social spending, which
only served to estrange the Christian Democrats further from their
working-class supporters. By 1986, the Salvadoran government was
spending less on schools and health care than it had a decade earlier.

The Reagan White House also limited Duarte's options by prohibiting him from entering into serious negotiations with the FMLN
to end the war through some sort of power-sharing deal. The one
effective political action taken by the United States was to threaten
to cut off funding if the military overthrew Duarte. Yet this did little to fortify civil society, for as one Salvadoran officer put it in 1986,
"we no longer need a coup because we already have power."[41] By
1989, the rebels were once again mounting impressive military operations. With no end in sight, the war had claimed the lives of well
over fifty thousand Salvadorans, the vast majority victims of government forces.

The Reagan administration began to distance itself from the in-
effectual Duarte. It turned instead to ARENA—the party it had just
spent the last five years and millions of dollars to prevent from

coming to power. With the Christian Democrats in disarray and the left out of the running, ARENA won the 1989 presidential elections handily.

So, for all the hype about fighting what counterinsurgent theorists call the "other war" and for all the talk of fortifying "frail government institutions" and eliminating poverty, U.S. policy at the end of the 1980s, after billions of dollars and tens of thousands of homicides, found itself where it started, resting on the twin pillars of a Jurassic oligarchy and a vengeful yet greatly fortified military—a "bunch of murderous thugs," as one U.S. diplomat described Washington's Salvadoran allies.[42]

THE GENOCIDE OPTION

After eleven years of war, a 1991 report commissioned by the undersecretary of defense for policy concluded that the "FMLN's infrastructure [remains] so dense" that "only a massacre could uproot it."[43] Not one massacre but many.

It was not clowns, mariachi bands, the provision of food, medicine, and education, or any of the other public relations schemes designed to win hearts and minds but, according to a 1991 Defense Department study, "lavish brutality" conducted by the death squads and security forces that prevented a guerrilla victory in El Salvador.[44] The White House insisted that its political initiatives were responsible for the containment of the insurgency, but a U.S. expert posted in El Salvador concluded that the "horrible lesson of the early 1980s is that terrorism works."[45] Benjamin Schwarz, the RAND analyst who produced the 1991 Defense report, today writes that all the "US military advisers and intelligence officers" whom he knew who were involved in the war understood that the containment of the rebels was "not the result of reform but the consequence of the murder of thousands of people."[46]

At the time, the Reagan administration generally avoided such honesty. But occasionally its members and hangers-on would come close to sanctioning terror. In her 1980 essay "The Hobbes Problem," Jeane Kirkpatrick writes that "traditionalist death squads" may be repugnant to Americans but they are deeply rooted in Salvador's political culture and are the only institution that can transform brute violence into legitimate authority.[47] From his perch at the *New York Times*, William Safire asked what "winning" would mean in El Salvador: "Is it supporting a military junta that kills the opposition but by its repressive nature produces more opposition that becomes necessary to kill? If need be, yes—considering the aggressive totalitarian alternative."[48]

But for the most part, the Reagan administration steered clear of such bluntness—as Cheney does today—and instead argued that it was political reform that saved the day. Part of this reform, the story goes, involved instilling a culture of respect for human rights in the military. In the early 1980s, as the bodies mounted, the White House went to great pains to demonstrate that "human rights" was part of the training it provided Salvadoran cadets, letting reporters see for themselves how the School of the Americas and other institutions were balancing the imperatives of national security with a respect for human life. "U.S. military advisors," wrote one *Newsweek* reporter who was allowed to sit in on a class, are "offering lessons in humanity: how to treat civilians fairly and how to take prisoners as well as tally body counts."[49]

Yet despite the military's appropriation of the language of human rights, the rehabilitation of counterinsurgency warfare doctrine in Central America in the 1980s entailed a return to the concept of counterterror developed two decades earlier—now turbocharged to reflect a real as opposed to an imagined insurgency. Human rights provided the idiom through which to gauge the correct degree of violence to be applied, as U.S. military preceptors schooled their Salvadoran charges in counterinsurgency while admonishing them to avoid, as Special Forces major Roger Slaughter told Salvadoran cadets in Fort Benning in 1982, "indiscriminate acts of violence." "An army cannot violate the individual rights of the people they are sworn to protect," said Slaughter. "You have to use aggressive restraint."[50] According to Colonel Waghelstein, the "idea" was "to minimize the collateral damage to the civilian population and to surgically apply combat power."[51] But "aggressive restraint," as honest military observers admitted in El Salvador, was a hard line to toe, and little, as a practical matter, separated "hot" from "cold" violence.

This calculus can be found in the so-called torture manuals distributed by the United States to Central and South American security forces in the 1970s and 1980s instructing them in interrogation techniques designed to induce psychological fear, sexual humiliation, and physical stress and cause sensory deprivation.[52] One Pentagon handbook distributed in at least five Latin American countries described at length "coercive" procedures designed to "destroy [the] capacity to resist." "Successful application," it coached, entailed learning how to cause the three Ds: "debility," "dependency," and "dread."[53]

In the course of the Central American conflicts, a number of torturers defected from their death squads to testify that they received their training directly from U.S. instructors.[54] After escaping from Honduras's notorious Battalion 316 in the mid-1980s, Florencio Caballero testified that American advisers worked closely with his unit to get it to abandon "physical" torture and adopt psychological methods.[55] Caballero was taught "to study the fears and weakness of a prisoner." "Make him stand up," he was told, "don't let him sleep, keep him naked and in isolation, put rats and cockroaches in his cell, give him bad food, serve him dead animals, throw cold water on him, change the temperature."

Just as the torture memos of today's war on terror parse the difference between "pain" and "severe pain," and "psychological harm" and "lasting psychological harm," these field manuals went to great length to regulate the application of suffering.[56] "The threat to inflict pain can trigger fears more damaging than the immediate sensation of pain," one handbook observed.[57] Yet as in Abu Ghraib, such distinctions in Central America were unsustainable. Once a threat is made and the suspect does not respond, one manual conceded, the threat "must be carried out."[58] One of Caballero's victims, Ines Murillo, who survived only because of her family's political connections, says she was subject to beatings and electric shocks to her body, including her genitals, given raw dead birds and rats for dinner, and forced to stand naked for hours without sleep and without being allowed to urinate, with freezing water poured over her at regular intervals for extended periods.

While terrorism worked in El Salvador to prevent an insurgent takeover of the state, the FMLN, after more than a decade in the trenches, remained undefeated. It was still able to mount serious military offensives and claim the loyalty of large sectors of both the rural and the urban population. When Washington in 1991, at the end of the Cold War, urged its Salvadoran clients to draw their war to a close, the rebels therefore bargained from a position of strength and were able to demand that any cessation of hostilities be contingent on the implementation of many of the initiatives long championed, at least rhetorically, by the United States—including land reform, reform of the judicial system, dismantling of the death-squad apparatus, and purging the military of some of its worst human rights offenders.

After twelve years of fighting, fifty to sixty thousand civilian deaths, another twenty to thirty-four thousand military deaths, and more than six billion of Washington's dollars, it took an unvanquished insurgency to force the kind of democratization that the United States had grudgingly supported as a means to defeat that insurgency in the first place.[59]

In Guatemala, the bloodshed was even worse than it was in El

Salvador. After the CIA overthrew Arbenz in 1954, Washington promised that it would turn the country into a "showcase for democracy." It instead created a laboratory of repression. Decades of counterinsurgent funding and training produced in Guatemala a highly skilled military, one that by the time of Reagan's inauguration was hurtling toward the most brutal phase of Central America's most brutal war. Between November 1981 and early 1983, the military swept through indigenous communities, committing over six hundred massacres and turning the rural highlands into a slaughterhouse.

Even as the genocide proceeded, Reagan and his advisers pushed hard to restore complete military aid, which had been partly cut by the Carter administration. In December 1979, before his campaign got fully under way, a delegation from the private American Security Council, which included men, such as John Singlaub, who would play a prominent role in Reagan's campaign and administration, had made contact with the military to reassure them that aid would be resumed once Carter was voted out. The message the team brought to Guatemala was: "Mr. Reagan recognizes that a good deal of dirty work has to be done."[60]

Once in office, Reagan lobbied to make good on his promise but there was no real urgency. Despite Carter's cutoff of military aid, American funding and training continued to flow to Guatemala, either through preexisting contracts not affected by the ban or through Agency for International Development money directed to support the military's effort to gain control of the countryside.[61] By late 1982, it was clear that the killing had succeeded in containing the insurgency, so the White House felt it didn't have to push Congress to restore aid to Guatemala with the same enthusiasm with which it advanced its Nicaraguan and Salvadoran policy.

Reagan still took every opportunity he could to laud the Guatemalan regime, even though his administration had full knowledge that troops had orders to "eliminate all sources of resistance" and were engaged in "large-scale killing of Indian men, women and children."[62] Just a day before the Guatemalan army committed a particularly gruesome massacre (over the course of three days soldiers in a small village called Dos Erres killed more than 160 people, including 65 children who were swung by their feet so their heads were smashed on rocks), Reagan met with Efraín Ríos Montt, the president of Guatemala and one of the principal architects of the genocide. Reagan complained to the press that his Central American counterpart, an evangelical Christian with strong ties to the fundamentalist movement in the United States, was getting a "bad deal" from his critics and assured reporters that Ríos Montt was "totally committed to democracy."[63]

Genocide may not have been an option in 1966 when strategists gamed for war in Central America, but by the early 1980s it had become an acceptable solution.

Taking the Revolution Out of the Hands of Revolutionaries

Mass slaughter in defense of national security was insufficient for a movement bent on restoring not just America's military authority in the world but its moral legitimacy as well. Since the initiation of the Cold War, there have existed true believers within the U.S. foreign policy establishment who have rejected the policy of "containment," arguing instead that Washington should take forceful action to "roll back" Communism. Ex-Trotskyist philosopher turned Office of Strategic Services consultant James Burnham was perhaps the first to popularize the Cold War as the "Third World War," providing a vocabulary that came to exemplify the passion of those who view the world as engaged in a perpetual struggle between the forces of darkness and light.[64] As early as 1947, Burnham called on Washington to "penetrate the communist fortress," to "reverse the direction of the thrust from the [Marxist] heartland," and to "undermine communist power in East Europe, northern Iran, Afghanistan, Manchuria, northern Korea, and China." In the 1950s, during the Korean War, a number of conservative Republicans and southern Democrats shed their isolationist skin to support General Douglas MacArthur's call to use 800,000 nationalist Chinese to reverse Communism in China, against the multilateral equivocators Harry Truman and Dean Acheson.

Others more directly involved in crafting the early Cold War were tempted by a similar vision of world crusade.[65] John Foster Dulles, Eisenhower's secretary of state, called for a "policy of boldness" and even claimed to have "rolled back" Soviet advances in Iran in 1953 and Guatemala in 1954.[66] Yet the realities of geopolitical power and nuclear rivalry sobered their vision, and while politicians like Dulles often acted with daring in areas of little consequence, in Guatemala, say, or Cuba, they proceeded with restraint in their dealings with Russia.

In the 1960s, though, frontline counterinsurgents operating in Southeast Asia took Kennedy's revolutionary rhetoric to heart, believing that in order to best their Communist rivals they had to adopt their tactics, style, and zeal. Men like Edward Lansdale, Ted Shackley, and John Singlaub modeled themselves as insurgent counterinsurgents: they organized secret "guerrilla" paramilitary armies among the Meo, Montagnard, and Hmong ethnic groups in Vietnam and Laos and celebrated heroic, bold deeds. They extolled an ethic of ends over means, which included justifying the use of torture, terror, and murder in the name of a higher ideal, and built a transnational counterinsurgent network—an "anti-Communist International" comprised of a sordid mélange of dictators, fascists, militarists, and drug runners.[67] In short, in Vietnam, they transformed anti-Communism from a parochial reflex into a world-historical paramilitary movement with pretensions no less universal than those of Marxism.

In 1972, Special Forces veteran and political scientist Sam Sarkesian captured the movement's sensibility when he said that the task of counterinsurgents was to "take the revolution out of the hands of the revolutionaries." (Sarkesian perhaps revealed the movement's sentiments a bit too well considering that he was referencing, without acknowledgment, a phrase from a 1923 book called *Das Dritte Reich*—The Third Reich—by Arthur Moeller van den Bruck, a German historian from whom the Nazis drew many of their ideas.)[68]

The 1979 revolution in Nicaragua proved to be tailor-made for those who wanted to transform America's foreign policy from containment to rollback. For over a year prior to the 1980 presidential elections, defense activists gathering around Reagan's candidacy used the revolution to assail Carter, attacking his human rights policy and tolerance for "ideological pluralism" as leading to the downfall of Somoza, who for decades served the United States as a loyal backstop against Communism. Beyond the "appeasers" in the White House, the Sandinistas themselves made useful foils. Rather than comprising hard-line Stalinists, as groups such as the Committee of Santa Fe claimed, the Sandinista front was made up of a coalition of progressive capitalists, socialists, Marxists, and Catholics. Its leaders were pragmatic, fully aware of the realities of hemispheric power. But they were also adamant nationalists who took seriously the principle of sovereignty, having observed Nicaragua's long and unfortunate dealings with the United States. They stood their ground, unwilling to forsake Cuba's friendship or reject its aid. While they had no desire to replicate Castro's sclerotic economy or polity, they were dedicated to making Nicaragua more humane through the creation of a mixed economy in which the state directed capital investment and redistributed wealth by providing health care and education. The more Washington tried to tutor them to genuflect to its reign, the more they moved to consolidate power, committed to avoid the mistakes of Guatemala in 1954, Brazil in 1964, and Chile in 1973. Their resolve was taken by Kirkpatrick and others as evidence of their totalitarianism—even though throughout the worst of the Contra war, the Sandinistas never violated civil rights or engaged in repression anywhere near to the degree that Somoza had.

Sandinista stubbornness, of course, is just what the hard-liners counted on, having reassembled Somoza's ill-famed National Guard into a counterrevolutionary force months before Reagan won the presidency, before, in fact, he had even captured his party's nomination in mid-1980. An American citizen, Nat Hamrick, described by one of his Nicaraguan allies as a "playboy type of adventurer, a fast talker," and John Carbaugh, a staffer in Jesse Helms's office who played an important role in vetting Reagan's national security and diplomatic appointments, made contact with a group of ex-National Guardsmen and Honduran military officers who hoped to organize a counterrevolutionary expedition based in Nicaragua's northern border. Hamrick made his living as a mail-order gun supplier, specializing in Chinese Mausers and Boer rifles. But he also had a business exporting hardwoods out of the Nicaraguan rain forest during the Somoza regime, and when the Sandinistas told him he could continue his operations, he turned his enterprise into an "intelligence-gathering network for the Defense Intelligence Agency."[69] Just after Reagan's election, Carbaugh and Hamrick brokered a meeting between would-be Contra leaders and representatives of the Argentine military junta—who took time out of their own campaign of "disappearing" tens of thousands of their compatriots. In agreeing to fund and train the Contras, Argentina acted not only out of ideological sympathy with the counterrevolutionaries but in hopes of improving diplomatic relations with the United States, which had grown strained under Carter.

Supplementing this public-private initiative was Major General Laurence Schweitzer, an assistant to the deputy army chief of staff during Carter's presidency who played a key role in bringing the CIA on board. Described as "brilliant, brave, and indefatigable, a zealous anti-Communist" and "pious Roman Catholic," Schweitzer, who during Vietnam repeatedly forsook the comfort afforded by his rank to engage in nighttime firefights, grew alarmed at the indifference with which he believed Carter's Joint Chiefs of Staff viewed the Central American crisis.[70] After Reagan's inauguration, the major general, now on the National Security Council, arranged a meeting between Honduran officers and William Casey, just nominated to head the CIA, in which the Hondurans pitched their idea of organizing fleeing members of Nicaragua's National Guard into a counterrevolutionary expedition that could destabilize the Sandinista government. With the State Department out of the loop, Casey signed on to the plan and covertly began to sponsor the fledgling organization. As talks between Washington and Managua broke down over democratization issues, the United States increasingly took a more public role in supporting the Contras.

Over the course of the next ten years, the Contras gestated in the undergrowth of empire. Their primary patrons were the irrepressible Oliver North, at the NSC, and the ineffable William Casey, head of the CIA, a team whose ascendance in the White House signaled the consolidation of the war party over Central American foreign policy. Thomas Enders was forced out of the State Department in 1983, while Secretary of State Shultz found himself increasingly isolated. Donald Regan, a Casey protégé, took over from James Baker, a Casey adversary, as Reagan's chief of staff.[71] John Poindexter, as obsessed with secrecy as was Casey, became head of the NSC. Norman Podhoretz's son-in-law Elliott Abrams, with no diplomatic experience, was made assistant secretary of state for inter-American affairs, Enders's old job, thus synchronizing the State Department with the CIA and the NSC.

Between 1982, when Argentina's disastrous Falklands war took them out of the game in Central America and left the CIA the principal sponsor of the Contras, and 1986, when the Iran-Contra story exploded in the press, Casey and North presided over the construction of an elaborate transnational support network designed to bypass congressional and public scrutiny. The network remobilized many of the clandestine operatives laid off at the end of the 1970s, insinuating them "back into newly revived covert operations, whether in governmental, private, or mixed roles."[72] It also included states such as Saudi Arabia, Taiwan, Panama, and Israel, conservative religious organizations like Pat Robertson's 700 Club and Sun Myung Moon's Unification Church, private security firms and arms merchants, retired military personnel, mercenaries, businessmen, ex-agents of the Iranian shah's secret police, and international drug traffickers. Grassroots organizations in America raised money to ship humanitarian aid to Contra bases in Honduras and Costa Rica, and foreign governments and mercenaries provided training and arms. Most infamously, North created an elaborate circuit of exchange that, with the help of Israeli arms traders, sold U.S. missiles to Iran at inflated prices, with the profits from the deal used to supply the Contras.[73] There is ample evidence, not the least of which comes from North's handwritten notes, that the CIA employed Latin American cocaine and marijuana dealers as middlemen, using their planes to ship arms to the Contras in exchange for easy access to American markets.[74]

Just as the counterinsurgency in El Salvador represented a disjuncture between the doctrine of political reform and the practice of terror, an enormous chasm existed between the idealism used by Reagan to justify support for the Contras and the actions his charges took on the ground. They were the "strangest national liberation organization in the world," remarked an adviser to the Joint Chiefs of Staff, "just a bunch of killers."[75] One high-level Contra official who worked closely with the CIA said that brigades would "arrive at an undefended village, assemble all the residents in the town square and then proceed to kill—in full view of the others—all persons suspected of working" for the government or the Sandinista party.[76] They "slaughter[ed] people like hogs," reported a member of a private mercenary outfit that provided support for the Contras after Congress cut off aid.[77] Other Contra leaders confessed to "damnable atrocities" and "hundreds of civilian murders, mutilations, tortures, and rapes," of which "CIA superiors were well aware."[78] Sexual violence was a favorite sport of Contra forces, who, according to a U.S. official, had a "tendency to kidnap young girls."[79] By 1985, the Contras had executed close to four thousand civilians, wounded an equal number, and kidnapped roughly another five thousand.[80] Human rights organizations accused them of "indiscriminate attacks, torture, and other outrages," while the CIA acknowledged that the "freedom fighters" had killed "civilians and Sandinista officials in the provinces, as well as heads of cooperatives, nurses, doctors, and judges."[81] Beyond the Contras, the CIA organized contract mercenaries from Ecuador, Guatemala, and El Salvador into units dubbed "unilaterally controlled Latino assets" to launch a sea war from a converted oil rig positioned in international waters off Nicaragua's Pacific shore, bombing coastal targets and mining the country's principal commercial port. By the end of the war, thirty thousand civilians had been killed, the overwhelming majority at the hands of the Contras.[82]

Applying the same rational-choice logic used in Salvador's counterinsurgency, the Nicaraguan counterrevolution was aimed not at establishing ideological legitimacy for the Contras or winning the allegiance of the majority of the population but simply making it too painful for the Sandinistas to govern. As one CIA training manual put it, the trick was to modulate between "implicit and explicit terror" to wear down the new regime through unpredictable yet persistent acts of brutality.[83] Hoping to show a wavering rural population that the Sandinistas could not establish effective sovereignty, the Contras razed cooperatives, schools, health clinics, and power stations and tortured, raped, and murdered civilians, including foreigners who were helping to rebuild Nicaragua. It was also hoped that the Contras would, at the very least, force the Sandinistas to devote scarce resources to the war and to impose draconian measures that would eat away at their legitimacy and, with luck, provoke them into attacking Honduras, which would then justify a U.S. response.[84]

Such terror succeeded not just in destroying the hopes for a more humane society raised by Nicaragua's 1979 revolution—the Sandinistas were voted out of office in 1990—but in helping to justify rollback as a legitimate, and feasible, objective of American diplomacy. The Contras were by no means the first anti-Communist insurgency sponsored by the United States. Similar policies had already been attempted in Guatemala in 1954, Cuba in 1961, and in Southeast Asia, Africa, and Afghanistan. But no other insurgency was championed for such a sustained period of time in such idealistic terms.

The more their atrocities were documented by the press and human rights activists, the more Reagan and his advisers heralded the Contras as freedom's foot soldiers, as the "moral equivalents of our founding fathers." What was first dubbed by columnist Charles Krauthammer as the "Reagan Doctrine"—a pledge not just to contain world Communism but to roll it back—was most fully elaborated in relation to Nicaragua. Central American hands Elliott Abrams and Constantine Menges, an NSC adviser and primary advocate of the 1983 invasion of Grenada, inserted the words into Reagan's 1985 State of the Union address that formed the heart of the doctrine: "We must not break faith with those who are risking their lives—on every continent, from Afghanistan to Nicaragua—to defy Soviet-supported aggression. . . . Support for freedom fighters is self-defense and totally consistent with the OAS and U.N. Charters. . . . I want to work with you to support the democratic forces whose struggle is tied to our own security."[85] Casey was the most aggressive proponent of rollback, envisioning the Contra supply network as a model for a global "off-the-books" operational system—what he called the "Enterprise"—directed by the government yet powered by private organizations, through which arms, money, and training would surreptitiously flow to anti-Communist insurgencies in Afghanistan, Cambodia, Ethiopia, Angola, Cuba, Mozambique, and Yemen.[86] To this list the Heritage Foundation added Laos, Libya, Iran, and Vietnam.[87]

Propelled by the back draft generated by defeat in Vietnam and using Central America as their staging ground, militarists rehabilitated the most repressive aspects of the covert operations and counterinsurgent doctrines of the 1950s and 1960s in order to reverse what they believed was a dangerous recession of American power in the world. By the end of the 1980s, the White House had expanded and increased funding for the Special Forces, had set up in the Pentagon a Special Operations Unified Command to conduct low-intensity warfare, and had created a new post of assistant secretary of defense for special operations and low-intensity conflict. By the time Reagan left office, despite the nominal sway of the Weinberger Doctrine, the United States was on the offensive, carrying out unconventional military operations throughout the third world.

There were of course other areas more pressing than Central America on the White House's foreign policy radar in the 1980s, particularly the Persian Gulf region of the Middle East. Yet no other region provided such a prolonged opportunity to reorient American militarism after the setback in Vietnam as did Central America, in ways that continue to resound in the initiatives taken after 9/11 by George W. Bush's administration.

It was in the exercise of Central American policy that conservative militants turned statesmen learned how to maneuver around their more cautious colleagues in the State Department and most consistently disregarded the opinion of multilateral institutions. When the International Court of Justice ordered the United States to pay Nicaragua billions of dollars in reparations for mining its harbor and conducting an illegal war of aggression, Washington balked and withdrew from the court's jurisdiction—a "watershed moment," according to legal scholar Eric Posner, in the United States's relationship with the international community, one that Bush's ambassador to the United Nations, John Bolton, has cited as evidence for why the United States should not support the new International Criminal Court.[88] It was in Central America that unconventional warriors learned to bypass congressional oversight by creating a semiprivate, international network to carry out a clandestine foreign policy and to undermine post-Vietnam efforts to limit the use of military power for other than clearly defined, limited objectives. And it was there that the New Right, now in power, began to instill a culture of loyalty to the cause and incuriosity about the world: "To raise a question was to be a negative thinker," complained CIA agent Nestor Sanchez of the administration's fixation on Central America.[89]

Central America also marked an important threshold in the moral evolution of U.S. foreign policy militarism. In coming to see themselves as revolutionaries, militarists justified any and all means in relation to ends. Yet their "revolution" offered little but free-market absolutism, which turned out to be a poor program for winning "hearts and minds." They became dependent nearly exclusively on intimidation. Washington did indeed take that "step toward the primitive" when in Central America it cast its lot with the most feverish end of the anti-Communist spectrum, men who slaughtered hundreds of thousands in the name of political liberalism. It moved even farther along in its journey in Afghanistan, when in order to force the Cold War to a conclusion the United States "unapologetically," according to George Crile's sympathetic history of the anti-Soviet jihad, equipped and trained "cadres of high tech holy warriors"—allies who wanted to roll back not just the USSR but the Enlightenment as well.[90]

Despite the New Right's impressive restoration of military power and global purpose, one impediment, wrote the Pentagon's legal adviser William O'Brien in 1984, still remained: the "unrelenting anti-militarism" of the "American home front," whose distaste for things like torture, extrajudicial assassinations, "dead or wounded children," and "starvation as a means of combat" continued to handicap American action in the world.[91] The conservative movement tackled this domestic antimilitarism head-on, bringing to the struggle the same passion it used to confront enemies abroad, as we shall see in the next chapter.

CHAPTER FOUR

Bringing It All Back Home:
The Politics of the New
Imperialism

FOR MANY OF THE POLICY and opinion makers who seized on 9/11 to promote their vision of an imperial America, placing the nation on a permanent war footing was as much a form of domestic collective therapy as it was an international crusade to reshape the world. "Nothing less than the soul of this country is at stake," Norman Podhoretz wrote a month after the attacks on the World Trade Center and Pentagon. "Nothing less than an unambiguous victory will save us from yet another disappointment in ourselves and another despairing disillusion with our leaders." The attacks provided a chance for Americans who "crave 'a new birth' of the confidence we used to have in ourselves and in 'America the Beautiful.'"¹ Such desires to overcome the factionalism and disenchantment that had plagued America since the 1960s were not confined to the political right, as many liberals likewise hungered for a renewed sense of national purpose. The *New Republic*'s Peter Beinart, for instance, called on Democrats to join the struggle against Islamic fascism and to rediscover their "fighting faith" in political liberalism. For their part, essayists Max Boot and Charles Krauthammer have expressed optimism that the brutality of a protracted global war on terrorism would finally form a callus over the national psyche, dulling the undue sensitivity to pain that spread in the wake of Vietnam.[2]

But decades before 9/11 raised hopes that a galvanized domestic constituency for perpetual war could at last be forged, Reagan's Central American policy offered the opportunity to contain, and begin to roll back, the antimilitarism that had infected U.S. political culture and institutions since the Vietnam War. More than any other twentieth-century conflict, Vietnam highlighted the porous border between foreign and domestic policy. Escalating protest, much of it linked to a reinvigorated internationalism, not only helped end the war but led to legislative measures that curbed the power of government security institutions, most notably the Central Intelligence Agency. At home, a deep skepticism shattered the governing consensus that had held sway for the first two decades after World War II. In what seemed a remarkably short period of time, the institutional pillars of society—universities, churches, newspapers, movies, Congress, and the judiciary—that had previously buttressed government legitimacy began to lean against it, advancing what some conservative critics came to deride as a permanent "adversary culture."[3] It was not just military defeat that brought about such a turnaround but also revelations of brutality committed throughout the third world in the name of national security and of perfidy conducted under the cloak of government secrecy and executive privilege.

By the end of the 1980s, defense intellectuals and activists had achieved a revolution in the mechanics and morals of special warfare doctrine abroad. But for their revolution to take hold, they knew they had to confront this culture of dissent at home. In the face of persistent and growing opposition to U.S. policies in El Salvador and Nicaragua, militarists countered with a series of actions that eroded the boundary between imperial policies and national politics. Making little distinction between foreign enemies and domestic opponents, the Reagan administration put in place what one government official described as a "psychological operation of the kind the military conducts to influence a population in denied or enemy territory."[4] The operation unfolded on three fronts.

First, to confront an adversarial press, tame a presumptuous Congress, and make inroads on college campuses, the administration orchestrated a sophisticated and centralized "public diplomacy" campaign that deployed techniques drawn from both the PR world and the intelligence community. Second, the White House either loosened or circumvented restrictions placed on domestic law-and-order surveillance operations against political dissidents, reviving tactics that the FBI and other intelligence agencies had used to intimidate the antiwar movement in the 1960s, tactics that were thought to have been repudiated by the Rockefeller Committee and other congressional investigations into domestic covert actions in the mid-1970s. Finally, and most consequentially, the administration built countervailing grassroots support to counter what seemed a permanently entrenched anti-imperialist opposition, mobilizing militarists and evangelicals on behalf of a hard-line foreign policy. Such a campaign allowed the White House to go forward with its Central American program. More critically, it also helped create the ideas and infrastructure that turned the Republican Party into a mass movement and transformed the New Right into the dominant political force in America today.

Media Education

In January 1983, Reagan signed National Security Decision Directive 77, creating a domestic interagency task force "designed to generate support for our national security objectives."[5] Five months later, the

Office of Public Diplomacy for Latin America and the Caribbean was born under the direction of Cuban émigré Otto Reich.

Public Diplomacy was officially charged with implementing a "new, nontraditional" approach to "defining the terms of the public discussion on Central American policy" and with "unshackl[ing] . . . public perception of policy from myths and cant."[6] In reality, it was the homeland branch of Casey and North's "Enterprise," staffed by psych-warfare operatives from the CIA and the U.S. Army's Fourth Psychological Operations Group.[7] In order to bypass the 1947 National Security Act, which prohibited the CIA from trying to influence domestic opinion, the office was placed under the nominal authority of the State Department. But Reich himself—despite being vouched for as "politically sound" by Jeane Kirkpatrick—was "review[ed] weekly" by Walter Raymond, a thirty-year CIA propaganda operative who sat on Reagan's NSC.[8]

To circumvent laws that barred the White House from spending money to lobby Congress, the office implemented, as Raymond put it, a "public-private strategy," coordinating the work of the NSC with PR firms, psychological warfare specialists, and New Right activists, intellectuals, and pressure groups. It contracted Republican-affiliated advertising firms such as Woody Kepner Associates and International Business Communications and supervised the fundraising and publicity activity of individuals and nongovernmental organizations such as Freedom House and Accuracy in Media.[9] The office also worked closely with conservative cadres such as Carl "Spitz" Channell, who as a private individual raised millions of dollars, mostly through front organizations like the National Endowment for the Preservation of Liberty, the American Conservative Trust, and the American Anti-Terrorism Committee. The money was used to fund "television ads, newspaper ads and grassroots activities" on behalf of the Contras.[10] Channell also funneled millions of dollars in private donations through a Swiss bank account to pay for weapons for the Nicaraguan rebels.

Congress proved more willing to cooperate with Reagan on his Salvadoran policy, so the office focused on Nicaragua, using polling data to identify Sandinista "negatives" and Contra "positives" and to compile "key words, phrases, or images" that could turn Americans against the Nicaraguan government.[11] A 1985 "action plan" formated according to the PR industry's "perception management" guidelines listed simple notions or phrases, many of them repeated multiple times with no elaboration, to help administration officials and their allies to frame the debate. The Sandinistas were "evil," Soviet "puppets," "racist and repress human rights," "involved in U.S. drug problems." The Contras were "freedom fighters," "good guys," "underdogs," "religious," and "poor."

The memo offered a few concepts that went beyond two or three syllables. The United States, it said, wanted not to "overthrow" the Sandinistas but only to change their "behavior." It was not "immoral" to support a "covert action." But mostly the memo chanted buzzwords with mantralike minimalism: "military buildup," "forced military conscription," "the drug connection," "Panama Canal," "human rights violations," "Communist connection," and "persecution of church groups."[12]

The office used the Nicaraguan campaign to shift the understanding of the threat facing America away from Communism, which no matter how vilified was part of the Western tradition and associated with the interests of a specific nation, toward the more capacious concept of "terrorism." In the 1980s, the United States found itself ever more involved in Middle Eastern politics, and the Reagan administration increasingly tied Nicaragua to troubles in that region.

Aside from equating the Sandinistas with the Nazis and charging Managua with fomenting "terrorism" in Costa Rica and El Salvador, Public Diplomacy operatives accused the Sandinistas of having "ties with the PLO, Libya, and terrorists," linking them, as Reagan did in a 1985 speech, with "Arafat, Qadhafi, and the Ayatollah Khomeini."[13] The office even indicted them for persecuting Jews.[14] Taking over the office from Reich in 1986, Robert Kagan recommended the distribution of reports that documented Sandinista "anti-Semitism"—supplemented with "glossy pictures" and presented in an "In Their Own Words" style—to "key Jewish journalists and interreligious publications."[15] Yet it was not the Sandinistas who traded in anti-Jewish sentiment. The American "media was controlled by Jews," said one CIA handler, according to a respected Contra leader, "and if we could show that Jews were being persecuted it would help a lot."[16] (In the 1960s the FBI likewise spread rumors that the Black Power movement was anti-Semitic in order to drive a wedge between it and Jewish intellectuals.)

Operatives worked at a breakneck pace. Over just a two-month period in early 1985 the office laid out a chronology of seventy-nine tasks to accomplish, among them:

- Assign U.S. intelligence agencies to research Sandinista violations of the Geneva Convention;
- Prepare themes to approach Congressmen based on listed perceptions;
- Encourage U.S. reporters to meet individual Contra fighters;
- Contact internal eyewitnesses/victims to testify before Congress about their abortive attempts to deal with Sandinistas;
- Prepare list of publicly and privately expressed Congressional objections to aiding Contras;
- Request that Zbigniew Brzezinski write a paper which points out geopolitical consequences of Communist domination of Nicaragua;
- Hold briefings for key Congressional members and staffers;
- Supervise preparation and assignment of articles directed to special interest groups at rate of one per week (examples: article on Nicaraguan educational system for National Educational Association, article by retired military for Retired Officers Association, etc.);

- Draft one op-ed per week for signature by Administration officials. Specify themes for the op-eds and retain final editorial rights;
- Conduct public opinion poll of American attitudes toward Sandinistas, freedom fighters;
- Martha Lida Murillo (9 year old atrocity victim) visit to Washington; possible photo-op with First Lady;
- Prepare list of key media outlets interested in Central American issues; identify specific editors, commentators, talk shows, and columnists;
- Call/visit newspaper editorial boards and give them background on the Nicaraguan freedom fighters;
- Prepare a "Dear Colleagues" letter for signature by a responsible Democrat which counsels against "negotiating" with the Sandinistas;
- Review and restate themes based on results of public opinion poll;
- Prepare document on Nicaraguan narcotics involvement;
- Publish and distribute "Nicaragua's Development as Marxist Leninist State";
- Sponsor media events for Central American resistance leaders;
- Congressional delegation visits during recess to Nicaraguan refugee camps in Honduras and Costa Rica;
- Administration and prominent non-government spokesman on network shows regarding Soviet, Cuban, East German, Libyan, and Iranian connection with Sandinistas;
- Distribute paper on geopolitical consequences [presumably the one that was requested of Brzezinski];
- Release paper on Nicaraguan drug involvement;
- Conduct telephone campaign in 120 Congressional districts. Citizens for America district activists organize phone-tree to target Congressional offices encouraging them to vote for Contra aid;
- Organize rallies featuring Central American spokesmen throughout the country in conjunction with Citizens for America activists;

- Organize nationally coordinated sermons about aid to the freedom fighters;
- Organize Washington conference "Central America: Resistance or Surrender" (Presidential drop-by?);
- Organize major rally in the Orange Bowl, Miami, attended by President Reagan; and [with no irony]:
- Release paper on Nicaraguan media manipulation.[17]

The administration produced a steady flow of white papers, briefings, talking points, pamphlets, and books on El Salvador and Nicaragua. For El Salvador, the job was primarily proving Cuban and Sandinista ties and rapidly refuting charges of atrocities committed by the Salvadoran military.[18] For Nicaragua, when the White House was not fabricating facts wholesale it was amplifying every statement and action made by the Sandinistas to prove their malfeasance. Documents with the titles "Mothers of Political Prisoners," "Religious Repression in Nicaragua," "Nicaragua and Cuba—Drugs," "In Their Own Words—Former Sandinistas Tell Their Story," "Human Costs of Communism," "Nicaragua in Quotes," "Inside the Sandinista Regime," and "Christians under Fire" were distributed either directly by the administration or by allied think tanks, ad hoc committees such as Citizens for America, CIA-front publishing houses, college organizations such as Young Americans for Freedom and Campus Crusade for Christ, the newly created National Endowment for Democracy, and an emerging network of alternative conservative news outlets, the most important at the time being the Christian Broadcasting Network and the Moon-owned *Washington Times*.[19]

The administration distributed its literature not just to New Right organizations but to "church groups, human rights organizations, lawyers, political scientists, journalists, etc.," each receiving "cover letters tailored" to their specific interests.[20] The Office of Public Diplomacy organized conferences on Central America and invited "leaders of special interest and public policy groups (think tanks, foundations, church groups, labor organizations, Indian and Black organizations, academics) with special interest in Latin America."[21] In its first year of operations, the office arranged more that 1,500 speaking engagements and distributed material to "1,600 libraries, 520 political science faculties, 122 editorial writers and 107 religious organizations"[22] It complied a comprehensive list of moral and political objections to Contra funding and drafted appropriate responses to each one, briefed the press and Congress on a regular basis, and wrote, or helped write, op-eds that were published in the *New York Times*, the *Washington Post*, and the *Wall Street Journal* under the bylines of administration officials, retired military officers, Contra leaders, foreign policy experts, and sympathetic scholars.[23]

The reduction of foreign policy to a series of emotionally laden talking points that linked the Sandinistas to any number of world evils manifested itself in the speeches of administration officials such as Jeane Kirkpatrick, William Casey, and Elliott Abrams. Nicaragua's connections with terrorism, Soviet nuclear submarines, religious and ethnic persecution, totalitarianism, Castro, East Germans, Bulgarians, Libya, Iran, even the Baader-Meinhof Gang—all were to be confronted with American purpose and resolve. Yet it was Ronald Reagan, listed by Public Diplomacy as an "asset" due to his communication skills, who best embodied the triumph of emotion over substance.[24] With little respect for history or fact, Reagan offered an image of the Nicaraguan struggle professionally tuned to resonate with popular fears and self-perceptions, presenting support for the Contras as keeping faith with America's "revolutionary heritage."[25] After all, the PR mavens at the Office of Public Diplomacy listed as their two most "exploitable themes" the idea that the Contras "are Freedom Fighters" fighting for "freedom in the American tradition" and the idea that American "history requires support to freedom fighters." Who could argue?

Revolution in the name of democracy became a marketing device. Office of Public Diplomacy memos stressed the need to refer to the insurgents not as "Contras" but as either "new revolutionaries" or "freedom fighters fighting in the American tradition." The war against the Sandinistas was to be called Nicaragua's "New Revolution." One memo suggested adopting as a logo for the Contras "a TORCH raised high by a hand, perhaps a shackled hand. It would signify a torch of freedom, like the Statute of Liberty's or the Olympic Torch, or the light of freedom at the end of the tunnel of darkness of Communism." Another idea was to commission a "song written about the freedom fighters and their struggle for freedom and democracy. Ideally, one which could be translated into either Spanish or English and sung by an American artist and can be made into a hit like the Ballad of the Green Berets. Such a song could generate publicity, especially if sung by a country western star." Other recommendations included the printing of T-shirts with messages in support of the freedom fighters. "One could be given to President Reagan," suggested one memo, as a spontaneous act to show popular support for his Central American policies. And on cue, Reagan accepted such a gift from a supporter, beaming as he held it high.[26]

The point of all this activity was not to create majority support for Reagan's Central American policy. White House director of communications Patrick Buchanan admitted as much at a 1986 Low-Intensity Warfare Conference when he said that the consensus that existed between 1941 and 1966 was gone and was not coming back: "There are many Americans out there . . . that will tell you that the great enemy of America is our support for right-wing dictatorships. . . . We do not have agreement among ourselves. We are not going to have agreement. We haven't had it for 20 years. And it seems to me there is no sense waiting for that agreement before acting."[27] The goal, rather, was to prevent an oppositional consensus from forming.

To that end, Public Diplomacy, much like rational-choice counterinsurgency, helped shift the debate in favor of the White House not by winning over domestic hearts and minds but by making it too costly for mainstream journalists and politicians to challenge policy.

By flooding the media with questionable facts and allegations, the Office of Public Diplomacy forced Reagan's opponents to dissipate their energies disproving allegations rather than making their own positive case for nonintervention. Confronted by government spokespeople and sympathetic experts ready to rebut unfavorable coverage, no matter how slight the criticism or how marginal the source, reporters came to dread the amount of fact checking it took to cover Central America.[28] "I work for a network very concerned with cost and image," complained Karen Burnes of ABC News in 1987. "It takes months and months," she said, to do a critical story on Reagan's Central American policy. Spending that much prep time on a story that would take up only five minutes of airtime, she said, was "not a way to be successful."[29]

By offering alternative interpretations, no mater how far-fetched, to discredit charges of atrocities committed by U.S. allies, Public Diplomacy muddied the waters and made it difficult, if not impossible, for human rights organizations to establish the facts of a case. In May 2005, *Newsweek* suffered the Bush administration's ire when it ran a story on tactics, including the desecration of the Koran, designed to humiliate Islamic prisoners in the global war on terror. But this wasn't the first time the magazine ran afoul of the White House for reporting critically on its foreign policy. In 1985, it had published an article documenting atrocities based not on an anonymous government source, as in the case of the controversial Koran report, but on color photographs provided by Frank Wohl, a Marine ROTC graduate and anti-Communist activist who was traveling with the rebels when he witnessed the execution of a prisoner of war. Using his account, *Newsweek* reported that:

> The victim dug his own grave, scooping the dirt out with his hands. Squatting in the hole, he ate some dry powdered milk, and

then lay down to die. No one gagged him. But he didn't scream. He crossed himself. Then a contra executioner knelt and rammed a Ka-Bar knife into his throat. A second enforcer stabbed at his jugular, then his abdomen. When the corpse was finally still, the contras threw dirt over the shallow grave—and walked away.[30]

The Office of Public Diplomacy sprang into action. The photos were authentic, yet Otto Reich argued that they must have been faked because the Contra uniforms were too clean. Wohl's conservative credentials didn't stop Oliver North from accusing him of being a Sandinista sympathizer. When asked about the killing by House Speaker Tip O'Neill, Reagan simply said, "I saw that picture, and I'm told that after it was taken, the so-called victim got up and walked away."[31]

Reich was a pedagogue, carrying out what he called "media education."[32] Instruction entailed personal visits to reporters whom he felt to be too sympathetic to either the Sandinistas or the Salvadoran rebels.[33] At an NPR studio, Reich let journalists know that his office had contracted a "special consultant service [to listen] to all NPR programs" on Central America—a serious threat to an agency that operated by government largesse. Reich later boasted that he had succeeded in getting reporters who he felt were too easy on the Sandinistas reassigned.[34] Following his visit, NPR hired conservative commentator Linda Chavez to provide "balance."[35] When the *Washington Post*'s John Lantigua proved too independent, Reich, through the right-wing advocacy organization Accuracy in the Media, started a rumor that he "was being furnished with live-in female Sandinista sex slaves in exchange for penning Sandinista agitprop."[36] According to journalist Robert Parry, himself the subject of innuendo, the "public diplomacy boys" during cocktail parties "would talk about American female journalists 'sleeping with Sandinistas.' "[37]

Congressional representatives who opposed Reagan on El Salvador or Nicaragua found themselves fighting for their political lives. "Attacking the President," Reich warned, "was no longer cost free."[38] During the 1980s the New Right, advised by PR firms under Public Diplomacy contract, focused much of its organizing work on unseating congressional antimilitarists, particularly those who opposed Reagan's Central American policy.[39] If you "cross" Reagan, said a Republican aide, "they're going to carve you up publicly"—a fate that befell Maryland congressman Michael Barnes during his senatorial bid.[40] International Business Communication, the Republican-linked PR firm, worked in tandem with Reich and Channell's American Anti-Terrorism Committee to execute a smear campaign that cost him the election. "Destroy Barnes," said the personal notes of one of Channell's operatives.[41]

Public Diplomacy combined the power of psych ops and PR tactics to blunt the distinction between foreign and domestic policy. The White House even timed Contra military operations to coincide with congressional votes on funding.[42] When its actions came to light, the office was condemned by both the Congress and the General Accounting Office as, in the words of an excised part of Congress's Iran-Contra report, "what a covert CIA operation in a foreign country might do."[43] Nonetheless, the administration considered the Office of Public Diplomacy such a stunning success that it "initiated" similar "methodologies" and "operations," as Elliott Abrams put it in 1986, "for Southern Africa and for terrorism issues."[44]

But the White House found that it could also control the press and Congress with less aggressive measures, for neither institution was quite as untamed as their reputations suggested. Aside from a few intrepid reporters in the mainstream and alternative press, such as Raymond Bonner and Robert Parry, the media cut the popular Reagan considerable slack. Ben Bradlee of the *Washington Post* describes a "return to deference" on the part of the press corps: "We were dealing with someone this time who really, really, really disapproved of us, disliked us, distrusted us, and that [we thought] we ought not give him any opportunities to see he was right."[45] Bradlee and his colleagues also responded to a perceived public fatigue with journalists "trying to make a Watergate out of everything." They "ease[d] off" the president, allowing him, and his reputation, to survive the Iran-Contra scandal, which by any sober account has to be ranked as one of the most egregious presidential violations of the public trust of the twentieth century.

A RETURN TO DEFERENCE

It was on the front line of the Central American conflicts that the Pentagon learned how to finesse the news at home by controlling reporters at the source. Defense strategists had analyzed the relationship between the press and the military after Vietnam and concluded that the problem in Southeast Asia was that journalists had become too independent in developing their own channels of information. In response, the Pentagon and the CIA granted privileged access to certain reporters in Central America, laying the groundwork for protocols that would be developed further in Grenada, Panama, and Iraq. John Waghelstein recounts that when he first arrived in El Salvador in the early 1980s he found that "many of the stories were written from within guerrilla-controlled areas and some of the eyewitness accounts had a pro-guerrilla bias."[46] He took "serious steps" to change this, conducting a "series of one-on-one backgrounders with a few of the more respected journalists" and holding an "informal weekly press session." "Good Salvadoran commanders were highlighted" and "problems were discussed candidly." He also authorized network camera crews to film the Salvadoran army in action. Such controlled access gave U.S. military advisers a way to establish cordial, respectful relations with the in-country press corps, allowing them not only to present their side of the war but to accustom select mainstream reporters to that access and make them loath to write anything that might jeopardize it.

It also created a bonding experience in which privilege was transformed into sympathy for the institution granting the access. Fred Barnes, now of the *Weekly Standard* but then of the *New Republic*, was even allowed to don a uniform and play "Contra for a Day." The only critical note in his chronicle of life among the anti-Communist insurgents was that the "coffee wasn't hot enough" and he had to sleep on a "plywood slab."[47]

Waghelstein thought his reforms changed the tenor of media coverage of El Salvador, with more time granted to the administration's point of view. But not all reporters could be brought into the fold, and he complained that the methods of journalists Raymond Bonner and John Dinges, whom he believed to be "dupes of a very sophisticated enemy," were "slipshod." It was Bonner who broke the story of the El Mozote massacre, which Washington vigorously denied for over a decade. Bonner's reporting met with a firestorm of criticism from the State Department and the *Wall Street Journal*, leading the *New York Times* to pull him out of El Salvador. "We finally got rid of that sonuvabitch," said one officer delighted to see him go.[48]

For their part, antimilitarists in Congress were no match for the alliance of Republicans and conservative Democrats more than willing to grant the administration the benefit of the doubt, especially when it came to foreign policy and especially in a region as inconsequential as Central America. Hard-liners like William Casey and Robert McFarlane wanted to challenge critics in the House and Senate directly on El Salvador and Nicaragua as a way of isolating and discrediting the legislative branch. But there was no need for confrontation. In El Salvador, Reagan's rhetorical support of his predecessor's reform program won over enough "responsible Democrats" to carry on the White House's policy.[49] Support for the Contras was trickier, but Congress was willing to challenge Reagan only so far.

Opponents of the administration's Nicaragua policy celebrated a number of minor victories in the early 1980s that limited support for the Contras but sometime around 1985–86—at the height of Public Diplomacy work—they noted that the public debate had gotten away from them.[50] Enough Democrats had come to accept the administration's analysis of the crisis: the Sandinistas were rogues and the Contras, however they came into being, deserved American backing. The much-debated Boland Amendment to the 1982 House Appropriations Bill—which prohibited the federal government from providing military support to the Contras "for the purpose of overthrowing the Government of Nicaragua" but allowed humanitarian aid to continue—was by no means as strict as the earlier Clark Amendment ban on funding anti-Communist rebels in Angola. In 1986, Congress approved $100 million to the Contras, and continued to support them in one form or another, even after the Iran-Contra scandal erupted.

The fallout from the scandal itself had largely been contained, as the Senate refused to investigate the assumptions driving the policy and instead focused on procedural violations. The special prosecutor's inquiry dragged on for years with little result, stonewalled by the Department of Justice—with John Bolton taking the lead in playing defense—and increasingly ignored by a press unwilling to bring down another president. Not only were those convicted or indicted pardoned, but many of the key players in the affairs—Abrams, Negroponte, Weinberger, and Reich—went on to take jobs in George W. Bush's administration. The anti-imperial moment was over.

PLAN OF ATTACK

The New Right came to power intent on overturning many of the checks placed on policing and intelligence gathering, either by Congress and the Justice Department or by the Warren Supreme Court, which had expanded the notion of individual rights in a way that greatly restricted the latitude law enforcement agencies had in carrying out investigations.[51] For law-and-order, national-security types, the Miranda requirement, restrictions on search and seizures, as well as on wiretapping, and congressional oversight of overseas covert operations were of a piece, symbols of the shackles that prevented intelligence and policy agencies from protecting against crime and foreign subversion.

In August 1979, an intelligence subcommittee of the Republican National Committee comprised of a group of ex-CIA and Pentagon officials and headed by Reagan's future NSC chief, Richard Allen, produced a twelve-page plan that called for the consolidation of the diverse intelligence agencies into a single apparatus that would "mobilize" the entire government on behalf of national security. The plan advocated diluting the Freedom of Information Act and weakening constitutional protections extended by the Warren Court. It also sought the removal of prohibitions against the sharing of information between the FBI and the CIA and for the creation of "joint teams of officers from both the domestic and foreign intelligence services."[52] The 1980 Republican platform followed up by criticizing the "ill-considered restrictions sponsored by Democrats, which have debilitated U.S. intelligence capabilities." Shortly after Reagan's victory, the Heritage Foundation likewise issued an agenda for a conservative government that would abolish the "new restrictions" that had resulted in "fragmentation of the mission between several [intelligence] agencies and technical disciplines, as well as division of jurisdiction between foreign and domestic matters."[53]

Much of this agenda, while today largely fulfilled in the Patriot Act and subsequent restructuring of intelligence services, was at the time considered too radical to implement.[54] But the Heritage Foundation also specifically called for the surveillance of solidarity organizations that lobbied in support of the "Sandinistas and other Latin American . . . terrorists."[55] Here the FBI obliged, launching in early 1981 an investigation of the newly formed Committee in Solidarity with the People of El Salvador (CISPES).

The impetus for the CISPES investigation came from the synergy created by the right-wing public/private network that revolved around the NSC, CIA, and Office of Public Diplomacy. The FBI launched its inquiry after the publication of an article by John Rees of the John Birch Society linking CISPES to the Salvadoran rebels. This article was based, in part, on documents made available to Rees by the CIA, which were purportedly captured from the FMLN.[56] Throughout the course of the investigation, the bureau also relied heavily on information supplied by Western Goals, an outfit created by Rees and other conservative activists. In the organization's own words, its purpose was to step in and "fill the critical gap left by the crippling of the FBI, the disabling of the House Committee on Un-American Activities, and the destruction of crucial governmental files [on dissidents and subversives]."[57] In coordination with the Office of Public Diplomacy, Western Goals—which had on its advisory board Contra activists John Singlaub and Carl Channell—created a database cataloging the names and personal information of activists in the nuclear freeze and Central American solidarity movement. It then made that information available to the FBI.

The bureau found no evidence that CISPES was "acting on behalf" of the Salvadoran rebels or "any other foreign principle," leading it not to call off but to expand its hunt, now under the rubric of "international terrorism." The investigation lasted for five years, involved all fifty-nine of the FBI's field offices, and collected information on over two thousand individuals and over one thousand groups. It generated 178 spin-off inquiries that reached into all branches of the anti-interventionist movement, including the Southern Christian Leadership Conference, the Inter-Religious Task Force on Central America, the Maryknoll Sisters, the United Auto Workers, and the congressional offices of Pat Schroeder, Christopher Dodd, Jim Wright, John Kerry, Lee Hamilton, and David Durenberger.

The FBI defined its mission less as a criminal investigation than as a battle campaign. It set out to, as one internal memo put it, "formulate some plan of attack against CISPES and specifically against individuals who definitely display their contempt for the U.S. government by making speeches and propagandizing their cause."[58] Agents observed rallies and churches, shadowed individuals, and intimidated activists. Designating CISPES a Soviet-front organization, the bureau forwarded the names and addresses of its members to the White House, the Secret Service, the Justice Department, and the State Department—not an insignificant act considering that Oliver North had drawn up plans to arrest and detain Central American activists indefinitely in the event of an American invasion of Nicaragua.[59] One woman was told by agents that she was "going around with a bunch of terrorists, and we want to help keep you clean."[60] Activists who traveled to Central America had their official documents and personal papers seized, their mail tampered with, and their landlords and employers questioned. Much of this surveillance, according to FBI director William Webster, was conducted at the request of the CIA and the NSC.[61]

Citizens were subjected to more than observation. Throughout the 1980s, Central American solidarity activists experienced nearly two hundred incidents of harassment and intimidation, many involving break-ins of their homes and offices.[62] Church leaders testified to Congress that the burglaries had a "chilling effect" on their political work. Yanira Corea, a twenty-four-year-old Salvadoran refugee, was kidnapped at knifepoint in front of CISPES Los Angeles headquarters by three men she identified as Salvadoran by their accents. The assault was but one of a wave of threats and attacks against political exiles carried out by Salvadoran death squads operating in the Los Angeles area. As they tortured and raped her, the assailants, whom one investigative reporter tied to a Salvadoran security unit linked to the CIA, questioned Corea about her political work and demanded the names of her associates.[63]

No government agency was ever linked to these crimes, but then none of them were ever solved. The bureau refused to investigate, claiming that they fell under local jurisdiction. But a number of victims—such as the International Center for Development Policy, which had its offices burgled twice and documents related to its inquiry into the Iran-Contra scandal removed—were singled out by Oliver North, who asked that the FBI keep tabs on them.[64] Despite the curious fact that in most cases files were rifled but no property was stolen, the bureau claimed to see no pattern to the break-ins.

It should have researched its own history, for the burglaries closely resembled illegal search and seizures carried out during J. Edgar Hoover's long reign. Indeed, one of Reagan's very first acts in office, inexplicable by any standard save a cynical one, was to grant unconditional pardons to two former bureau officials convicted of authorizing the burglary of the homes of antiwar protesters in the early 1970s. The agents were prosecuted by Carter's attorney general as part of the fallout from the Church and Rockefeller committees, which documented FBI harassment and illegal surveillance of antiwar activists. Reagan not only exonerated the officers but praised them for acting "on high principle to bring an end to the terrorism that was threatening our nation." Vindicated, the agents described their exoneration as "the biggest shot in the arm for the intelligence community for a long time"—"A very fine thing for the present FBI," which would allow it to do its "job 100 percent."[65]

COMMITTEE ON THE (EVER) PRESENT DANGER

For conservative activists, both in and out of the government, taking defensive action through media manipulation and surveillance of dissidents was not enough. Just as militarists in the 1980s pushed the United States beyond a policy of containment to rollback, leaders of the New Right, in the vanguard of an emerging governing coalition, worked to change the terms of the debate by creating their own grassroots mobilization for an increasingly martial and imperial foreign

policy. Their efforts to enforce an aggressive Central American policy addressed three key constituent groups: civilian Cold War policy
and opinion makers, militarists, and the Christian right.[66]

The Central American conflict breathed new life into policy
lobby groups, bringing right-wing nationalists together with liberal
anti-Communists—often referred to today as "neoconservatives"—
in common cause. Already by the late 1970s, the first generation of
neocons had begun to join with the nationalist right through ad hoc
and standing organizations such as the Committee on the Present
Danger, Coalition for a Democratic Majority, and the Committee to
Maintain a Prudent Defense Policy (which introduced the young
Richard Perle and Paul Wolfowitz to venerable Cold War warriors
such as Dean Acheson and Paul Nitze). They derailed SALT II,
raised the alarm over America's abandonment of Taiwan to embrace
China, and demanded that Washington support Israel and respond
forcefully to third-world revolutionary nationalism. The alliance
deepened as liberals such as Daniel Patrick Moynihan and Nathan
Glazer lost their fondness for the New Deal welfare state and grew
increasingly disaffected with the "nihilism," as Irving Kristol put it,
of the New Left. Some became contemptuous of the Democratic
Party and fed up with a "new class of liberal verbalists"—academic
and intellectual parasites who thrived on a bloated bureaucracy and
a permanent adversarial culture.[67]

But it was Reagan's Central American policy that provided the
opportunity for a more committed and unified engagement among
the different branches of the conservative foreign policy establishment. Old Cold War workhorses like the American Security Council (a McCarthy-era group originally set up by right-wing opponents
of America's entry into World War II) and New Right organizations
like Western Goals, Citizens for America, and the Freedom Research Foundation began to focus much of their attention on Central America, as did the storied Congress for Cultural Freedom,
composed of liberal and socialist anti-Communists. The congress

recycled many of its members, including civil rights activist Bayard
Rustin and playwright Tom Stoppard, into the newly formed Committee for the Free World, which also included Donald Rumsfeld,
Seymour Martin Lipset, and Jeane Kirkpatrick. The new organization announced its existence with a paid ad in early 1981 in the *New
York Times* to "applaud the American policy in El Salvador," understood by the group's "intellectuals and religious leaders" to be nothing less than defense of the "values, the achievements and the
institutions of Western Civilization."

The second constituency, the militarists, became key players in
setting up the clandestine Contra supply operation. Retired general
John Singlaub raised millions of dollars for the rebels, creating a
funding network that brought Saudi Arabia, Taiwan, and South Korea together with conservative financiers in the United States such as
Bert Hurlbut, president of the First Texas Royalty and Exploration
Company, and Joseph Coors, the beer magnate and financial patron
of much of the right-wing activism that emerged in the 1970s.[68]
Singlaub's organizing work largely drew on his connections in the
Unification Church–affiliated World Anti-Communist League, of
which he was the president. Made up of "fascists, militarists, [and]
right wing terrorists," the league dates from the beginning of the
Cold War and represented, according to one of its own members, a
"world of ideological fanaticism, racialism, ignorance and fear
which is almost beyond the comprehension of the average American."[69] One reporter observed that death squads in Latin America
were essentially local franchises of the league, a characterization
that though exaggerated is not far off the mark.[70] Singlaub also established the private Institute for Regional and International Studies, located in Boulder, Colorado, and headed by an editor of *Soldier
of Fortune* magazine, to provide military training to the Contras and
to Salvador's security forces, as well as to paramilitary organizations
in the Philippines. Other mercenary groups included the Florida-
based Air Commandos Association, composed of about sixteen hun-

dred Special Forces veterans, the Alabama-based Civilian Military Assistance group, and the Washington-based GeoMiliTech, a military consulting firm that had sent a five-million-dollar arms shipment to the Contras in 1985.[71] (These outfits were the precursors to the private defense contractors like DynCorp and Blackwater who today do security and logistical work for the U.S. military and its allies in places like Iraq, Afghanistan, and Colombia.) Just as the Civil War produced a generation of itinerant soldiers, many of them from the losing side, who put their energies into informally expanding U.S. power in Central America and the Caribbean, Vietnam resulted in a legion of mercenaries who worked the trouble spots of the American empire.

The third constituency for a Central American hard line came out of the religious New Right. While American expansion has long been bound up with notions of religious purpose and moral meaning, the relationship between evangelicalism and support of imperial militarism has not always been harmonious. Of course, throughout the whole of the twentieth century, evangelicals had continued to proselytize abroad, understanding their missionary work in Latin America and elsewhere as contributing to biblical fulfillment.[72] And in the conflict-ridden third world, they often found themselves siding, out of either conviction or expedience, with violent anti-Communist regimes. But as part of their general retreat from secular politics, American evangelicals, even as they accepted the tenets of anti-Communism, tended to stay out of international politics. They even, according to Andrew Bacevich, who has written on American militarism, developed something of an "anti-war tradition." This began to change in the 1960s, when preachers like Billy Graham increasingly drew connections between the crisis at home and the crisis abroad, particularly in the third world. As did secular neoconservative declinists, evangelical theologians such as John Price and Jerry Falwell interpreted defeat in Vietnam as a signal moment of world history in which the United States stood at the precipice of spiritual collapse. They pushed the evangelical movement not only to fight what would become known as the culture wars—the campaign against the Equal Rights Amendment, abortion, gay rights, and so forth—but to get more involved in foreign affairs as well.

From the mid-1970s, Christian organizations would begin to play a more prominent role in international politics, supporting causes associated with America's resurgent nationalist right. Some worked with the American Security Council to oppose disarmament treaties and defend Ian Smith's white government in Rhodesia. Jerry Falwell and other ministers traveled to Taiwan and Israel, developing close ties with Prime Minister Menachem Begin.[73] But it was in Central America, which brought together a hodgepodge of improbable sects such as Sun Myung Moon's Unification Church and Pat Robertson's 700 Club, where the New Christian Right would receive its first sustained international apprenticeship.

Grassroots Christian groups such as Gospel Outreach and Transworld Mission had been sending charitable aid to Central America's military governments since the early 1970s but greatly increased their activity following the 1979 Sandinista revolution. At the request of the White House, Pat Robertson used his Christian Broadcasting Network to raise money for Efraín Ríos Montt, the evangelical Christian who presided over the Guatemala genocide. Most of the Guatemalan relief aid raised by evangelicals in the United States, by groups such as the California-based charismatic Full Gospel Business Men's Fellowship, went to help the military's efforts to establish control in the countryside in the wake of its campaign of massacres. In Honduras, Gospel Crusades, Inc., Friends of the Americas, Operation Blessing, World Vision, the Wycliffe Bible Translators, and World Medical Relief shipped hundreds of tons of humanitarian aid to Contra and refugee camps, where they established schools, health clinics, and religious missions. Phyllis Schlafly's Eagle Forum sent "Freedom Fighter Friendship Kits" to the Nicaraguan rebels, complete with toothpaste, insect repellent, and a Bible. In El Salvador, Harvesting in Spanish, Paralife Ministries, the National Association of Evangelicals, the Nicaraguan Freedom Fund (affiliated with the Unification Church), and the Christian Anti-Communism Crusade broadcast radio programs, handed out Bibles, ran schools, established medical and dental clinics, and provided moral education to the soldiers. In Nicaragua, groups like Christian Aid for Romania and Transworld Missions used the cover of humanitarian aid to organize Christian opposition to the Sandinistas. In the United States, Campus Crusade for Christ and the Moon-affiliated Collegiate Association for the Research of Principles countered the fast-growing student movement opposed to Reagan's Central American policy.

THE ECONOMICS OF SATAN

It was more than anti-Communism that created such an odd coalition in Central America. The fact that both the Central American left and their supporters in the United States drew inspiration from Christianity provided an ideological challenge to conservatives. In Central America, the socialism of the revolutionary movements was motivated by liberation theology—a current in Catholicism that challenged Latin American militarism and sought to achieve social justice through a redistribution of wealth—as much as it was by Marxism. Many high-ranking members of the Sandinista party were avowed Catholics and even ordained priests. At home, the solidarity movement that opposed Reagan's foreign policy was largely Christian. Groups such as the Religious Task Force on El Salvador, the Ecumenical Program on Central America and the Caribbean, the U.S. Catholic Conference, and the National Council of Churches actively mobilized hundreds of thousands of citizens in opposition to Reagan's policy. For their part, the Quakers organized an underground railroad that gave refuge to exiles fleeing persecution in El

Salvador, publicly breaking federal immigration laws.[74] So when Jeane Kirkpatrick remarked that the three U.S. nuns and one lay worker who were raped, mutilated, and murdered by Salvadoran security forces in 1980 were "not just nuns, they were political activists," she was being more than cruel—she was signaling her disapproval of a particular kind of peace Christianity.

A shared opposition to the socialist values of liberation theology—which Rousas John Rushdoony, the founder of Christian Reconstruction, the influential branch of the evangelical movement that seeks to replace the Constitution with biblical law, described as the "economics of Satan"—united mainstream Protestants and pulpit-thumping fundamentalists.[75] For instance, the Institute on Religion and Democracy, organized in 1981 by intellectuals associated with the American Enterprise Institute, presented itself as a reformist, liberal organization that supported the administration's efforts at political reform in Central America. Yet IRD allied with evangelicals like Jimmy Swaggart, Jerry Falwell, and Pat Robertson and worked with Oliver North and Otto Reich to discredit not only explicitly leftist Christian groups but established organizations, such as the National Council of Churches, that were critical of Central American policy.[76] With the support of PR firms contracted by the Office of Public Diplomacy, the Institute on Religion and Democracy, for instance, engaged in a mass mailing campaign to the Catholic rank and file to "generate some heat"—that is, to drive a wedge between liberal Catholic bishops and their supposedly more conservative flock.[77]

The power of liberation theology, along with other variants of peace Christianity, resided not just in its political analysis of global poverty but in its ethical imperative that to be a good Christian one had to do more than dispense charity; one had to transform the structural causes of inequality and violence. In Latin America, nuns, priests, and lay Christians were not only presenting democracy and capitalism as antithetical values but turning to revolution as a way to bring about social justice on earth.

Liberation theology threatened to undermine the New Right's long struggle to affirm unbridled capitalism's inextricable relationship to human freedom.[78] It was not enough, therefore, for mainstream Christian conservatives and fundamentalists simply to discredit liberal religious organizations. They had to go on the offensive and make the case that corporate capitalism "mirrors God's presence" on earth, as Catholic theologian Michael Novak put it.[79]

In other words, well before "political Islam" became the paramount spiritual enemy for the New Right, it singled out Christian humanism for attack. In a series of books and articles challenging the major tenets and proponents of liberation theology, theologians connected with the American Enterprise Institute and its affiliated Institute on Religion and Democracy, such as Novak and Lutheran pastor (now Catholic) Richard Neuhaus, elaborated a set of ideals specific to capitalism that they believed complemented the Christian understanding of free will.[80] To those who said that capitalism embodied the worst of acquisitive individualism, Novak, who presented himself as a political liberal, countered with his "theology of the corporation," which held up the business firm as "an expression of the social nature of humans."[81] He dedicated much of his work to refuting liberation theology's insistence that third-world poverty could be blamed on exploitation by the first world. Instead of examining economic and political relations, he contended that Latin America's failure to modernize must be blamed on indigenous cultural factors dating back to the Spanish Crown's seventeenth-century counterreformation, which placed strictures on capitalist development.[82]

As did their mainstream coreligionists, fundamentalists formulated their free-market moralism as a quarrel with liberation theology—which they described as a "theology of mass murder" and the "the single most critical problem that Christianity has faced in all of its 2000-year history."[83] They of course dismissed Novak's liberalism but like him saw capitalism as an ethical system, one that corresponded to God's gift of free will. Man lives in a "fundamentally scarce world," Christian economist John Cooper argued, not an abundant one only in need of more equitable distribution, as the liberation theologians would have it.[84] The profit motive, rather than being an amoral economic mechanism, is part of a divine plan to discipline fallen man and make him produce. Where Christian humanists contended that people were fundamentally good and that "evil" was a condition of class exploitation, Christian capitalists such as Amway's Richard DeVos, head of the Christian Freedom Foundation, insisted that evil is found in the heart of man. Where liberation theology held that humans could fully realize their potential here on earth, fundamentalist economists argued that attempts to distribute wealth and regulate production were based on an incorrect understanding of society—an understanding that incited disobedience to proper authority and, by focusing on economic inequality, generated guilt, envy, and conflict. God's Kingdom, they insisted, would be established not by a war between the classes but by a struggle between the wicked and the just.

Like Novak, evangelicals sought to rebut liberation theology's critique of the global political economy. Third-world poverty, according to evangelical economist Ronald Nash, has a "cultural, moral, and even religious dimension" that reveals itself in a "lack of respect for any private property," "lack of initiative," and "high leisure preference." Some took this argument to its logical conclusion. Gary North, another influential Christian economist, insisted that the "Third World's problems are religious: moral perversity, a long history of demonism, and outright paganism." "The citizens of the Third World," he wrote, "ought to feel guilt, to fall on their knees and repent from their Godless, rebellious, socialistic ways. They should feel guilty because they are guilty, both individually and corporately."[85]

Evangelical Christianity's elaboration of a theological justification for free-market capitalism, along with its view of an immoral third world, resonated with other ideological currents within the New Right, laying the groundwork for today's embrace of empire as America's national purpose. In a universe of free will where good work is rewarded and bad works are punished, the fact of American prosperity was a self-evident confirmation of God's blessing of U.S. power in the world. Third-world misery, in contrast, was proof of "God's curse." David Chilton, of the Institute for Christian Economics, a think tank affiliated with the Reconstructionist branch of the evangelical movement, wrote that poverty is how "God controls heathen cultures: they must spend so much time surviving that they are unable to exercise ungodly dominion over the earth."[86]

Mainstream theologians like Novak would not use such stark terms, yet the sentiment is not far removed from their logic. "God has made no special covenant with America as such," conceded the Institute on Religion and Democracy's mission statement, written by Richard Neuhaus. Nonetheless, "because America is a large and influential part of his creation, because America is the home of most of the heirs of Israel of old, and because this is a land in which his church is vibrantly free to live and proclaim the gospel to the world, we believe that America has a peculiar place in God's promises and purposes." The IRD therefore annointed America the "primary bearer of the democratic possibility in the world today."[87] Such an opinion nestled comfortably with evangelical notions of America as a "redeemer nation."

The apocalyptic and universalist passions of conservative Christianity melded with other, secular elements in the Reagan coalition. Many fundamentalists supported Reagan's resuscitation of America's revolutionary heritage on behalf of, as Rushdoony put it, a "conservative counter-revolution."[88] Others, such as Gary North, understood themselves as leading a Christian "anti-Humanist revolution."[89] They shared with neocons and militarists a sense that America had grown dangerously weak and scorned the purposelessness of détente and the naivete of rapprochement with Communist China. As it did for militarists, the "Churchill versus Chamberlain drama" loomed large in evangelical internationalism, used to frame all foreign policy debates in terms of resolve and appeasement.[90] Where neocons called for renewal of political will, evangelicals believed that America's revival would come about through spiritual rebirth. Their sense of themselves as a persecuted people, engaged in a life and death end-time struggle between the forces of good and evil mapped easily onto the millennialism of anti-Communist militarists, particularly those involved in Central America. Many of these militarists— Singlaub, Casey, Vernon Walters, and North (whom Falwell likened to Jesus Christ himself)—were themselves members of conservative Protestant congregations or of ultramontane sects within the Catholic Church, such as Opus Dei and the Knights of Malta.

GOING ON THE OFFENSIVE

The ties between the White House and conservative groups focused on Central America were tight and grew tighter still as a result of their work. Reagan's assistant Faith Ryan Whittlesey presided over a White House Outreach Working Group on Central America, which coordinated the efforts of the NSC and CIA with those of more than fifty private organizations, including Jerry Falwell's Moral Majority, Pat Robertson's Freedom Council, Phyllis Schlafly's Eagle Forum, and the Heritage Foundation.[91] John Singlaub, described by TV journalist Mike Wallace as the "virtual director" of the Contra war, headed the 1984 Defense Department panel that recommended increased use of unconventional warfare tactics; he also solicited Contra aid from Asian dictators and served as the NSC's primary fund-raiser on Nicaragua.[92] Many of the right-wing foreign policy lobbying groups, such as Western Goals and Citizens for America, began to work closely with the NSC and the Office of Public Diplomacy, disseminating information, assisting on political campaigns,

keeping tabs on dissidents, and raising money to buy arms and supplies for the Contras and other anti-Communist struggles around
the world. Christian economists such as Gary North, Richard De-
Vos, and Rousas John Rushdoony, along with Robertson, Falwell,
Schlafly, and North, himself a member of the charismatic Church of
the Apostles, founded the Council for National Policy, which, as the
religious right's steering committee in the 1980s, was deeply involved in North's Central American exploits. Christian businessmen
funded the myriad organizations that worked closely with the NSC
and the Office of Public Diplomacy to sway public opinion and congressional votes in favor of Reagan's policy in El Salvador and
Nicaragua. They raised money for arms and humanitarian work and
joined with Opus Dei and other conservative Catholics to form a
broad front to counter peace Christianity.

The White House, through the offices of Oliver North, supervised much of the Christian mobilization.[93] In 1984, the administration made it easier for evangelical groups to synchronize their
activities with USAID. It pushed through Congress a law that
allowed the Defense Department to use its planes and ships to
transport privately raised humanitarian aid and established a "coordinator for humanitarian assistance." These measures effectively reversed a 1976 ban that prohibited the CIA from entering into
contractual relations with missionaries.[94] At the same time as the
FBI was launching its "plan of attack" against CISPES, the Internal
Revenue Service was granting tax-exempt status to Singlaub's Council for World Freedom and other New Right "humanitarian" organizations.

Central American policy, as well as the grassroots mobilization
that supported it, became the linchpin that helped hold the Reagan
coalition together. Contrary to the antigovernment rhetoric that accompanied Reagan's rise, all components of his political base believed in a strong government. The Christian right, propelled by
victory in the fight against the Equal Rights Amendment, wanted to

reorient the state away from promoting and protecting individualism and secularism to defend family morality, to overturn *Roe v. Wade*, and to stop the advance of gay rights. Neocons sold a vision of America as a world enforcer of liberal morals. And economic elites, while committed to free enterprise in the abstract, wanted the government to continue investing in technology and infrastructure, particularly through expanded defense spending, and to impose law and order. They all agreed on the need for a strong foreign policy, either to fight Bolshevism, to encourage open markets, or to protect overseas interests.

This coalition gave Reagan a tripartite mandate to pursue an anti-Communist foreign policy, restore traditional morality, and end the welfare state—a directive he at best only partly fulfilled. He implemented a tax reform, which began to weaken the redistributive capacity of the state, yet was largely unable to dismantle social entitlements. He named close to half the judges serving in the lower federal courts, appointed two Supreme Court judges, and elevated William Rehnquist to chief justice, actions that would pay dividends in the years to come. But abortion remained legal, affirmative action in force, and school prayer unconstitutional.

It was foreign policy, as Sara Diamond, who has written on the rise of the Christian Right, has argued, that "offered the greatest opportunities" for maintaining the "flourishing alliance" between the administration and its potentially rancorous base.[95] But even here, there was conciliation (Reagan's befriending of Gorbachev), humiliations (withdrawal from Lebanon), and setbacks (sanctions on South Africa). By midpoint in Reagan's second term, the Right had had enough of his timidity, condemning their president as an appeaser and "useful idiot" of the Soviet Union for his willingness to negotiate arms reductions with Moscow.[96] But on Central America—a region whose unimportance made it critically important—there was no compromise. Designed and executed by the hardest of the hardliners in his administration, Reagan's policy toward the poor, powerless region gathered together the disparate passions of the conservative alliance into a single mission. It melded diverse constituencies together, organizing them into a dense, interlocking network of action groups and social movements, uniting mainstream conservatives with militants from the carnivalesque right. Respectable intellectuals and religious leaders from the Committee for the Free World and the Institute for Religion and Democracy and capitalists from the Business Roundtable found themselves making common cause with World Anti-Communist League revanchists, evangelicals such as Falwell, Robertson, and Schlafly, end-timers like Tim LaHaye, and Moonies from the Nicaraguan Freedom Fund.

But for an emerging movement getting a sense of its own power, Central America was too small a prize. Reagan first fully enunciated that it was American policy to support "freedom fighters" throughout the world in his 1985 State of the Union speech, specifically referring to the insurgencies in Nicaragua and Afghanistan. Others in his administration such as William Casey, Jeane Kirkpatrick, and George Shultz quickly followed, giving form to what would become known as the Reagan Doctrine. "A revolution is sweeping the world today—a democratic revolution," were the words Shultz used to begin his 1985 speech to the San Francisco Commonwealth Club detailing the new policy.

Though the administration, concerned with maintaining regional stability and balance-of-power relations, largely let its oratory outstrip its actions—except where the Contras and the mujahedeen were concerned—New Right activists took seriously the idea of world revolution, a revolution they saw themselves leading both at home and abroad. Throughout 1985 and 1986, conservatives, many of them grouped around the Heritage Foundation, pushed the White House to make good on its promise to support insurgencies from Cambodia to Laos, Libya to Angola, Ethiopia to Mozambique, Cuba to Yemen. When no action was forthcoming, they attacked the State Department and demanded Shultz's resignation.[97]

They also took matters into their own hands. From the network built to support the Nicaraguan Contras, militarists, idealists, and religionists, together with hard-liners in the NSC, CIA, and Office of Public Diplomacy, moved to extend operations across three continents. As they did for Central America, evangelical activists raised money to ship clothes, Bibles, medical supplies, and guns.[98] Beyond supplying aid and weapons, militants began to coordinate a "Democratic International" to fight the "Soviet Empire"—apparently modeled on the storied Third International of Communism's heyday. In June 1985, Contra supporter and head of Citizens for America Lewis Lehrman, heir to the Rite Aid pharmacy fortune, convened a "freedom fighter" summit in rebel-held Angola that brought together anti-Communist rebels from Nicaragua, Angola, Afghanistan, and Laos (the Cambodians were invited but didn't show up) to sign a unity pact. At a mass rally in a soccer stadium, Lehrman (today a member of the Project for the New American Century) presented the rebel delegates with a copy of the Declaration of Independence and read aloud a letter from Reagan, praising the revolutionaries— including the mujahedeen—as part of a worldwide revolution whose "goals are [America's] goals."[99]

This transformation of conservative activists into world revolutionaries entailed adopting an ethics of absolutism, sacrificing any qualms they may have had about means at the altar of ends. The violence of counterinsurgent war stoked the fires of evangelical Manichaeanism, leading Falwell, Robertson, and others to ally with the worst murderers and torturers in Central and Latin America. "For the Christian," wrote Rus Walton, a fundamentalist activist, "there can be no neutrality in this battle: 'He that is not with Me is against Me' (Matthew 12:30)."[100] Robertson befriended Guatemala's Efraín Ríos Montt and Salvador's Roberto D'Aubuisson—who was behind the murder of, among untold others, Archbishop Oscar Romero— celebrating both men on his Christian Broadcasting Network. And more than a dozen New Christian Right organizations, including the Moral Majority and the Pro-Life Action Committee, presented D'Aubuisson with a plaque in 1984, honoring his "continuing efforts for freedom."[101]

Many of the death-squad members were themselves conservative religious ideologues, taking the fight against liberation theology to the trenches. Guatemalan security forces regularly questioned their prisoners about their "views on liberation theology," as they did when they tortured one Clemente Díaz Aguilar, who turned out to be an evangelical himself, having been mistaken by his captors for a political dissident.[102] Others report being tortured to the singing of hymns and reciting of prayers.[103] Some evangelicals excused such suffering. "Killing for the joy of it was wrong," a Paralife minister from the United States comforted his flock of Salvadoran soldiers, "but killing because it was necessary to fight against an anti-Christ system, communism, was not only right but a duty of every Christian."[104]

As the involvement of evangelicals in world affairs continued, they started to align their theology to incorporate elements of both the idealism and the unflinching realism that today prevail among foreign policy elites. Mimicking Jeane Kirkpatrick's Hobbesian hardheaded belief that the war had to be won before society could be reformed, John Eidsmoe insisted that in El Salvador "the best way to promote freedom is to first of all win the war, then work for human rights."[105] "Our government," Falwell wrote in 1980, sounding like George W. Bush in 2002, "has the right to use its armaments to bring wrath upon those who would do evil by hurting other people."[106] And not just defensively but preemptively: "We must go on the offensive," wrote Walton in 1988. Just as today's imperialists believe that Washington can impose democracy at the point of a gun, evangelicals in the 1980s called on the United States to pursue a policy of "confrontation," as Christian activist Francis Schaeffer put it, "loving confrontation but confrontation."

Central America, in other words, was the crucible that brought together missionary Christianity, free-market capitalism, and American hard power. William J. Murray, a prominent evangelical activist and the chairman of the Religious Freedom Coalition, a Christian humanitarian aid group that today focuses its energies on the Middle East, is a strong backer of Bush's foreign policy. He got his overseas start in Central America in the 1980s, as head of Freedom's Friends, set up to counter, in his words, "those priests in Nicaragua, with their Liberation theology," who "are among the most murderous torturers in the world." "Most relief organizations will help left-leaning groups only," Murray complained. But he was launching "what can be called a Christian, anti-Communist movement and we will help the freedom fighters. Let's face it, food and medicine have become political tools, and we're the ones willing to use them against the evil of communism."[107]

After Reagan left office and the Central American crises wound down, the concordance between evangelicals and secular idealists would begin to fracture. Prominent fundamentalists like Pat Robertson distrusted George Herbert Walker Bush, who epitomized the kind of East Coast liberal Atlanticism that the right had rebelled against. Bush's call to create a "New World Order" didn't help matters, stoking conspiracies of jackboots and black helicopters flying under the flag of the United Nations. Robertson even suggested that Saddam Hussein was tricked into invading Kuwait in order to justify a war that would help install that order.[108] Yet many fundamentalists extended their increasingly confident engagement in world affairs well beyond Central America, with congressional Christian conservatives like Virginian representative Frank Wolf and Kansas senator Sam Brownback consistently pushing the U.S. government to deal with global humanitarian issues such as AIDS, sex trafficking, slavery, religious freedom, malaria, and genocide prevention. After 9/11, evangelical internationalists once again joined with a now fully empowered cohort of neocons to convert George W. Bush's realism into hard Wilsonianism and to "remoralize" America's role in the world.[109]

⌣

When asked just after Bush's second inauguration to name the most important achievement of his administration's first term, Vice President Dick Cheney pointed not to the liberation of Afghanistan and Iraq or to tax cuts or his energy policy but to the "restoration" of the "power and authority of the president" since the "low point" of the late 1970s.[110] As we have seen, this restoration of presidential authority began in full in the 1980s with the election of Ronald Reagan and was inescapably bound up with another restoration, that of American power in the world.

American diplomacy had to be reestablished on an ethical foundation—one that rejected both the amoralism of Henry Kissinger's realpolitik and the guilt-wracked moralism that seemed to have overtaken the Democratic Party, a foundation that conformed to America's sense of itself as a purpose-driven nation. This ideological reloading of the Cold War during its endgame manifested itself in the Republican Party's unexpected embrace of human rights, democracy, and nation building as a vital state concern and in the resurrection of the notion that America was engaged in a metaphysical battle—nothing less than World War III—against not another state but an existential evil, the antithesis of everything the United States was said to stand for in the world. Such conceits empowered those who pushed the United States to go on the global offensive, to move from a policy of containment to rollback to, in the minds of some, global democratic revolution. This renewal of U.S. dominance likewise meant rehabilitating unconventional warfare tactics, learning how, after the disaster of direct involvement in Vietnam, to outsource the violence needed to maintain its imperial perimeter.[111]

The restoration of American power in the world also entailed the realignment of domestic politics to support, not obstruct, an aggressive foreign policy. More than just an instrumental campaign to clamp down on protest, the operation run by defense activists on behalf of Reagan's Central American hard line heralded the political empowerment of the New Right, with its financiers, intellectuals, and activists pledged to transform America's domestic and foreign policies. Reagan's actions in Central America routed the diverse currents of this movement into a common stream, focusing the drive both to militarize and to moralize diplomacy and bringing together for the first time the constituencies that today stand behind George W. Bush.

But there is another dimension to this restoration of American power in the world, one hardly commented on in the voluminous writing on the Bush Doctrine and the new imperialism. It is the economic dimension, the subject of the next chapter.

CHAPTER FIVE

The Third Conquest of Latin America: The Economics of the New Imperialism

S AY WHAT YOU WILL about the White House's bungled postinvasion political plan for Iraq, its economic program was coherent and consistent. Even before the bombs began to fall on Baghdad, the administration contracted a consulting firm to put into place, as a Coalition Provisional Authority spokesman gushed during a press conference, "an unbelievably liberalized economy."[1]

Immediately after his arrival (and before handing the reins to old Contra hand John Negroponte), L. Paul Bremer, America's proconsul during what was hoped would be the consolidation stage of the occupation, imposed a package of economic reforms that institutionalized corporate power. He eliminated or lowered tariffs to no more than 5 percent, reduced the top personal income and corporate tax rate to a flat 15 percent, curtailed the right of labor to organize and strike, removed restrictions on foreign corporate ownership, allowed foreign businesses unlimited repatriation of profits, laid off public-sector employees, and privatized state industries. The U.S.

occupation has imposed on Iraq a massive state intervention on behalf of multinationals, insured by U.S. taxpayers and subsidized by the U.S. defense budget.[2] Not for nothing is the U.S. First Cavalry Division in Iraq carrying out "Operation Adam Smith," aimed at teaching Iraqis—despite their centuries-long fame as entrepreneurs, traders, and merchants—business practices that conform to the new global corporate order.[3] Bremer's "Iraqi Order 81" even prohibited Iraqi farmers from saving heirloom seeds from one year to the next, obliging them to buy them anew each season from corporations like Monsanto and Dow Chemical—so much for the 2002 National Security Strategy's promise that free trade would "unleash the productive potential of individuals in all nations."

It was a "stunning example" of free-market nation building, wrote the *Wall Street Journal*, one that made "Iraq's economy one of the most open to trade and capital flows in the world, and put it among the lowest taxed in the world, rich or poor."[4] Whatever the motivations of either the occupation or the insurgency, the dismantling of state industries, abolition of food subsidies, and throwing open of Iraq to imports and foreign capital stoked the fires of resentment, conscripting thousands of unemployed men into the ranks of the armed opposition.[5]

Of course, the promotion of capitalism has long been a concern of American foreign policy, yet the kind of capitalism advanced by the Bush Doctrine is innovative, at least in its arrogant disregard for the lessons of history. It is a militarized and moralized version that under the banner of free trade, free markets, and free enterprise often makes its money through naked dispossession. It was in Latin America where this brutal new global economy was initially installed, beginning in the 1970s, resulting in what could be called the region's "third conquest"—the first being led by Spanish conquistadores, the second by American corporations starting in the nineteenth century, and the last by multinational banks, the U.S. Treasury Department, and the International Monetary Fund.

But for a brief period in the twentieth century, the violence and instability bred during the "second conquest" forced Washington, as we have seen, to blunt its imperial edge. Starting in the 1930s, American policy makers began to realize that the kind of extreme free-market free-for-all imposed on countries like Mexico, the Dominican Republic, and Nicaragua produced cyclical political and financial crises. Violent conflict, such as that which erupted during the Mexican Revolution and Sandino's guerrilla war, compelled Washington to begin to tolerate, and then sponsor, a version of reform capitalism abroad, one that partially subordinated corporate rights to the diplomatic needs of stability. The more farsighted among the political establishment understood this subordination as required both to protect America's expanding geopolitical interests and to create a stable climate that would benefit the general interests of overseas investors.

During the Cold War, concern with stability increasingly expressed itself through the promotion of economic development, in the hope that prosperity would weaken the appeal of Marxism and radical nationalism. Presidents from Truman to Carter answered Communism's charge that capitalism produced third-world poverty by endorsing a vision of development similar to the one executed in Mexico after its revolution, in which the state would play an active role in the economy in order to lessen the volatility of commodity and capital markets. Harry Truman committed the United States to working with U.N. agencies and other nations to support a "constructive program for the better use of the world's human and natural resources" so as to help overcome, collectively, the misery in which so many of the world's citizens lived. "Guarantees to the investor," said Truman in his 1949 inaugural address, "must be balanced by guarantees in the interest of the people whose resources and whose labor go into these developments. The old imperialism—exploitation for foreign profit—has no place in our plans. What we envisage is a program of development based on the concepts of democratic fair-dealing."

To be sure, American politicians, particularly as U.S. power grew after World War II, never stopped celebrating the glories of economic freedom and private property. Starting in the mid-1960s, a noticeable shift took place in U.S. economic diplomacy toward Latin America. Where possible, Washington downplayed New Deal and Alliance for Progress–style reform and encouraged free trade, deregulation, and private investment. And even those American businesses supportive of political liberalism at home continued to push for open markets and to oppose anything that smacked of radical economic nationalism. These corporate elites did, after all, help to bring down reformist presidents in Guatemala, Brazil, and Chile.

But the U.S. government also allowed, grudgingly, for policies that would encourage economic diversification and cultivate a middle class, including price and wage controls, labor protections, the nationalization and subvention of certain key industries and utilities, and tariffs to protect local manufacturing. Walt Whitman Rostow, an adviser to Kennedy and Johnson and a zealous defender of the Vietnam War, believed that the endpoint of third-world modernization would be a welfare state. The purpose of society, Rostow wrote in his classic *Stages of Economic Growth*, was not "compound interest forever." Human beings, he said, were not "maximizing" units but "pluralist" beings who deserve to live in dignity.[6] This tolerance of what in other countries has been called social democracy was erratic, often self-serving, and not nearly enough to mitigate other destabilizing aspects of American economic and political diplomacy. Yet it did allow Washington's Cold War policy to correspond somewhat with the interests and visions of foreign politicians and economic elites, to enter into long-lasting alliances, and to bring its rhetoric more into line with the context of the world it was trying to reform—to promote, in short, a vision of economic progress in which the world moved forward together.

From the moment he came to power, George W. Bush, in contrast, promoted not reform capitalism but raw capitalism, one that glorified the unregulated days before Franklin Roosevelt's New Deal, before even Theodore Roosevelt's trust-busting progressivism. "The McKinley era" is where Grover Norquist, president of Americans for Tax Reform and a central player in the Bush coalition, hopes to take us, "absent the protectionism."[7] In the early twentieth century, Woodrow Wilson blended capitalism with Calvinism to save nineteenth-century political liberalism, with its ideal of free individuals, from the suffocating power of corporate monopolies. In the early twenty-first century, Bush used the idea of "freedom"—resonant for both Christian and secular conservatives—to save corporate power from the suffocating regulations of twentieth-century political liberalism.

How we have come full around to the free-market absolutism now being imposed on Iraq is the back story of our times, indispensable to understanding the power of the new imperialism. And just as Latin America played a critical role in the reconstitution of the ideological, military, and political foundations of the American empire following the crisis of the 1970s, the region provided the main venue for the economic transformation that today underwrites that imperialism. In important ways the road to Iraq passes through Latin America, starting first in Chile.

THE ROAD FROM SERFDOM

Milton Friedman had no idea that his six-day trip to Chile in March 1975 would generate so much controversy. He was invited to Santiago by a group of Chilean economists who over the previous decades had been educated at the University of Chicago, in a program set up by Friedman's colleague Arnold Harberger. Two years after the overthrow of Salvador Allende, with the dictatorship unable to get inflation under control, the "Chicago Boys" began to gain real influence in General Augusto Pinochet's military government. They recommended the application of what Friedman had already taken to calling "shock treatment" or a "shock program"—immediately halting the printing of money to finance the budget deficit, cutting state spending 20 to 25 percent, laying off tens of thousands of government workers, ending wage and price controls, privatizing state industries, and deregulating capital markets. "Complete free trade," Friedman advised.[8]

Friedman and Harberger were flown down to "help to sell" the plan to the military junta, which despite its zealous defense of the abstraction of free enterprise was partial to corporatism and the maintenance of a large state sector. Friedman gave a series of lectures and met with Pinochet for forty-five minutes, during which the general "indicated very little indeed about his own or the government's feeling." But Friedman noted that the dictator, responsible for the torture of tens of thousands of Chileans, seemed "sympathetically attracted to the idea of a shock treatment."

Friedman returned home to a firestorm of protest, aggravated by his celebrity as a *Newsweek* columnist and ongoing revelations about Washington's and corporate America's involvement in the overthrow of Allende. Not only had Nixon, the CIA, and ITT, along with other companies, plotted to destabilize Allende's "democratic road to socialism," but now a renowned University of Chicago economist, whose promotion of the wonders of the free market was heavily subsidized by corporations such as Bechtel, Pepsico, Getty, Pfizer, General Motors, W. R. Grace, and Firestone, was advising the dictator who overthrew him on how to complete the counterrevolution—at the cost of skyrocketing unemployment among Chile's poor. The *New York Times* identified Friedman as the "guiding light of the junta's economic policy," while columnist Anthony Lewis asked: if "pure Chicago economic theory can be carried out in Chile only at the price of repression, should its authors feel some responsibility?" At the University of Chicago, the Spartacus Youth League pledged to "drive Friedman off campus through protest and exposure," while the student government, replicating the Church Commission that was just then investigating U.S. crimes in Chile, convened a "Commission of Inquiry on the Friedman/Harberger Issue." Everywhere in the press the name Friedman was paired with the adjectives *draconian* and *shock*, with small but persistent protests dogging the professor at many of his public appearances.

In letters to various editors and detractors, Friedman downplayed the extent of his involvement in Chile, fingering Harberger as more directly involved in the mentoring of Chilean economists. While defensive, he nevertheless reveled in the controversy and the frisson of being ushered into speaking engagements via kitchens and back doors to avoid demonstrators. He enjoyed exposing the double standard of "liberal McCarthyism," pointing out that he was never criticized for giving similar advice to Red China, the Soviet Union, or Yugoslavia. In recounting an episode in which a man was dragged out of the Nobel award ceremony after shouting "Down with capitalism, freedom for Chile," Friedman delighted in noting that the protest backfired, resulting in his receiving "twice as long an ovation" as any other laureate.[9]

Friedman defended his relationship with Pinochet by saying that if Allende had been allowed to remain in office Chileans would have suffered "the elimination of thousands and perhaps mass starvation, . . . torture and unjust imprisonment." But the elimination of thousands, hunger, torture, and unjust imprisonment were exactly what was taking place in Chile at the moment the Chicago economist was defending his protégé. Allende's downfall came because he refused to betray Chile's long democratic tradition and invoke martial law, yet Friedman nevertheless insisted that the military junta offered "more room for individual initiative and for a private sphere of life" and thus a greater "chance of a return to a democratic society." It was pure boilerplate, but it gave Friedman a chance to rehearse his understanding of the relationship between capitalism and freedom.

Critics of both Pinochet and Friedman took Chile as proof positive that the kind of free-market absolutism advocated by the Chicago School was only possible through repression. So Friedman countered by redefining the meaning of freedom. Contrary to the prevailing postwar belief that political liberty was dependent on some form of mild social leveling, he insisted that "economic freedom is an essential requisite for political freedom." More than his monetarist theorems, this equation of "capitalism and freedom" was his greatest contribution to the rehabilitation of conservatism in the 1970s. Where pre–New Deal conservatives positioned themselves in defense of social hierarchy, privilege, and order, postwar conservatives instead celebrated the free market as a venue of creativity and liberty.[10] Such a formulation today stands at the heart of the conservative movement, having been accepted as commonsense by mainline politicians and opinion makers. It is likewise enshrined in Bush's National Security Strategy, which mentions "economic freedom" more than twice as many times as it does "political freedom."

While he was in Chile Friedman gave a speech titled "The Fragility of Freedom" in which he described the "role in the destruction of a free society that was played by the emergence of the welfare state." Chile's present difficulties, he argued, "were due almost entirely to the forty-year trend toward collectivism, socialism and the welfare state, . . . a course that would lead to coercion rather than freedom."[11] The Pinochet regime, he argued, represented a turning point in a protracted campaign, a tearing off of democracy's false husks to reach true freedom's inner core. "The problem is not of recent origin," Friedman wrote in a follow-up letter to Pinochet, but "arises from trends toward socialism that started forty years ago, and reached their logical—and terrible—climax in the Allende regime." He praised the general for putting Chile back on the "right track" with the "many measures you have already taken to reverse this trend."

Friedman understood the struggle to be a long one, and indeed some of the first recruits for the battle of Chile had been conscripted decades earlier. With financial funding from the U.S. government's Point Four foreign aid program and the Rockefeller Foundation, the University of Chicago's Department of Economics set up scholarship programs in the mid-1950s with Chile's Catholic and public universities. Between 1957 and 1970, about one hundred select students received close, hands-on training, first in an apprenticeship program in Chile and then in postgraduate work in Chicago. In principle, Friedman and his colleagues opposed as a market distortion the kind of developmental largesse that funded the exchange program, yet they took the cash to finance their department's graduate program. But they also had a more idealistic purpose.

Starting in the 1950s, Latin America, particularly the Southern Cone countries of Argentina, Chile, and Brazil, had become a laboratory for developmentalist economics. Social scientists such as the Argentine Raúl Prebisch, head of the U.N. Economic Commission on Latin America, expanded Keynesianism—after John Maynard Keynes, who elaborated the dominant postwar economic philosophy that envisioned an active role for the state in the workings of the market—beyond its focus on managing countervailing cycles of inflation and unemployment to question the terms of international trade. Chronic inflation, as understood by Prebisch and other Latin American economists, was not a reflex of a given country's irresponsible monetary system but a symptom of deep structural inequalities that divided the global economy between the developed and the undeveloped world. Volatile commodity prices and capital investment reinforced first-world advantage and third-world disadvantage. Economists and politicians across the political spectrum accepted the need for state planning, regulation, and intervention. Such ideas not only drove the economic policies of developing nations but echoed through the corridors and conference rooms of the United Nations and the World Bank, as well as in the nonaligned movement's 1973 call for a New International Economic Order.

It was the Chicago School's vision of hell, the New Deal writ large across the world stage. These ideas "fell like a bomb" on those who had long stood against Keynesianism at home only to see its authority spread globally.[12] The Chilean scholarship program was intended to counter such a vision. "University of Chile economists have been followers of Keynes and Prebisch more than of Marx," wrote William Benton, a former president of the University of Chicago and the State Department's director of overseas education programs. "The Chicago influence," he said, would "introduce a third basic viewpoint, that of contemporary 'market economics.'"[13]

Students returned to Chile not just with a well-rounded education in classical economics but with a burning dedication to carry the faith to benighted lands. They purged the economics departments of their universities of developmentalists and began to set up free-market institutes and think tanks—the Center for Social and Economic Studies, for example, and the Foundation for Liberty and Development—funded, as their counterparts in the United States were, by corporate money. These Chicago alumni understood their mission in continental terms, as a commitment—in the words of one of them, Ernesto Fontaine—"to expand throughout Latin America, confronting the ideological positions which prevented freedom and perpetuated poverty and backwardness."[14]

The program, which brought up students from universities in Argentina as well, exemplifies the erratic nature of both public and private U.S. diplomacy, conforming as it does to competing power interests within American society. At the same time that Kennedy was promoting Alliance for Progress reform capitalism, he was training and funding the men and institutions that would constitute the continent's dense network of death squads. At the same time that Chase Manhattan, Chemical, Manufacturers Hanover, and Morgan Guaranty were promoting, through the establishment of the Trilateral Commission, a more conciliatory economic policy in the third world, they were cutting off credit to Chile—in accordance with

Nixon's directive, making its economy "scream."[15] And at the same time that every American president from Truman to Nixon was embracing Keynesianism, the University of Chicago's Economics Department, with financial support from the U.S. government, had turned itself into a free-market madrassa that indoctrinated a generation of Latin American economists in the need to spearhead an international capitalist insurgency.

Throughout the turbulent 1960s and 1970s, though, the revolution seemed to be forever deferred. In the late 1960s, the Chicago Boys had drawn up the platform of Allende's nationalist opponent in the 1970 election, which included many of the proposals that would eventually be implemented under Pinochet. But Allende won, so Chile had to wait. In 1973, the military junta in Brazil, which took power in 1964, invited Friedman down for advice, which it took for a while. A severe recession and skyrocketing unemployment followed. Friedman pronounced this first application of "shock therapy" an "economic miracle."[16] But the generals, wisely it seems, demurred, returning to their state-directed program of industrialization, which, while failing to curb inflation, lowered unemployment and laid the foundation for Brazil's current economic dominance of Latin America. Richard Nixon, too, early in his first term, showed promise, but then he raised tariffs, introduced wage and price controls, and, with an eye to the 1972 election, declared himself a Keynesian and opened up the money spout. Nixon was an "enormous disappointment," reflected Friedman.[17]

That left Pinochet, not the most reputable of characters but willing to go the distance. Chile became, according to *Business Week*, a "laboratory experiment" for taming inflation through monetary control, carrying out, said *Barrons*, the "most important modifications implemented in the developing world in recent times."[18] American economists may have been writing "treatises" on the "way the world should work, but it [was] another country that [was] putting it into effect."

A month after Friedman's visit, the Chilean junta announced that inflation would be stopped "at any cost."[19] The regime cut government spending 27 percent, practically shuttered the national mint, and set fire to bundles of escudos. The state divested from the banking system and deregulated finance, including interest rates. It slashed import tariffs, freed prices on over two thousand products, and removed restrictions on foreign investment. Pinochet pulled Chile out of a number of alliances with neighboring countries intended to promote regional industrialization, turning his own country into a gateway for the introduction of cheap goods into Latin America. Tens of thousands of public workers lost their jobs as the government auctioned off, in what amounted to a spectacular transfer of wealth to the private sector, over four hundred state industries. Multinationals were not only granted the right to repatriate 100 percent of their profits but given guaranteed exchange rates to help them do so. In order to build investor confidence, the escudo was fixed to the dollar. Within four years, nearly 30 percent of all property expropriated not just under Allende but under a previous Alliance for Progress land reform was returned to previous owners. New laws treated labor like any other "free" commodity, sweeping away four decades of progressive union legislation. Health care was privatized, as was the public pension fund.

GNP plummeted 13 percent, industrial production fell 28 percent, and purchasing power collapsed to 40 percent of its 1970 level. One national business after another went bankrupt. Unemployment soared.

Yet by 1978 the economy rebounded, expanding 32 percent between 1978 and 1981. Though salary levels remained close to 20 percent below what they were a decade earlier, per capita income began to climb again. Perhaps even a better indicator of progress, torture and extrajudicial executions began to taper off. With hindsight, however, it is now clear that the Chicago economists, despite the credit they received for three years of economic growth, set Chile on the road to near collapse. The rebound of the economy was a function of the liberalization of the financial system and massive foreign investment. That investment, it turns out, led to a speculative binge, monopolization of the banking system, and heavy borrowing. The deluge of foreign capital did allow the fixed exchange rate to be maintained for a short period. But sharp increases in private debt—rising from $2 billion in 1978 to over $14 billion in 1982—put unsustainable pressure on Chile's currency. Pegged as it was to the appreciating U.S. dollar, the value of the escudo was kept artificially high, leading to a flood of cheap imports. While consumers took advantage of liberalized credit to purchase TVs, cars, and other high-ticket items, savings shrank, debt increased, exports fell, and the trade deficit ballooned.

In 1982 the economy fell apart. Copper prices plummeted, accelerating Chile's balance of trade deficit. GDP plunged 15 percent, while industrial production rapidly contracted. Bankruptcies tripled and unemployment hit 30 percent. Despite his pledge to hold firm, Pinochet devalued the escudo, devastating poor Chileans who had availed themselves of liberalized credit to borrow in dollars or who held their savings in escudos. The Central Bank lost 45 percent of its reserves, while the private banking system collapsed. The crisis forced the state, dusting off laws still on the books from the Allende period, to take over nearly 70 percent of the banking system and reimpose controls on finance, industry, prices, and wages. Turning to the IMF for a bailout, Pinochet extended a public guarantee to repay foreign creditors and banks.

But before the economic crisis of 1982, there were the golden years between 1978 and 1981. Just as the international left flocked to Chile during the Allende period, under Pinochet the country became a mecca for the free-market right. Economists, political scientists, and journalists came to witness the "miracle" firsthand, holding up Chile as a model to be implemented throughout the world. Representatives from European and American banks poured into Santiago, paying tribute to Pinochet by restoring credit that was denied the heretic Allende. The World Bank and the Inter-American Development Bank extolled Chile as a paragon of responsibility, advancing it forty-six loans between 1976 and 1986 for over $3.1 billion.

In addition to money men, right-wing activists traveled to Chile in a show of solidarity with the Pinochet regime. William Rusher, the publisher of the *National Review*, along with other cadres who eventually coalesced around Reagan's 1976 and 1980 bids for the Republican nomination, organized the American-Chilean Council to counter critical press coverage of Pinochet in the United States. "I was unable to find a single opponent of the regime in Chile," Rusher wrote after a 1978 pilgrimage, "who believes the Chilean government engages" in torture. As to the "interim human discomfort" caused by radical free-market policies, Rusher believed that "a certain amount of deprivation today, in the interest of a far healthier society tomorrow, is neither unendurable nor necessarily reprehensible."[20]

Friedrich von Hayek, the Austrian émigré and University of Chicago professor whose 1944 *Road to Serfdom* dared to suggest that state planning would produce not "freedom and prosperity" but "bondage and misery," visited Pinochet's Chile a number of times. He was so impressed that he held a meeting of his famed Société du Mont Pélerin there. He even recommended Chile to Margaret Thatcher as a model for completion of the free-market revolution she was leading in Britain. The prime minister, at the nadir of Chile's 1982 financial collapse, agreed that Chile represented a "remarkable success" but believed that Britain's "democratic institutions and the need for a high degree of consent" made "some of the measures" taken by Pinochet "quite unacceptable."[21]

Like Friedman, Hayek glimpsed in Pinochet an avatar of true freedom, who would rule as a dictator only for a "transitional period," only as long as needed to reverse decades of state regulation. "My personal preference," he told a Chilean interviewer, "leans toward a liberal dictatorship rather than toward a democratic government devoid of liberalism."[22] In a letter to the *London Times* he defended the junta, reporting that he had "not been able to find a single person even in much maligned Chile who did not agree that personal freedom was much greater under Pinochet than it had been under Allende."[23] Of course, the thousands executed and tens of thousands tortured by Pinochet's regime weren't talking.

Hayek's University of Chicago colleague Milton Friedman got the grief, but it was Hayek who served as the true inspiration for Chile's capitalist crusaders. It was Hayek who depicted Allende's regime as a way station between Chile's postwar welfare state and a hypothetical totalitarian future. Accordingly, the junta justified its terror as needed not only to prevent Chile from turning into a Stalinist gulag but to sweep away fifty years of tariffs, subsidies, capital controls, labor legislation, and social welfare provisions—a "half century of errors," according to Finance Minister Sergio de Castro, that were leading Chile down its own road to serfdom.

"To us, it was a revolution," said government economist Miguel Kast, an Opus Dei member and follower of both Hayek and AEI theologian Michael Novak.[24] And indeed the Chicago economists had set out to effect, radically and immediately, a "foundational" conversion of Chilean society, to obliterate its "pseudo-democracy" (prior to 1973, Chile enjoyed one of the most durable constitutional democracies in the Americas).[25]

Where Friedman made allusions to the superiority of economic freedom over political freedom in his defense of Pinochet, the Chicago group institutionalized that hierarchy in a 1980 constitution named after Hayek's 1960 treatise *The Constitution of Liberty*. The new charter enshrined economic liberty and political authoritarianism as complementary elements. The drafters justified the need for a strong executive such as Pinochet not only to bring about a profound transformation of society but to maintain it until there was a "change in Chilean mentality." Chileans had long been "educated in weakness," said the president of the Central Bank, and a strong hand was needed to "educate them in strength."[26] The market itself would provide tutoring: when asked about the social consequences of the high bankruptcy rate that resulted from the shock therapy, Admiral José Toribio Merino replied that "such is the jungle of . . . economic life. A jungle of savage beasts, where he who can kill the one next to him, kills him. That is reality."[27]

Before such a savage nirvana of pure competition and risk could be attained, a dictatorship was needed to force Chileans to accept the values of consumerism, individualism, and passive rather than participatory democracy. "Democracy is not an end in itself," said Pinochet in a 1979 speech written by two of Friedman's disciples, but a conduit to a truly "free society" that protected absolute economic freedom. Friedman hedged on the relationship between capitalism and dictatorship, but his former students were consistent: "A person's actual freedom," said Finance Minister de Castro, "can only be ensured through an authoritarian regime that exercises power by implementing equal rules for everyone."[28] "Public opinion," he admitted, "was very much against [us], so we needed a strong personality to maintain the policy."[29]

Jeane Kirkpatrick was among those who traveled to Chile to pay their respects to the pioneer, lauding Pinochet for his economic initiatives. "The Chilean economy is a great success," the ambassador said. "Everyone knows it, or they should know it."[30] She was dispatched by Reagan shortly after his 1981 inauguration to "normalize completely [Washington's] relations with Chile in order to work together in a pleasant way," which included removing economic and arms sanctions and revoking Carter's "discriminatory" human rights policy.[31] Such pleasantries, though, didn't include meeting with the relatives of the disappeared, commenting on the recent deportation of leading opposition figures, or holding Pinochet responsible for the 1976 car bomb execution of Orlando Letelier, Allende's ambassador to the United States, in Washington's Dupont Circle—all issues Kirkpatrick insisted would be resolved with "quiet diplomacy."

Absent the struggles surrounding religion, race, and sexuality that give American politics their unique edge, Chile had largely fulfilled the New Right agenda of defining democracy in terms of economic freedom and restoring the power of the executive branch. Under Pinochet's firm hand, the country, according to prominent Chicago graduate Cristián Larroulet, became a "pioneer in the world trend toward forms of government based on a free social order."[32] Its privatized pension system, for example, is today held up as a model for the transformation of Social Security, with Bush having received advice from Chilean economist José Piñera, also a Chicago student, in 1997.[33] Pinochet "felt he was making history," said Piñera. "He wanted to be ahead of both Reagan and Thatcher."[34]

AMERICA ON THE MARCH

And trailblazer he was, harbinger of a brave and merciless new world. But if Pinochet's revolution was to spread throughout Latin America and elsewhere, it first had to take hold in the United States. And indeed, even as the dictator was "torturing people so prices could be free," as Uruguayan writer Eduardo Galeano once mordantly observed, the insurgency that would come to unite behind Ronald Reagan was gathering steam.

Reagan's failed bid in 1976 for the Republican nomination was originally organized around the constituencies that stood behind Barry Goldwater's quixotic presidential campaign a decade earlier—protectionist textile, footwear, and steel industries, independent oilmen, small businesses and domestic banks, and a rising class of Sunbelt Christian capitalists. On its own, this movement was not strong enough to breach the ramparts of America's political establishment. In order to grow, therefore, it did what Jeane Kirkpatrick accused the Sandinista revolution of doing: it marshaled followers in the name of an aggressive foreign policy against an external enemy, both to solidify its core constituency and to draw new groups into its orbit.

The Reagan revolution's initial social base had deep chauvinist roots, led as it was by activists who saw themselves as opposed not only to the East Coast corporate elites who dominated the Republican Party, internationalists like Henry Kissinger and Nelson Rockefeller, but to the political liberalism of the Democratic Party. It is hard to imagine a group more removed from the cosmopolitan CEOs who sat around the mainstream corporate Business Roundtable than the evangelical Christian capitalists who organized the Council on National Policy. The Council's members included Pat Robertson, Bob Jones, president of Bob Jones University, founder of Christian Reconstruction Rousas John Rushdoony, Amway's Richard DeVos, John Bircher Nelson Bunker Hunt, conservative philanthropist Joseph Coors, right-wing direct-mail tactician Richard Viguerie, "Onion King" Othal Brand, ex–Ku Klux Klan leader Richard Schoff, and Sun Myung Moon publisher James Whalen. The two confederacies clashed not only over trade issues, with the latter tending toward protectionism and the former toward free trade, but over values. The members of the Council on National Policy saw themselves as deeply grounded in America, and they condemned the lack of patriotism on the part of the internationalists, who would sell out America to the Russians if it meant higher corporate profits. The differences between the two groups revealed themselves in such campaigns as the 1986 boycott of Chevron, organized by Pat Robertson and other Christian capitalists and activists to protest the multinational petroleum company's deal with Angola's Marxist government to begin oil production. Organizers of the boycott even distributed Wanted flyers that accused Chevron's CEO, George Keller, of providing "aid and comfort" to "America's Soviet Enemy in Cuban-Occupied Angola."[35]

Such campaigns did not mean that Christian capitalists were isolationists. On the contrary, their anti-Communism made them ardent expansionists. Much of the financial and moral support for Reagan's military buildup and renewed international aggression, for example, came from a network of unabashedly conservative and evangelical entrepreneurs, affiliated with Sunbelt capitalists or with traditional manufacturing, who were finding their political voice through organizations like the Religious Roundtable and the Council on National Policy. Texas oilmen like ultraconservative Nelson Bunker Hunt purchased arms and helicopters for the Contras and funded Singlaub's World Anti-Communist League.[36] Senator Jesse Helms of North Carolina zealously defended tariffs and subsidies on behalf of his state's textile and tobacco industries. Yet he was also the point man for the militarists on foreign policy nominations, ensuring that all aspirants (recall Helms's obstruction of Thomas Enders's appointment as assistant secretary of state for inter-American affairs) were sufficiently committed to carry out a belligerent policy—one that contributed to the opening up of the world's economy. Likewise, the stepped-up political engagement with the world on the part of evangelicals provided them with opportunities to increase their overseas economic interests. At the time of his boycott of Chevron, Pat Robertson, for example, had been working closely with Angola's anti-Communist rebels, parlaying his close connections with African dictators into vast forestry and diamond-mining holdings for his African Development Corporation.[37]

The militarists on the front lines of the conflicts in Central America and other third-world hot spots, such as Oliver North and John Singlaub, were ideologically and politically affiliated not with the corporations that commanded the heights of world capitalism but with traditional protectionists and the new evangelical entrepreneurs who organized the Council for National Policy, of which both North and Singlaub were members. Yet an alliance with some of Latin America's most violent avengers, such as El Salvador's Roberto D'Aubuisson, placed them in the vanguard of trade liberalization, for the elimination of Latin American nationalists was a necessary step in the advancement of open markets. At a Washington dinner sponsored by a phalanx of right-wing organizations in honor of D'Aubuisson—responsible for the murder of thousands of Salvadorans—one cadre complained that "death squads have a very negative connotation" that was preventing the laureled executioner from getting "across his message of free enterprise, anticommunism, freedom of exports and imports."[38]

Throughout the 1970s, just as this praetorian wing of the Republican Party was gaining ground and becoming more internationalist, their establishment enemies, the corporate and political liberal elites who set American foreign and domestic policy, were turning mean. At the beginning of the decade, with U.S. corporations no longer enjoying the advantages of an expanding, noncompetitive global economy, they began to withdraw their support for what had been the twin pillars of the New Deal coalition that had governed America for decades: the welfare state at home and reform capitalism abroad. The long postwar idyll in which U.S. firms could set prices, extract profit, and decide investment strategy largely free from serious international competition had drawn to an end. More of the American economy was integrated into the world, with the international trade proportion of America's GNP steadily increasing. For a brief moment in the early 1970s, it was hoped that détente, by opening Russia to foreign capital, would offset decreasing corporate profits due to increasing global competition. But U.S. banks found that the USSR had quickly reached the upper limit of how much capital investment it could absorb, while Western Europe proved better placed than the United States to trade with Russia and its satellites.

The death of New Deal liberalism came in 1973, when the United States was hit by the twin blows of sharply rising oil prices and a seventeen-month recession, described by political scientists Thomas Ferguson and Joel Rogers as "the longest and deepest economic downturn the United States had experienced since the great

Depression."[39] The contraction led to a sharpened sense of class consciousness and unity of action among corporate leaders—many of whom had previously supported the New Deal coalition but now rapidly increased their funding of conservative political action committees, advocacy advertising, ad hoc lobbying groups, and right-wing policy and legal think tanks dedicated to the dismantling of economic regulations and social entitlements. The number of pro-business political action committees jumped from 248 in 1974 to 1,100 in 1978.[40] The Olin, Smith Richardson, and Scaife funds, representing chemical, pharmaceutical, and petrochemical interests, paid scholars and journalists to produce, as corporate activist William E. Simon, Nixon's undersecretary of the Treasury, put it, "books, books, and more books" to rejoin the "relationship between political and economic liberty."[41]

Corporate foundations and individual capitalists also began to bankroll an ever metastasizing number of committees, coalitions, institutes, councils, journals, and magazines that, while each treating specific symptoms—SALT II, the Panama Canal treaty, the MX missile system, the Strategic Defense Initiative, Cuba, South Africa, Rhodesia, Israel, Taiwan, Central America—were all broadly committed to remedying the "Vietnam syndrome" and establishing American supremacy in the world.[42]

As part of this backlash, opinion and policy makers set their sights on third-world economic nationalism, which was increasingly identified as an obstacle to economic recovery. America, wrote retired general Maxwell Taylor in 1974, was threatened by a "turbulent and disorderly" third world. "As the leading affluent 'have' power," he said, "we may expect to have to fight for our national valuables against envious 'have-nots.'" Carter's secretary of defense, Harold Brown, made the connection between domestic revival and overseas expansion explicit. "The particular manner in which our economy has expanded," he said, "means that we have come to depend to no small degree on imports, exports and the earnings from overseas investments for our material well-being."[43] But now U.S. dependence was threatened, as a number of countries, such as Cuba and, briefly, Chile, tried to pull out of America's orbit, while others threw up obstacles to foreign investment. Between 1970 and 1980, for example, the number of state-owned industries in Brazil and Mexico increased from just over three hundred to more than a thousand.[44]

With détente offering no relief from the crunch generated by increased global competition and a third world hostile to U.S. capital investment, the Forbes 500 knights of the Business Roundtable made their peace with the renascent right and set out to retake the third world.[45] Putting aside their qualms about a potential inflationary risk, non–defense industry CEOs joined in the call for a renewed arms buildup. Executive officers from corporations that used to be squarely in the Democratic camp began to work closely with right-wing think tanks and policy institutes such as the American Enterprise Institute and the Heritage Foundation, which promoted both a dramatic expansion of America's military might abroad and the shredding of the New Deal at home.[46]

Some businesses and intellectuals from the multilateral wing of corporate America offered tepid dissent to Reagan's aggressive foreign policy. But increasingly, the cosmopolitans and the chauvinists came together over the need to project American power, broadly into the third world and especially into Latin America. Even David Rockefeller, an archinternationalist and the bête noire of the conservative right, got on the bandwagon. A week after Reagan's 1980 victory, he toured Chile, Argentina, Brazil, and Paraguay to reassure the generals that, unlike Carter, the new president "will deal with the world as it is" and not as it should be, promising them that the United States would soon restore full diplomatic and military relations with them no matter what their record on human rights.[47]

By the early 1980s, then, America had undergone a rapid transformation in the class and political relations that defined how it acted in the world. The previous decade's protracted recession both weakened and provoked the northeastern establishment—the internationalist core of the New Deal coalition and the liberal wing of the Republican Party. At the same time, the economic base of the New Right began to expand, as steep rises in commodity prices emboldened agricultural, mineral, and independent oil interests in the South and the West, bringing them together with manufacturers demanding protection, defense contractors, an emerging network of Christian capitalists, and a steady flow of corporate defectors from the Democratic Party. A number of these conservative constituencies, particularly those from the South and Southwest, could draw on their ties with fundamentalists and right-wing populist movements to back up their free-market and foreign policy initiatives with grassroots power and theological justification. As economic internationalists joined with militarists and Christian capitalists to defeat world Bolshevism, avenge Vietnam, and push for open markets, the restoration of America's global military power and the restoration of laissez-faire capitalism were increasingly understood to be indistinguishable goals. This fusion of the goals of corporate America with the passion and ideas of a nationalist backlash created a perfect storm of resurgent American expansionism—an expansionism that would force on the rest of the world the kind of economic regime first institutionalized in Chile.

CHANGING THE RULES OF THE GAME

Reagan took office juggling diverse interests, with commentators at the time criticizing the incoherence of his policies, particularly when it came to defining what, exactly, was Reaganomics. After all, any program that executes supply-side across-the-board tax cuts, massive increases in defense spending, and a tight-money austerity program to tame inflation can only be described as Whitmanesque in its contradictions. Reagan presided over a budget-breaking arms buildup and tax giveaway. "The hogs," observed budget director David Stockman, "were really feeding. The greed level, the level of opportunism, just got out of control."[48] But Reagan also continued the austerity program initiated by Carter's Federal Reserve chair, Paul Volcker, which meant that not everybody got to nuzzle up to the trough. Interest rates were kept at a ruthlessly high level, kicking off a two-year recession. Volcker didn't take his foot off the brake until the summer of 1982, when Mexico threatened to default on its international loans.[49]

The effect of what seemed to be a confused economic policy was, in retrospect, a cohesive transformation of American society and diplomacy—the institutionalizing of a perpetual system of global austerity that rendered political liberalism, both domestic and international, not viable.

Reagan's policies halted and then began the reversal of what some economists had identified as a dangerous trend—namely, the democratization of wealth brought about by union power, a progressive corporate and personal tax code, education spending, low unemployment, and social welfare programs. Over the course of the previous three decades, the amount of income claimed by the nation's top 1 percentile dropped from 16 to 8 percent.[50] Reagan's tax cuts and increased defense spending reversed this process, creating permanent budget shortfalls and slowing bleeding New Deal and Great Society programs. When unsustainable deficits compelled Reagan to raise revenues, he did so by largely shifting the burden to payroll taxes, which only helped to further weaken support for government programs—understandably so since real wages had begun to decline for many working-class families. Tight money led to rising unemployment and to the gutting of organized labor's bargaining power. Automatic cost-of-living salary increases, job security, and guaranteed pensions were thereby consigned to the ash heap of history. Corporations began the scuttling of America's industrial base, moving production to the Southwest and overseas.

In the international realm, high U.S. interest rates forced European governments anxious to stem the flight of capital to the dollar to respond in kind. They even compelled French president François Mitterrand to turn, according to Reagan's NSC international economics adviser, "full circle" and impose "severe austerity measures," thus ending France's experiment in democratic socialism—and what at the time was the chief ideological challenge to Reaganomics in the developed world.[51] Similar monetary pressure also helped bring conservative governments to power in West Germany and Japan.

In the third world, the global recession overwhelmed national governments. Even before the "Volcker shock," third-world loans were increasingly directed not at capital investment and infrastructure but at papering over growing deficits. Since 1973, rising energy costs had broken the budgets and trade accounts of developing countries, forcing them to borrow more and more money—which London and New York banks, engorged with petrodollars, were only too happy to lend (the percentage of foreign earnings in the thirteen largest U.S. banks increased from just under 19 to nearly 50 percent between 1970 and 1976).[52]

Between 1973 and 1980, third-world debt grew from $130 to $474 billion.[53] With poor nations already staggering under such a debt load, rising U.S. interest rates and an appreciating U.S. dollar turned out to be a deathblow to even the mildest kind of third-world development strategy, as advocated by Alliance for Progress types. Since both third-world debt and currency reserves were denominated in American dollars, for every point the U.S. Fed raised its rate, $2.5 billion was added to the interest of outstanding loans; for every 20 percent the dollar appreciated, another 20 percent was added to the balance.[54] And as interest payments on loans increased by over 50 percent between 1980 and 1982, the recession greatly reduced first-world demand for third-world products, with commodity prices falling nearly 30 percent from 1981 to 1982.[55]

While devastating for the people who lived in the countries involved, the crisis was seen as a "blessing," as William Ryrie, executive vice president of the International Finance Corporation, put it, for America's financial and political leaders.[56] The "debt crisis afforded an unparalleled opportunity," wrote Jerome Levinson, a former official of the Inter-American Development Bank, that allowed the U.S. Treasury to achieve "the structural reforms favored by the Reagan Administration," which included a "commitment on the part of the debtor countries to reduce the role of the public sector as a vehicle for economic and social development and rely more on market forces and private enterprises."[57] As interest payments on third-world debt soared—growing between 1970 and 1987 from less than $3 billion to over $36 billion—governments, starting first in Latin America, yielded to the IMF's demand to emulate the Chilean example. In exchange for refinancing, they cut subsidies, lowered tariffs, slashed social spending, sold off national industries, and devalued their currencies.

Henry Nau, Reagan's NSC adviser for international trade, described the global crisis provoked by Volcker's austerity program not as an unfortunate consequence of the induced recession but as an intended effect, one that reflected a "coherent analysis and attack on the major economic ills" of the 1970s.[58] With the United States losing its edge in the postwar system of industrial capitalism to European, Japanese, and third-world producers, Reaganomics dispensed with the competitive challenge by changing the rules of the game. Abandoning America's postwar promise to act as a global stabilizer, Reagan used monetary policy as a club to assert America's national interest on the world stage, institutionalizing an international system of financial and speculative capitalism that allowed the United States to maintain its primacy even as its industrial base was eroding.

Reagan in Cancún, or the Third Conquest of Latin America

Reagan unveiled the outline of this new system at the International Meeting on Cooperation and Development, held in Cancún, Mexico, in late 1981.[59] At the time, discussions of the international economy were still permeated with the language of developmentalism. Throughout the preceding decade, third-world leaders had expanded on ideas elaborated by the Argentine economist Raúl Prebisch, who headed the U.N. Economic Commission on Latin America, to propose a radical restructuring of the terms of global trade. Their vision of a New International Economic Order included increasing financial assistance to developing countries, negotiating the transfer of first-world technology and industry to poor nations, lowering tariff barriers to third-world manufacturing, recognizing each state's full sovereignty over its natural resources and economic activities (which would legitimate industrial expropriations and nationalizations), and setting just prices for ten core commodities—cocoa, coffee, tea, sugar, hard fibers, jute, cotton, rubber, copper, and tin. A majority of third-world countries called for the establishment of new international institutions, such as an affiliate to the World Bank that would help make energy costs more manageable for non-OPEC countries, and began to organize themselves as a single bloc to press their interests on the floor of the U.N. General Assembly.

In the months leading up to the economic forum in Cancún, Canadian and European politicians seconded such proposals. Canadian prime minister Pierre Trudeau and West German chancellor Willy Brandt suggested increasing development aid from $26 billion to $50 billion a year. At the bicentennial celebration of the Battle of Yorktown in September 1981, François Mitterrand urged America to open its markets to third-world products, to help renegotiate crushing debt, to set stable prices for primary products, and to enter into "global negotiations" that would recognize the "legitimacy" of third-world grievances.

But the economic ground under such proposals had already evaporated. "Trade, not aid," is how Reagan's Treasury secretary, Donald Regan, said development would take place, backed up by a 15 percent cut in U.S. foreign assistance. In a run-up speech to the Cancún meeting in Philadelphia, Reagan chided those who "mistake compassion for development and claim massive transfers of wealth somehow will produce new well-being." Reagan agreed with his critics that "development is human fulfillment" but lectured that such development would be achieved not through regulation or redistribution but by "free people" building "free trade." The *Boston Globe* urged the president to avoid repeating in Mexico such "doctrinaire one-liners and homespun homilies about the virtues of free enterprise, the necessity of self-reliance and the need of underdeveloped countries to emulate the methods of American capitalism."

But homespun became the core of America's economic policy in the third world. In Cancún, Reagan rejected outright the call to create new institutions and establish fixed commodity prices, along with other nonmarket mechanisms to promote third-world industrialization. Development, he said, would come about by "stimulating international trade, . . . opening up markets," and rolling back regulations to "liberate individuals by creating incentives to work, save, invest, and succeed." Without a "sound understanding of our domestic freedom and responsibilities . . . no amount of international good will and action can produce prosperity."

This was a radical break with past U.S. policy, one that had been based on the strategy that the Cold War would be won by providing a more equitable and successful model of development than did the Soviet Union. In contrast, Reagan in Cancún exalted the unrestrained market as both the end and the means of reform, laying out a vision of the world not as a kind of global welfare state but as a competitive arena. Success was the responsibility not of a community of nations but of each nation alone. Rather than encouraging nations to travel together on a "path to equity," as Raúl Prebisch called on the world's leaders to do, the new system would have winners and losers. And since throughout the previous two decades a generation of Latin America's democrats and economic nationalists had been exiled, executed, or tortured into silence by U.S.-backed military regimes, there were few left to argue.

Compelled by the debt crisis, one country after another implemented a program that was the mirror opposite of what was called for in the nonaligned movement's program for a New International Economic Order. They slashed taxes, drastically devalued their currencies, lowered the minimum wage, exempted foreign companies from labor and environmental laws, cut spending on health care, education, and other social services, did away with regulations, smashed unions, passed legislation that allowed up to 100 percent repatriations of profits, cut subsidies designed to protect national manufacturing, freed interest rates, and privatized state industries and public utilities. Rather than fostering unified efforts to set commodity prices and force fairer terms on the industrialized world, as poor countries were just beginning to do, the debt crisis forced a race to the bottom to attract foreign capital. It was every nation for itself.

In Latin America, the sale of state enterprises was one of the largest transfers of wealth in world history. In the second half of the nineteenth century and early part of the twentieth, Latin America experienced what some historians have described as a "second conquest."[60] The first was, of course, the plundering of American gold and silver by the Spanish and Portuguese. The second entailed the initial phase of U.S. corporate expansion, as extractive firms like United Fruit Company, Standard Oil, and Phelps Dodge turned to the region as a source of raw materials and agricultural products, coming to control most of the continent's railroads, electric companies, ports, mines, and oil fields. "When the trumpet blared everything on earth was prepared," wrote the Chilean poet Pablo Neruda, capturing the

Job-like scope of this dispossession, "and Jehovah distributed the world to Coca-Cola Inc., Anaconda, Ford Motor and other entities."

The third conquest, beginning full scale in the early 1980s, was no less epic. Railroads, postal service, roads, factories, telephone services, schools, hospitals, prisons, garbage collection services, water, broadcast frequencies, pension systems, electric, television, and telephone companies were sold off—often not to the highest but to the best-connected bidder. In Chile, everything from "kindergartens to cemeteries and community swimming pools were put out for bid."[61] Between 1985 and 1992, over two thousand government industries were sold off throughout Latin America.[62] Much of this property passed into the hands of either multinational corporations or Latin America's "superbillionaires," a new class that had taken advantage of the dismantling of the state to grow spectacularly rich.

In Mexico, even as the average real minimum wage plummeted, the number of billionaires, according to *Forbes*, increased from one in 1987 to thirteen in 1994 and then nearly doubled the next year to twenty-four. Much of this wealth was concentrated during an orgy of "unprecedented corruption," as a PBS documentary described the privatization program of Carlos Salinas, the Mexican president who sold off over a thousand state industries, many of them to his political cronies. Today, the assets of Carlos Slim Helú, whose acquisition of Mexico's national telephone system catapulted him into the rank of Latin America's richest men, equal that of the seventeen million poorest Mexicans.

Free marketeers today single out state industries as hothouses of corruption and waste yet, as historian Mark Alan Healey and sociologist Ernesto Semán observe, a "vast web of bribes, subsidies, deals and swindles" accompanied the selling off of Latin American "state assets, involving many top government officials and major corporations like IBM, Citibank, and Telefónica"—all winked at by Washington and the IMF. In Argentina, the government agreed to absorb much of the debt of the privatized companies, many of which, such as Aerolíneas Argentinas, were disassembled and had their profitable assets resold. Much of the money from these transactions, write Healey and Semán, "vanished into a tangle of private accounts and offshore banks"—a disappearing act, it should be added, made possible through the magic wand of the financial deregulation that went with privatization.[63] Even Pinochet, despite his reputation for severe rectitude, used his close ties with Riggs Bank and other U.S. financial houses to squirrel away millions of illicit dollars in hundreds of accounts and offshore shelters.[64]

In Chile, public enterprises were sold at roughly 30 percent below value on terms, according to one economist, "extremely advantageous to the buyers," many of whom had close connections with the Chicago alums and with military officers.[65] In Bolivia, between 1995 and 1996, the government auctioned off the oil company, the telephone system, the national airline, and the electric company. Much of the national railroad was dismantled and sold for parts.[66] The following year, the World Bank informed Bolivia that future debt relief was dependent on unloading its water company as well, which it duly did to Bechtel. Nearly overnight, families getting by on barely sixty dollars a month were told that their water bill would average fifteen dollars a month, a 200 percent hike. Bolivians were even outlawed from capturing rainwater for their personal use. The whole deal disquietingly echoed the fate of the Caribbean nation in Gabriel García Márquez's *Autumn of the Patriarch*, which suddenly found itself no longer an island, having had its surrounding sea sold off to dark-suited U.S. businessmen.

Latin America did not agree to be a laboratory experiment in free-market absolutism solely because of the execution of a generation of economic nationalists. The allure of cheap consumer goods, along with the promise of better service that the privatization of public utilities was supposed to bring, enticed a small but politically important urban population, while the transfer of first-world production facilities to the third world offered relatively high wages to a small segment of the working class. Moreover, advanced industrial countries like Mexico and Argentina were having trouble generating or attracting enough capital to either modernize state industries or move private manufacturing beyond the light industrialization stage. Likewise, the quadrupling of energy costs in the 1970s had led to unsustainable trade and budget shortfalls, forcing governments to borrow not for investment but to cover deficits. In a number of countries, inflation, always present, accelerated to astronomical levels.

But the abandonment of state-directed development programs—which doesn't necessarily have to imply closed markets and internally directed manufacturing strategies—resulted less from their intrinsic shortcomings than U.S. leaders' political choice to use the dollar as a weapon. Economists like Prebisch argued that Latin America's capital shortage was in essence a political problem and therefore could be solved with political solutions, such as the creation of an international organization to subsidize energy costs for poor countries.[67] It also can be argued that it was the very success of state-directed developmentalism that led to its downfall. Impressive levels of economic growth from the 1950s to the early 1970s—much higher and certainly more evenly distributed than anything seen since—produced new social groups demanding increased political and social democracy, demands to which the region's ruling classes, under the cover of the Cold War and with tech support provided by the Pentagon, responded with wholesale slaughter.

There were alternatives to the global system of permanent austerity and speculative capitalism put in place by the Reagan administration, but as the emerging victor in the Cold War, Washington was free to choose to ignore them.[68]

FREE MARKETS AND FREE SOCIETIES

George H. W. Bush entered the White House committed to consolidating the economic policies initiated by Reagan in Latin America. He took office in 1989, in the middle of what political scientists like to call Latin America's "transition to democracy." In South America, the threat of revolutionary nationalism that prompted Kennedy to arm the death squads and Johnson and Nixon to make their peace with anti-Communist military regimes had been extinguished. In the 1980s, Washington began to encourage the dictators of pacified countries to yield to civilian rule, and by the time Reagan left office, nominally democratic elections had taken place in Argentina and Brazil. As the Cold War wound down, Bush was able to step up this process. He allowed El Salvador to negotiate an end to its civil war and even agreed to draw down the Contra war—as long as the Sandinistas, exhausted after a decade of bloodletting, agreed to hold an election that they could not win (especially since Bush let it be known that U.S. support of the Contras would resume if they did win).

Yet aside from Castro's Cuba, one major obstacle remained to finishing the pacification of Latin America: Panama's corrupt and brutal dictator, Manuel Noriega. Noriega, of course, had been a longtime ally of the United States, providing such important services that the Carter administration in 1979 blocked a federal prosecutor from indicting him on drug charges. But with the Cold War coming to an end, his arms smuggling, drug trafficking, and money laundering—activities that throughout the 1980s were key in raising money and providing weapons to the Contras—had become liabilities. So in December 1989, just a month after the Berlin Wall came down, Bush took him out.

At the time, observers took Operation Just Cause, as the Panama invasion was dubbed, as a textbook application of the Weinberger and Powell doctrines, which sought to avoid the mistakes of the Vietnam War by ensuring that when the United States committed to military action it would do so with overwhelming force and with a clear objective and exit strategy. Colin Powell was thought to be the dove in George H. W. Bush's White House. Yet it was he who as the chair of the Joint Chiefs of Staff vigorously advocated for the invasion—the largest combat deployment of U.S. troops since Southeast Asia. In retrospect, Just Cause represented an important step on the road to Baghdad. Not only was the invasion the first deployment of the U.S. military since World War II in a conflict not related to the Cold War, it was the first deployment specifically taken in the name of democratic nation building. With air support provided by super high-tech stealth bombers, nearly thirty thousand U.S. troops easily overran Panama's ragtag security forces, captured Manuel Noriega, and installed a new democratic government—all within three weeks' time. Just Cause not only broke with Washington's decades-long policy of delegating hemispheric administration to Latin American surrogates but helped, according to James Mann in his history of Bush's war cabinet, "overcome resistance within the Pentagon itself to the use of force," thus serving as a warm-up act to the first Gulf War.[69]

After Panama, Washington began encouraging Latin America's remaining dictators, such as Pinochet in Chile, to yield to elected governments and urging terror states such as Guatemala and El Salvador to negotiate ends to their civil wars. By the end of George H. W. Bush's presidency, every country in the hemisphere except Cuba was nominally democratic, prompting talk of a Free Trade Agreement of the Americas. And while the first wave of economic restructuring was imposed by military regimes, Latin America's return to constitutional rule did not signal an abandonment of IMF-imposed austerity. The violence visited on nationalists and socialists during the Cold War made the region's new democratic leaders all too aware of the costs of challenging Washington's authority. Desperate for investment and burdened with undercapitalized state industries and services, they didn't depart from laissez-faire absolutism but extended and institutionalized it.

Finally, it seemed, the abstraction of free markets and free people was made manifest. Advocates of economic liberalism could wash the stink of Pinochet off themselves, vindicated by the fact that even Chile had turned democratic. The "proof is available for all to see," wrote Friedman following the 1990 restoration of democratic rule in Chile, "the sound operation of a free-market economy in a free society."[70]

In the United States, the idea of free trade—or neoliberalism—had gained broad bipartisan support among America's political and economic leaders, who helped extend the model inaugurated in Latin America to Eastern Europe and the rest of the third world. Desperate to regain the favor of the capital-intensive, outward-oriented industries that had been the heart of the Democratic New Deal coalition, Bill Clinton made "globalization" the centerpiece of his foreign policy, signing more than three hundred trade agreements, ratifying the North American Free Trade Agreement and the World Trade Organization, and committing his administration to "open other nations' markets." Clinton talked about trying to strike a just balance between the demands of private enterprise and demands that development take place in an equitable manner, similar to Truman four decades earlier. Yet his much hyped environmental and labor side accords to treaties like NAFTA, which promised to humanize free trade, had little teeth matched up against the protections afforded to property and corporate rights. In Latin America, the main effect of all this new international commercial jurisprudence was to ratify—and make nearly impossible to reverse—the dispossession that took place during the previous two Republican administrations.

Clinton had the good fortune to inherit a "largely pacified third world," and so he was able to use an earlier language of political liberalism and multilateral cooperation to sell free trade.[71] But he, along with other leaders of the Democratic Party, had converted from New Deal principles to embrace both free-market absolutism and American militarism. His administration, therefore, served as a bridge between Reagan's resurgent nationalism and George W. Bush's revolutionary imperialism.

Clinton's foreign policy advisers, for example, were eager to use armed force, both to advance U.S. interests and to distance themselves from the taint of Carter's Hamlet-like dithering. "What's the point of having this superb military that you're always taking about," Secretary of State Madeleine Albright famously taunted Colin Powell, "if we can't use it?"[72] After an easy victory in Panama and successfully countering attempts to downsize its budget and pull back its global reach in the wake of the Cold War, the military high command had no answer. And so it consented to participate in an ever-growing array of peacekeeping, human rights, and nation-building operations. The historian Andrew Bacevich points out that the Clinton administration greatly expanded the concept of defense to include both the maintenance of a free-trade global economy and the policing of global crises—even when those crises were not directly connected to threats to the United States. It was under Clinton that the idea of "national security" ballooned into "global security." And it was under Clinton that the United States moved from a policy of "containment" and "rollback" to "enlargement," whereby Washington would use its now unipolar power to expand the "world's community of free nations."[73]

⌣

So even before 9/11, three central planks of the Bush Doctrine—the promotion of free-trade capitalism as the only acceptable road to development, the tendency to view America's interests as the world's interests, and a willingness among Washington's political classes to use military force to advance those interests—were already in operation. Bush's predeccesor was so eager to use military power that even Paul Wolfowitz, in 2000, praised the Democrats for their new-found toughness. "American forces under President Clinton's command have been bombing Iraq with some regularity for months now," he wrote approvingly, "without a whimper of opposition in the Congress and barely a mention in the press." But he complained that Clinton's commitment to militarism was "facile and complacent," lacking a sense of purpose and focus.[74]

It was up to George W. Bush, following the attacks on the World Trade Center and the Pentagon, to hitch predatory capitalism more tightly to America's military might and sense of historical mission. Clinton preached with an evangelical optimism the glories of globalization. Today, the idea is now pure fire and brimstone, baldly linked to martial power. As the 2002 National Security Strategy preemptively puts it, in case anyone begins to think differently, there is only one "*single* sustainable model for national success: freedom, democracy, and free enterprise." "Free trade," it says, is "true freedom."

CHAPTER SIX

Globalization's Showpiece: The Failure of the New Imperialism

G EORGE W. BUSH ENTERED the White House in 2001 sounding very much like an old-fashioned Republican pragmatist, promising to hold close to the Powell Doctrine and use the military only in response to clear threats to America's national interests. During the presidential campaign, he famously called on America to act with humility in the world and rebuked the Clinton administration for squandering America's armed forces in expeditions all over the globe.

Yet Bush led a transformed Republican Party, one that reflected the realignment of America's domestic and foreign politics brought about by the rise of a nationalist and expansionist right. The party was beholden as never before to a mobilized Christian base, which in Central America in the 1980s had begun to shed the insularity that had characterized the evangelical movement during most of the twentieth century. Fundamentalist leaders now saw themselves as playing a providential role in pushing America to redeem the world.

For their part, the party's most vital intellectuals spoke the language not of past Republican diplomats, of caution, pragmatism, and balances of power, but of change, action, and moral renewal. As such, they joined with evangelicals in believing that American power could mend the world. Republicans had likewise long abandoned their economic isolationist roots to become aggressive promoters of corporate overseas expansion, beginning with Reagan's skillful mobilization of nationalist anger to restructure the global economy to the benefit of U.S. financial interests. And well before Clinton's humanitarian interventions, militarists affiliated with the party in the 1980s advanced a vision of unconventional warfare in Central America in which democracy and nation building would flow from the barrel of a gun.

Even before the attacks on the World Trade Center and the Pentagon had fulfilled the wishes of the neocons, who just a year earlier had dreamed of a "catastrophic and catalyzing event," a "new Pearl Harbor" that would galvanize American values, all of the ideas that would justify Bush's march on Baghdad had come to prevail—and not just, it should be added, in the Republican Party but broadly throughout the bipartisan foreign policy establishment. What Bush did in the wake of 9/11 was to harness the force of American revanchism, accelerated by the anger generated by the attacks, and to link it to the "messianic idealism" that had long played a role in propelling America outward.[1] "I was lifted up by a wave of vengeance and testosterone and anger, I could feel it," is how George W. Bush described the passions that after 9/11 raised him from a candidate promising a "humble" foreign policy to a president who wanted to "rid the world of evil" and build "free and open societies on every continent."[2]

But as the triumphal note sounded on the road to war in Iraq, our new imperialists should have considered Latin America. The region, after all, has often been used to showcase what American power can achieve in the world. And with the Cold War over,

NAFTA in place, and elected governments in every country save Cuba, Latin America was held up by Democrats and Republicans alike as the crown jewel of the so-called Washington Consensus, which holds that free trade combined with constitutional rule will produce a peaceful, prosperous world. Compared with the "uncertainty of the rest of the world," said Southcom commander Barry R. McCaffrey in 1995, stability reigned among our southern neighbors.[3] "We have a lot to be proud [of]," agreed Secretary of Defense William S. Cohen two years later. The "Western Hemisphere has a lot to teach the world as the world reaches for the kind of progress we have made."[4]

Let's take a closer look at that progress.

ACCEPTABLE BY AMERICAN STANDARDS

At the beginning of the twenty-first century, wealth inequality in Latin America was at an all-time high, with three decades of IMF diktats doing little to provide better health care, education, or nutrition. In fact, stacked up against the previous developmental model, the new economic regime heralded by Milton Friedman and his colleagues and imposed by Reagan and his successors failed miserably. Taking Latin America as a whole, between 1947 and 1973—the heyday of state developmentalism—per capita income rose 73 percent in real wages. In contrast, between 1980 and 1998—the heyday of free-market fundamentalism—median per capita income stagnated at 0 percent.[5] By the end of the 1960s, 11 percent of Latin Americans were destitute, defined as those who live on today's equivalent of two dollars a day. By 1996, the total number of destitute grew to a full third of the population. That's 165 million people.[6] As of 2005, 221 million lived below the poverty level, an increase of over 20 million in just a decade.[7] Additional burdens were placed on the poor as governments, starting in the 1980s, shifted their revenue base from progressive income tax on wealth and profit to either sales or the equivalent of payroll taxes.[8]

In terms of specific countries, Argentina and Mexico both followed IMF and U.S. Treasury Department guidelines nearly to the letter, lowering inflation, reducing the gap between spending and income, deregulating the financial sector, privatizing state industries and services, and liberalizing trade. And both went to great pains to ensure a stable fiscal environment to attract investment. In 1991, Argentina took monetary policy out of the hands of politicians, setting up a currency board that all but replaced the peso with the dollar and ceded financial sovereignty to Alan Greenspan, Paul Volcker's successor at the Federal Reserve.[9] In 1988, Mexico began to dismantle the large public sector that had emerged out of the Mexican Revolution. It once again tethered its fortunes to the United States through trade negotiations that would eventually yield the 1992 NAFTA accord.[10]

As expected, shock therapy produced prolonged recessions, wrenchingly high unemployment, and dramatic reductions in social services. In Argentina, the industrial labor force contracted by a third. Poverty increased, made worse by the shredding of what was one of Latin America's most reliable social safety nets.[11] But shock therapy also eventually led to lower inflation rates and to economic growth that made it seem, to some, that the pain was worth it. The early 1990s were boom years, and Argentina's and Mexico's economies expanded at a steady clip. Billions poured into the two nations, either in the form of new loans (to cover persistent trade deficits) or as private capital to take advantage of the opportunities offered by financial deregulation and privatization. Mexico loosened environmental and labor laws along its northern border to turn the region into a vast assembly zone for medium- to high-technology products, where workers pieced together parts manufactured elsewhere for reexport to the U.S. market. Maquiladoras, as these reprocessing plants are called, today employ over a million Mexicans and bring in more than $10 billion in foreign exchange. For its part, Argentina sold much of its industrial plant and nearly 100 percent of its banks to foreign corporations.

Mexico was the first to give, buckling under the weight of one too many high-interest, short-term dollar-denominated bonds issued to cover a trade deficit that was spiraling out of control and to prop up an overvalued peso. On December 18, 1994, after well-connected Mexicans converted billions of pesos into dollars, the government devalued, and then devalued again. The banking system began to melt down as capital fled. It was saved from complete collapse by a last-minute $50 billion loan brokered by Clinton and Greenspan that, according to conservative economist Lawrence Kudlow, was in effect a "bailout of U.S. banks, brokerage firms, pension funds and insurance companies" that had heavily invested in Mexico.[12] Clinton could have saved on transaction fees and deposited the money directly into Wall Street's coffers.

Washington's rescue stabilized the peso and allowed the economy to recover, yet structural problems remained, including high rates of nonproductive speculative investment, declining wages in proportion to growth, and staggering levels of poverty. Most disruptive, the importation of cheap goods decimated domestic manufacturing and small-scale farming, which could not compete with U.S. agro-industry. Half a million peasants were driven off their land, as cheap corn flooded the market.[13] And since NAFTA compelled the state to slash food subsidies, "free trade" actually increased the cost of meeting basic nutritional requirements. While Mexican officials insisted that the peasant sector was doomed anyway—a self-fulfilling prophecy since the state directed meager resources to sustain it—the NAFTA model provided no mechanisms to incorporate displaced peasants into the new global economy, except pushing them to travel north to supply cheap labor to service the American economy.

Then it was Argentina's turn. For those who insisted on blaming the disappointment of neoliberalism not on the theory itself but on the failure of Latin American politicians to implement it correctly, Argentina, as old Committee of Santa Fe hand Roger Fontaine put it in 1996, provided "a clear example of how it can be accomplished."[14]

And what an example it was, ushering in, according to one observer, the "worst peacetime economic collapse in recorded history."[15] Since the Argentine peso was pegged to the dollar, deficit spending to expand the economy was off limits. The only way to grow was to bring in foreign currency, through privatization, investments, loans, or trade earnings. But by the mid-1990s, there was very little left to privatize, foreign investment was mostly short-term speculation, while an overvalued dollar worsened balance-of-trade accounts. That left borrowing and more borrowing. But with the country in recession since 1998, Argentina, despite ever more draconian cuts in social services, found it impossible to pay its debt. In 2002, the country defaulted, scrapped its currency board, and devalued the peso. The number of those living below the poverty line rose to 58 percent of the population—twenty-one million people, ten million of whom were totally destitute.

For its part, Brazil, comprising a third of Latin America's population and generating a third of the continent's GDP, escaped some of the harshest experiences of its neighbors. Brazil's economic might was largely due to the success of the state-developmentalist model the free-market program was intent on dismantling, which despite generating chronic inflation and high external debt greatly expanded the country's industrial base. Consequently, Brazil proved more reluctant to dance to the IMF's tune. Notwithstanding significant privatization, the state remained heavily involved in the economy, retaining control of 40 percent of its financial sector. And despite years of dictatorship followed by civilian presidents implementing neoliberal prescriptions, the country never launched an all-out assault on the power of organized labor as did Chile and Argentina.

Financial crisis hit in 1998, precipitated by the Asian meltdown, yet it was nowhere near as brutal as what occurred elsewhere in Latin America. Because it retained considerable financial autonomy from the U.S. Treasury—Brazil was not "dollarized" to the degree Argentina and Mexico were—it had more latitude to devalue without provoking a run on its banks.

And what of desperately poor Bolivia? By 1985, with inflation spiraling out of control at an annual percentage rate of 23,000, the country, unable to meet the interest on its debt, prostrated itself before the IMF. In exchange for divesting from the public sector and for submitting to shock therapy, the government was allowed to reschedule its debt payments and take out new loans. Inflation fell and the economy stabilized and even grew, but poverty rose to inhumane levels, engulfing 97 percent of the rural countryside.[16] Cheap imported food hammered the peasantry, which began to suffer from high levels of malnutrition and infectious diseases, while low-priced manufactures led to the shuttering of over a hundred factories. Unions were busted and labor protections eviscerated, contributing to rising unemployment and longer work weeks for those lucky enough to hold on to their jobs. "Working harder," write economists Carlos Arze and Tom Kruse, many Bolivians "barely manage[d] to maintain themselves even at the same level of poverty."[17]

The imposition of the neoliberal program led directly to the escalation of Bolivia's drug crisis. The decimation of the peasantry and the mining industry left no alternative for thousands of indigenous peasants and laid-off workers other than moving down to the country's tropical Chaparé region, where they established small-scale coca farms. And while growing, selling, and chewing coca leaves are legal in Bolivia—an important part of Quechua and Aymara culture for centuries—much of this new cultivation provided the raw material for the processing of cocaine for export. At the same time, financial liberalization made it easier to launder drug and other forms of illicit profit through Latin America's banking system. Just as coca production came to sustain what was left of rural society, coca dollars propped up Bolivia's banking system, always at the point of collapsing from unsustainable balance-of-trade deficits.

There was, of course, Chile, still the lodestar for free-market true believers. The figures were impressive. Since 1990, the economy seemed to have avoided the pitched cycles of expansion and contraction that whipsawed Chileans under Pinochet to attain a steady 7 percent growth rate through much of the decade. Inflation fell to single digits, while unemployment and underemployment declined. Millions prospered, as the number of those living in poverty decreased from 39 to 23 percent. Indices surrounding health, education, and life expectancy improved considerably, especially compared with figures during the Pinochet years and in other Latin American countries.[18]

But much of this growth was attained by transforming the country into a workhouse, whipping ever-higher rates of productivity out of the labor force. By 2004, workers in Santiago, Chile's capital, were logging an average of 2,250 hours per year, the world's record and fifty hours more than their second-place counterparts in Kuala Lumpur, Malaysia.[19] This, of course, is the fulcrum of the neoliberal model: instead of progressive taxation, the provision of government welfare, and planned development to generate employment, the burden of improving aggregate living conditions is placed on an expanding economy, which means not only extracting more profit from workers but leaving that profit to accumulate in fewer hands.

After a decade of celebrated growth, in 2002 three million Chileans—one in five—were living in poverty, with 83 percent of the population reporting that their lot had not improved under democratic rule. One indication that the Chilean model was coming up short was that its privatized pension plan not only failed to provide dignified pensions for many retirees but, as the *New York Times* recently reported, was unable to match the annuities Chileans would have received if the system had remained in government hands.[20]

Much of the success Chile did enjoy actually stemmed from breaking with free-market dogma. After the economic collapse of 1983, Pinochet opted for a more pragmatic economic strategy, one that assertively used the state to promote exports and made liberal use of regulatory laws still on the books, including some enacted by the vilified Allende government. Chile imposed a number of restrictions, including financial penalties, on the currency market, buffering its economy from the market panics that plagued its neighbors.[21] And while more than a million Chileans climbed out of poverty by 1992, the reason had less to do with the virtues of market orthodoxy than with the willingness of post-Pinochet center-left governments to capitalize on large reserves of popular support in the years immediately after the dictatorship by taxing the new rich in order to pay for education, health, and welfare.

In Central America, so "colossally important" to U.S. interests, according to Jeane Kirkpatrick, the situation was much worse.

Washington spent roughly ten billion dollars in Nicaragua and El Salvador throughout the wars of the 1980s yet refused to take responsibility for postwar reconstruction. Instead, it delegated the jobs of demobilizing combatants and enacting political and judicial reform to the United Nations. While the United States financed some of these efforts, it quickly turned its attentions elsewhere, mostly to Colombia and the war on drugs. To this day, Washington's involvement in Central America has remained largely limited to issues of illegal immigration and drug trafficking, with few steps taken to fulfill Reagan's thunderous pledges of democracy and development other than the promotion of a Central American Free Trade Agreement.

What has become of the region now that Washington has moved on? Political terror has certainly abated. Nicaragua, Guatemala, and El Salvador are all nominally constitutional democracies, holding regularly scheduled elections. Yet the devastation that began a quarter century ago has actually accelerated.[22]

A few years ago, the U.S. and Western media paid much attention to a United Nations report that highlighted the growing gap in education and development between the Middle East and the rest of the world. For neoconservatives, the report was proof positive of the need for increased U.S. involvement in the Middle East. Had they— or their allies in the media—bothered to compare countries like Iran and Syria, both slated for imperial reform, with Central America, they might have thought twice about the wisdom of their policies. In terms of education, for example, illiteracy in Iran (20.6% of total population) and Syria (23.1%) is much lower today than in Guatemala (29.4%) and Nicaragua (32.5%), where illiteracy rates have sharply increased since the electoral defeat of the Sandinistas in 1990.

In Iran, 40 percent of the population lives in poverty, while in Syria that number is approximately 20 percent. In contrast, 60 percent of the inhabitants of Nicaragua, Guatemala, Honduras, and El Salvador—roughly 20,000,000 people—live below the poverty level, a situation that has grown worse since the wars ended.[23] In Guatemala, almost six million people survive on less than two dollars a day. After Haiti, Nicaragua is the poorest country in the hemisphere. In Guatemala, there are thirty-eight deaths for every thousand live births—a rate more than five times greater than that of the United States. At the same time, wealth inequality is at an all-time high.[24] Privileged elites live in garrison communities, with private heavily armed security guards protecting them from the constant threat of kidnapping for ransom. In the countryside, hunger, infectious disease, and malnutrition are endemic and starvation has become common.[25] Environmental degradation—deforestation, soil erosion, poisoned water, and polluted air—has reached crisis proportions. Panama fares no better, plagued as it is by corruption, violence, high unemployment, and severe malnutrition. The country has the "fourth-worst distribution of wealth in the world," with the "average poor Panamanian mak[ing] 40 times less than the average rich Panamanian."[26]

For many, the only viable escape from such wretchedness is to travel north to Mexico or the United States, but increased U.S. border patrols—in response to the war on terror—have made that route more hazardous than ever. Of course, they could always enlist in the U.S. Army. This is what José Gutíerrez did. Having lost his parents in Guatemala's thirty-six-year counterinsurgency, Gutíerrez survived life on Guatemala City's streets as an orphan, a two-thousand-mile trek through Mexico into the U.S., and L.A.'s juvenile court system only to become—along with three fellow marines, all of them Mexican citizens—one of America's first fatalities in the Iraq war.[27]

As long as Central America doesn't act up, as it did in the 1980s, such misery is all that its citizens can hope for living in an American imperium. In 2003, RAND Corporation analyst James Dobbins summed up this situation clearly in terms of Panama: "Panama is far from perfect, but perfectly acceptable by American standards," he said. "It's not the worst regime in the region, its behavior doesn't challenge U.S. interests in any fundamental way, it's acceptably democratic and thus not out of tune with the hemisphere as a whole."

All through "acceptably democratic" Central America, even in reputable Costa Rica, violent crime has skyrocketed. In El Salvador, the murder rate is 120 per 100,000 inhabitants. In Guatemala City, more than seven hundred women, mostly from poor families, have been kidnapped, tortured, raped, and then stabbed to death since 2001. The police have made few arrests, and the killings go on, unexplained and unsolved. Sixty people are murdered each week in Guatemala City, principally in connection with car thefts, kidnappings, illegal timbering, bank robbery, and, most important, drugs. The isthmus has become the key transit point for drugs coming into the United States from the Andes, with high-ranking military officers moonlighting as import-exporters. A clandestine globalization has fueled this violence, with gangs such as the Salvatruchas and

Mara 18 operating throughout El Salvador, Guatemala, Honduras, and Los Angeles. It is estimated that these gangs are responsible for 10 percent of the region's homicides. In Guatemala, while political repression nowhere near approaches the level it did in the 1970s and 1980s, shadowy groups affiliated with the military operate in much the same way that the death squads did in the 1980s. Reinforced with information supplied by a never-disbanded wartime intelligence apparatus, they do the frontline work for gangster cliques headed by military officers. Mostly involved in common crime, they occasionally eliminate activists demanding land reform or attempting to bring to justice those responsible for political repression. More recently, in place of a national policy that could mitigate poverty and curb crime, death squads have reportedly been resurrected for "social cleansing," ridding the streets of delinquents through execution.[28]

In Latin America, as throughout much of the rest of the world, desperation increases as the poor, cast out of either the formal or the peasant economy, cram into what the security experts are now calling "feral cities"—creating slums on a vast scale incapable of meeting even the most basic needs of their inhabitants.[29] At best, the energy of the dispossessed is channeled into movements demanding a social-democratic redistribution of wealth, as happened in Bolivia and Argentina during their recent meltdowns. At worst, the poor seek remedy through more vengeful outlets, such as right-wing nationalism, religious fundamentalism, or street-gang brutality. Most likely, they join the ranks of the forgotten, victims or perpetrators of the kind of violence, unimaginable for those lucky enough to live in prosperous nations, that takes place in Rio de Janeiro, say, or the cities of Central America—violence that on any given day outstrips, with the possible exception of Iraq, all the more sensational acts of terrorist violence occurring throughout the world combined.

These are the results of the "experiment" that began three decades ago with the imposition of a radical free-market economy first on Chile and then on most of the rest of Latin America. Emancipated from laws and regulations that could force a more equitable distribution of wealth, which in turn would spur demand, it is an economy that can only make a profit by increasing productivity and driving wages downward. It is an economy that allows the United States to maintain its economic primacy even as its industrial base has eroded. Washington is able to leverage its consumption power, military might, and the fact that most of the world's national reserves and transactions are still denominated in dollars to wield monetary policy from a position of strength, to in effect borrow at low interest rates and lend at high ones, with the differential papering over its own increasingly unsustainable debt burden. It is an economy that yields enormous profit for U.S. financial institutions, mostly in the form of interest. And it has tragic human costs: UNICEF estimates that thirteen children die every minute in the third world as a result of moneys being siphoned off from social services to finance debt. This is certainly as morally urgent, not to mention remediable, an issue as any humanitarian concerns that may motivate the new imperialism.[30]

The Return of Latin America's Left

One would expect opposition to have formed against the kind of wretchedness that engulfs Latin America, and it has. Since 1976, over a hundred food riots have broken out in major cities protesting IMF-imposed reduction or abolition of the state subsidies that helped make basic provisions affordable for hard-strapped millions.[31] But riots have been just the first volley in what has grown into a broader international campaign. Bolivians have marched to retain control over their water and gas; Amazon Indians have fought the patenting of medicinal plants by major pharmaceutical corporations; Ecuadorians have sued oil companies for poisoning their environment; Mexican Mayans launched an armed insurgency the day NAFTA was to take effect; Guatemalan peasants have protested the disastrous effects of a World Bank–financed mega-dam on their communities. These are just a few examples of the political activism that has turned Latin America into the vital center of the Global Justice Movement, or what the press often calls the antiglobalization movement.

By early 2004, this grassroots mobilization had begun to attain significant political influence, helping to elect center-left presidents critical of free-market orthodoxy in one country after another: Hugo Chávez in Venezuela, former steelworker and union leader Luiz Inácio Lula da Silva in Brazil, Néstor Kirchner in Argentina, and Tabaré Vázquez in Uruguay. In Bolivia, starting in the 1990s, massive revolts led by Quechua and Aymara Indians opposing the selling off to transnational corporations of natural resources such as water and natural gas have paralyzed this landlocked country for weeks at a time, bringing down two presidents in 2003 and 2005. In Ecuador in 2005, popular protests overthrew a president who promised to resist the IMF but then capitulated to its dictates, replacing him with one who pledged to humanize the country's oppressive economic system. In Nicaragua, the Sandinistas, while riddled with divisions and but a shade of their former idealistic selves, now control nearly all of the country's municipal and state governments. Farther north, the popularity of Andrés Manuel López Obrador, Mexico City's mayor and the front-runner in the upcoming 2006 elections, has suggested that Latin America's new-left renaissance could reach all the way to the United States's doorstep.[32]

Globalization's cheerleaders inevitably dismiss as reactionary the dissent brewing in what was to be globalization's showcase, much as *New York Times* columnist Thomas Friedman famously dismissed the coalition behind World Trade Organization protests as a "Noah's ark of flat-earth advocates." But Friedman is mistaken, for it is these movements that are fighting for a more tolerable, tolerant, and democratic future. Recall that 165 million Latin Americans, one in three, live on less than two dollars a day, victims of social violence perpetuated by their inclusion in—not their exclusion from—a free-market global economic order that is still, despite the mounting evidence of its toxic effects, being prescribed as a tonic for the world's ills. Journalist Naomi Klein is right when she argues that Latin America's anti–corporate globalization movements—Brazil's rural activists demanding land, Argentina's unemployed, Bolivia's *cocaleros*—"are actually waging the real war on terrorism—not with law and order but by providing alternatives to the fundamentalist tendencies that exist wherever there is true desperation."[33]

Latin Americans, of course, have been plugged into the world economy since the days of slave ships and gold mines, so their skepticism regarding the benefits promised by the Washington Consensus can be excused. In this latest phase of globalization, it is not integration they resist but the particular kind of corporate integration that has been forced on them. If there is one overarching objective shared by the diverse and often opposing constituencies that make up Latin America's new left, it is a desire to wriggle at least somewhat free of U.S. control.

Latin Americans do not reject so much the ideal of "free trade" as the particular version of it promoted under the aegis of the Washington-backed Free Trade Agreement of the Americas. Far from advancing fair trade, provisions in the proposed FTAA would tighten the already stringent intellectual property rules, particularly those favoring pharmaceutical industries, found in the World Trade Organization, with the price of essential medicines, including AIDS drugs, most likely doubling.[34] The treaty would also greatly expand NAFTA's Chapter 11 clause, which allows corporations to sue governments over actions that would diminish *potential* future profits. In Mexico, these lawsuits have led to the evisceration of environmental, health, and labor legislation and have hamstrung efforts by local politicians to hold industries accountable to safety standards. And rather than leading to commercial integration among American nations, the FTAA as it is now designed would actually impede integration, offering a combination of incentives and penalties to compel nations to deal exclusively with the United States, thus ratifying Latin America's status as a U.S. province within the globalized economy. Call it "market polygamy," whereby the United States can have multiple partners but each of those partners must remain subordinate to it.

FIVE WARS INTO ONE

"Should I become president," Bush pledged during the 2000 presidential campaign, "I will look south, not as an afterthought, but as a fundamental commitment of my presidency." He promised to "listen" to Latin American leaders and not "bully" them to conform to U.S. expectations.

But after 9/11, bully is what he did. When Venezuelan president Hugo Chávez began to criticize the IMF model, the White House openly backed the plotters who attempted to depose him in spring 2002. The return of the heavy-handed tactics that the United States practiced during the Cold War angered Latin American governments, which were anxious that such actions would further weaken an already fragile hemispheric democratic order. That it was Otto Reich, the old Iran-Contra hand and Central American crusader who was leading the charge against Chávez didn't help matters.[35] Washington drew even more criticism after Chávez beat back the plotters in a remarkable eleventh-hour return to the presidential palace. Much as the disastrous 1961 Bay of Pigs invasion increased Fidel Castro's prestige and radicalized hemispheric politics, this 2002 failed coup attempt in Venezuela galvanized popular hostility toward the Bush administration and catapulted Chávez into the role of champion of the underdog, one of the most admired politicians in all of Latin America.

Relations went from bad to worse. When Mexico hesitated in

supporting Bush's invasion of Iraq, he threatened "discipline," while a U.S. diplomat hinted that Mexicans living in the United States could face internment, as did Japanese Americans during World War II.[36] When the Caribbean Community (CARICOM) likewise objected to the war, the irrepressible Reich was blunt: "I would urge CARICOM to study very carefully not only what it says, but the consequences of what it says." "What do I tell a member of Congress," he asked, "if I go asking for increased access for Caribbean products, for example, and he says, 'Well, they did not support us in our time of need'?"[37] When Latin American countries ratified the International Criminal Court treaty, the Bush administration, threatening to cut millions in economic aid, strong-armed many of them into signing bilateral deals exempting U.S. citizens from the court's jurisdiction.[38] And when Brazil began to organize against the Free Trade Agreement of the Americas, Robert Zoellick, the U.S. foreign trade representative and now number two at the State Department, said it could try selling its products to Antarctica.[39]

Washington was too tied down in the Middle East to afford to let these diplomatic skirmishes turn into a full-fledged firefight. So while the State Department continued to laud Latin America as a model for the United States's civilizing mission, the Defense Department, which has a larger budget and staff devoted to Latin America than does State, quietly began to remilitarize hemispheric relations.

In contrast to Clinton's Pentagon, which viewed the region optimistically, Bush's saw problems previously presented as discrete issues—drugs, arms trafficking, intellectual property piracy, migration, and money laundering, what Moisés Naím, the editor of *Foreign Policy*, describes as the "five wars of globalization"—as part of a larger unified campaign against terrorism.[40] Latin American nations "appear" to be peaceful and stable, said Bush's Southcom commander, Gary Speer. But appearances can be deceptive, for "underlying this perception of tranquility are the multiple transnational threats of terrorism, drug and arms trafficking, illegal migration, and organized crime." "Terrorists, drug traffickers, hostage takers, and criminal gangs," Donald Rumsfeld told a 2004 meeting of Latin American defense ministers in Quito, Ecuador, "form an anti-social combination that increasingly seeks to destabilize civil societies."[41] These threats, the Pentagon liked to point out, knew no borders and were "increasingly linked as they share common infrastructure, transit patterns, corrupting means, and illicit mechanisms."[42] "Legal boundaries," said Speer's successor, James Hill, "don't make sense anymore given the current threat."[43]

After 9/11, the Bush administration added critics of neoliberalism to its growing list of hemispheric security concerns. "Radical populism" was increasingly considered by Southcom to be an "emerging threat" that could link up with Islamic fundamentalism, while Venezuela's Hugo Chávez and Bolivia's peasant activist turned president Evo Morales were singled out as potential terrorists who took advantage of "deep-seated frustrations of the failure of democratic reforms to deliver expected goods and services."[44] In 2005, as mobilization against the Central American Free Trade Agreement increased in Nicaragua, Guatemala, Costa Rica, Honduras, and El Salvador, Bush met with the region's five presidents in the White House and identified "leftist groups"—not poverty, not gang violence, not military and government corruption—as the chief danger facing Central America.[45] During the Cold War, the region's security forces took such cues as death warrants. And indeed, violence against political activists throughout the isthmus immediately began to rise.

The paranoia of the national security state often leads to fulfillment of its own worst-case predictions. In a recent report prognosticating Latin America's future, the National Intelligence Council, an advisory group to the CIA, NSC, and Pentagon made up of military and academic national security experts, fretted that indigenous movements, such as those found in Bolivia protesting corporate control of gas reserves, could "evolve into more radical expressions," converging "with some non-indigenous but radicalized movements— such as the Brazilian 'landless,' the Paraguayan and Ecuadorian peasants, and the Argentine 'picketers.'" "In this scenario," the report went on, "by 2020 the groups will have grown exponentially and obtained the majority adherence of indigenous peoples in their countries, and a 'demonstration' or 'contagion' effect could cause spillover into other nations. The resulting indigenous irredentism would include rejection of western political and economic order maintained by Latin Americans of European origin, causing a deep social fracture that could lead to armed insurgency, repressive response by counter-insurgent governments, social violence and even political and territorial balkanization."[46] Did someone say, "Clash of Civilizations"?

Under the aegis of the "war on terror" (with terror now including anything from pirated DVDs to peasants protesting the Bechtel Corporation), Washington pushed for the construction of a "new architecture of hemispheric security" that would integrate Latin American security forces more tightly into the U.S. military's command structure.[47] As it did during the Cold War, the Pentagon urged Latin American countries to involve their armies in domestic policing. The number of military personnel trained by the United States grew 52 percent just between 2002 and 2003. The Pentagon pushed regional militaries to establish control over what it called "ungoverned spaces"—urban shantytowns where gangs operated, borders, coastlines, and rivers where arms, drug, and human smuggling took place, and jungle and rural areas where guerrillas and terror cells could take root.[48] Such a vision of international security implied a major expansion of the role of the armed forces in domestic affairs, eroding the fragile firewall between police and military operations that human rights activists had fought so hard to erect since the end of the Cold War. In June 2005, for instance, Washington encouraged Central American nations to create a regional "rapid response" team composed of military and police units that could deal with cross-border drug trafficking and gang violence—an operation that harkens back to the 1960s, when U.S.-created rapid response units turned themselves into death squads.

Forced back into the U.S. fold after the wars of the 1980s, Central America had little choice but to submit to Washington's instructions. But South American militaries responded with greater ambivalence. They were, of course, not averse to accepting economic aid or more training. The Brazilian army initiated antigang efforts, and a number of Central American countries launched joint military and police patrols.[49] But high-level officers bristled at completely subordinating their troops to the Pentagon's command.

When Rumsfeld pushed for deeper military integration at the 2004 Quito summit, Chile's defense minister objected, arguing that the United Nations was the "only forum with international legitimacy to act globally on security issues." His Argentine counterpart shot back that he and the other delegates were "very good at taking care of our borders," adding that "terrorism is a concern but not a top priority." The former head of Ecuador's armed forces, General René Vargas, understood Rumsfeld's proposal as an attempt to "consolidate control" over his country's oil and water. "In Latin America," Vargas retorted, "there are no terrorists—only hunger and unemployment and delinquents who turn to crime. What are we going to do, hit you with a banana?"[50]

HARD POWER IN THE ANDES

In the Andes, "transnational threats" have indeed fused into one generalized crisis—but this crisis can be traced to the doorstep not of terrorism or Islamic extremism but of the free-market fundamentalism peddled by the IMF–Wall Street–Treasury Department combine.

In response to escalating coca production and cocaine processing in Bolivia—a crisis brought on, as we saw above, by the imposition of neoliberalism—Washington launched in the late 1980s a
hardnosed coca eradication program. The Bolivian military, working closely with agents from the DEA and the Narcotics Affairs Section of the U.S. embassy, as well as with private security firms
contracted through USAID, has largely targeted small and vulnerable family farms at the bottom of the coca production ladder, producing little long-range effect on large-scale cocaine trafficking.[51]
Around sixty peasant activists have been killed by security forces
since the late 1990s. Homesteads are torched, hundreds wounded,
and many detained and tortured.[52] Under the terms of the notorious
Law 1008, which Bolivia's congress adopted under intense pressure
by the U.S. government, thousands of people have been arrested for
drug-related crimes on little or no evidence and held indefinitely
without being charged or tried. That the enforcers and prosecutors
of the law receive part of their salaries directly from the U.S. embassy provides a strong incentive to show their patrons results for the
money.[53]

As in Central America during the 1980s, a zealous commitment
to free enterprise has blinded the United States to options in Bolivia
that could create substitute employment and generate sustained, humane development, such as land reform or efforts to strengthen
peasant cooperatives.[54] USAID subcontracts out much of its work to
corporate-connected "development firms" like the Washington-
based Development Alternatives Inc., which has close ties to U.S. financial, agribusiness, and telecommunications industries. These
firms work exclusively with Bolivia's private sector, promoting the
kind of laissez-faire "market-based incentives" that accelerated rural
dispossession and indigence in the first place.[55]

But it is Colombia that lies at the heart of the crisis in the Andes.
The country annually produces an estimated six hundred tons of cocaine and heroin for the U.S. market, while its four-decade-long

stalemated civil war kills as many as eight thousand people a year. With taxes collected from coca producers, the Marxist Revolutionary Armed Forces of Colombia fields tens of thousands of foot soldiers; right-wing paramilitary armies, funded by wealthy planters and large drug traffickers and closely tied to the military, operate with near impunity. Reform politicians and political activists not directly involved in the war are executed with brutal regularity. Over four thousand unionists have been assassinated since the late 1980s. Added to these figures are over eighty daily killings related to common crime, giving Colombia the world's highest murder rate. The country also has the world's third-highest internally displaced population, as rural violence drives hundreds of thousands of migrants into contested territory, urban shantytowns, or adjacent countries. The conflict zone touches on all of Colombia's neighbors—Ecuador, Peru, Panama, Brazil, and Venezuela—and the potential for escalation is high, with porous borders providing easy transit for weapons and drugs and combat spilling over into foreign territory.

Since 1989, when George H. W. Bush first militarized the "war on drugs," U.S. troops have steadily expanded their presence in the Andes, establishing airfields and training centers to work with Colombian, Bolivian, Ecuadorian, and Peruvian security forces on fumigation and interdiction maneuvers. Southcom provides radar and intelligence assistance to Andean militaries, while U.S. agents instruct national police forces and intelligence agencies in counternarcotics operations.

Throughout the 1990s, American personnel were prohibited from helping Colombia's security forces to fight the insurgency. U.S. money and weapons were restricted to antidrug operations. But 9/11 removed this proscription. As another example of how the Bush administration has collapsed all public policy problems into the war on terror in order to bypass any oversight that may hinder its actions, the White House successfully urged Congress to include in its global counterterrorism funding bill authorization to fight a "unified campaign" in Colombia, making no distinction between narcotics traffickers, Marxist rebels, and Islamic terrorists.[56] "We see more clearly than ever the interdependence between the terrorists that threaten American lives and the illegal drugs that threaten American potential," was how Attorney General John Ashcroft summarized Bush's Colombia policy. "Lawlessness that breeds terrorism," he reasoned, "is also a fertile ground for the drug trafficking that supports terrorism."[57]

For all the region's importance and potential for escalation, hardly any U.S. aid goes to alleviating the poverty that even the Pentagon admits fuels the war and the drug trade. Needless to say, land reform, planned industrialization, and sustainable rural development are off the table. Without viable alternative employment, small-scale poppy and coca cultivators, when fumigation wipes out their harvest, either join the rebels or push farther into the jungle to cut down more of the rain forest. Even the Council on Foreign Relations, far from a radical critic of U.S. foreign policy, has complained about Washington's indifference to social reform, as well as its refusal to draw on Colombia's neighbors to help negotiate a peaceful political solution to the conflict.[58]

The council goes on to worry that a reliance on "hard" counternarcotics and counterterror tactics has worsened the crisis in the Andes and furthered human suffering. Like the legislation put in place in Bolivia, U.S.-drafted draconian drug laws are used to incarcerate Colombian peasant activists for lengthy periods with little legal recourse. There has been a rise in extrajudicial executions, along with other human rights violations, committed by U.S.-backed security forces not just in Colombia but throughout the Andes.

Of course, none of the 3.3 billion dollars earmarked for Colombia is supposed to go to the country's infamous death squads. But as in Central America in the 1980s, the distinction between the official armed forces and paramilitary vigilantes is nominal. Death squads are organized and funded by drug traffickers and large landowners who enjoy close relations with military officers.[59] And just as the United States first urged the Colombian military in the 1960s to create shadowy paramilitary groups that could operate outside of an established chain of military command, the Pentagon in the early 1990s again advised the Colombian armed forces to create a "more efficient and effective" intelligence network by keeping their operations "covert" and "compartmentalized" and by not putting orders "in writing."[60] One such intelligence unit has been accused of killing labor activists, community leaders, and journalists. And evoking memories of the clandestine operation that illegally supplied arms to the Contras, two U.S. Special Forces officers were arrested by Colombian police in Bogotá in 2005 for supplying over thirty-six thousand rounds of ammunition to a paramilitary group.[61]

The war on drugs has not decreased narcotic production and trafficking, any more than the global war on terror has decreased global terror. But it has served to quietly project the United States's military presence beyond Central America and the Caribbean into South America at a time when new political movements are openly challenging Washington's authority and contesting U.S. corporate control of the continent's natural resources. Even though the Pentagon transferred Southcom operations from Panama to Miami in 1999, it has since created new bases and airstrips in Peru, Ecuador, Bolivia, and Colombia, stationed troops as far south as Paraguay, and worked to establish footholds in Brazil and Argentina.[62]

Despite its extended reach in South America, the U.S. military increasingly outsources much of its work to private security firms—the corporatized heirs to the freelance mercenaries who helped execute Reagan's Central American wars.[63] Flying its own mini–air force, the Virginia-based DynCorp, as per the terms of its $600 million contract, transports equipment and personnel from one country to another, carries out reconnaissance and search and rescue missions, and conducts fumigation flights.[64] Also run out of Virginia, Military Professional Resources Inc., headed by retired generals, admirals, and CIA agents, won a $6 million bid to provide logistical support to the Colombian military and police. These firms operate with minimal oversight and no accountability, applying highly toxic herbicides with little precision, often destroying legitimate crops and contaminating water supplies. In a surveillance flight over the Amazon, agents from Aviation Development Corp., a private company that operates out of Maxwell Air Force Base in Alabama, advised Peru to shoot down a plane that turned out to be carrying not drugs but U.S. missionaries.[65] And in September 2001, ten thousand Ecuadorian peasants filed a class-action lawsuit against DynCorp for indiscriminate fumigation with untested chemicals, which ruined their food harvests, poisoned adults, and killed children and livestock.[66]

⌣

Over the course of nearly two hundred years, two broad arcs of hostility have defined U.S.–Latin American relations. One began in the early nineteenth century, with the first stirrings of the American empire. Marked by decades of nearly continuous warfare, this bout of conflict finally came to an end in the early 1930s, when Washington renounced the right to engage in unilateral armed intervention. The second round began in full with the CIA's 1954 Guatemalan coup and was characterized by dirty wars, death squads' covert operations, and political disappearances—all carried out in supposed defense of liberal democracy against Communist tyranny. This round ended when the Cold War ended, as Latin American nationalists and democrats, spent from the bloodletting, accommodated themselves to the free-trade order promoted by Washington.

Today, the United States and Latin America stand at the threshold of a third period of conflict, as Washington promotes an economic model that produces not development and stability but desolation and crisis. As such, the United States is once again relying on hard power to protect its interests and guard against the resurgence of a new, continent-wide democratic left. The hopes of this resurgence were summarized in a joint statement issued by Presidents Lula of Brazil and Kirchner of Argentina in Buenos Aires in October 2003. Dubbed the Buenos Aires Consensus to set it off from the so-called Washington Consensus that unrestrained free-market capitalism is the only viable model of development, the statement is hardly a radical program. In addition to confirming a commitment to free trade, it repeatedly stresses the importance of both political multilateralism and economic regional integration as a way of giving Latin America "greater autonomy" and protecting against the "destabilizing flows of speculative financial capital" and the "interests of the blocs of more developed countries." While the two presidents commit themselves to the hemispheric consolidation of democracy, they declare that democracy is meaningless without a commitment to end "poverty, unemployment, hunger, illiteracy and disease, which effectively constitute a loss of autonomy and dignity for those afflicted, obstructing them from fully exercising their rights and freedoms as citizens." Globalization, they say, has indeed "widened the horizon of possibilities for humanity." But it has also "generated unprecedented concentrations of wealth." While acknowledging the need to maintain a favorable investment climate, the presidents insist on the right to implement "fairer tax and spending initiatives" so as to promote not just economic growth but also the "equitable distribution of its benefits."

This is not Castro exhorting the youth of the third world to take up arms against Yankee imperialism. It is not Allende defending to his death Marxist humanism. Nor is it Central American revolutionaries attempting to inaugurate a new Christian socialism. But the vision laid out in the document does represent both a political and an economic challenge to Washington's understanding of inter-American "development and security cooperation," which is increasingly looking like its Colombian policy writ large.

Whatever its slim chance of success, the Buenos Aires Consensus, along with other challenges to market fundamentalism and its misery, is a reminder of the most important lesson taught by the history of the United States in Latin America: democracy, social and economic justice, and political liberalization have never been achieved through an embrace of empire but rather through resistance to its command.

Iraq Is Not Arabic
for Latin America

OVER THE COURSE OF MY WRITING this book, as the troubled oc-cupation of Iraq dragged on, Central America kept showing up in the oddest ways. Here was Elliott Abrams—the man who in the 1980s so twisted the concept of human rights that it could justify the homicidal activities of the Contras and the Salvadoran military—being appointed by Bush to lead a global crusade for democracy. There was Dick Cheney in the vice presidential debate telling the electorate that El Salvador, with 50 percent of its population below the poverty level, was a model for what his administration hoped to achieve in Iraq. William Kristol, editor of the conservative *Weekly Standard*, showed up on TV to hail Central America as an "amazing success story." Responding to accusations that John Negroponte's in-volvement in the cover-up of hundreds of executions while he was ambassador to Honduras made him unfit to serve as intelligence czar, the *National Review* praised Reagan's policy in Central and South America as a "spectacularly successful fight to introduce and sustain Western political norms in the region."[1] "By the end of or shortly after Reagan's term," the magazine said, "Argentina, Brazil, Chile, and Uruguay had democratized. Nicaragua held elections won by the opposition, and El Salvador became a model in the region. That John Negroponte was crucial to the policy that affected the revolution should be a recommendation, not a criticism."[2]

Such assertions suggest that a reconsideration of the Borges remark that began this book is in order. To be fair, Latin America, given its current grim reality, is not quite the camel not in the Koran. It is not so much that the history of the United States in Latin America is ignored because of its familiarity but rather that it is misrepresented because it challenges all that our new imperialists hold dear.

Candid assessments of what the United States achieved in Latin America—or at least how it was achieved—do occasionally percolate into the consciousness of pundits and policy makers. "Fifty-five Special Forces trainers in El Salvador," journalist Robert Kaplan wrote recently, "accomplished more than did 550,000 soldiers in Vietnam."[3] And indeed, as the situation in Iraq worsened, the Pentagon turned to the "Salvador option," which meant relying on local paramilitaries to impose order.[4] But once unleashed, these militias, as they did in El Salvador and elsewhere in Latin America, escaped U.S. control. "Hundreds of accounts of killings and abductions have emerged in recent weeks," reported the *New York Times* in November 2005, "most of them brought forward by Sunni civilians, who claim that their relatives have been taken away by Iraqi men in uniform without warrant or explanation. Some Sunni men have been found dead in ditches and fields, with bullet holes in their temples, acid burns on their skin, and holes in their bodies apparently made by electric drills. Many have simply vanished." Ayad Allawi, Iraq's first postinvasion prime minister, claimed that human rights violations had grown worse under the U.S. occupation than during Saddam's rule. Otherwise known as death squads, similar paramilitaries in Central America had the effect of accelerating minor conflicts into full-scale genocidal wars. Needless to say, this history does nothing to douse the maddened zeal with which the new imperialists embrace the idea that the United States has not only the right but the ability to order the world. On the contrary, Kaplan offered his insight as a recommendation to the Department of Defense as part of a ten-point program on how to win the war on terror.

The reported "amazing success" of Central America continues to leave its imprint on U.S. diplomacy. Thus Senator Trent Lott argued in favor of the 1998 "Iraqi Liberation Act," which made the removal of Saddam Hussein official U.S. policy and was passed unanimously by the Senate, by reminding his colleagues of the success of the Reagan Doctrine and U.S. patronage of the Nicaraguan Contras. At the "height of the Cold War," Lott argued, "we supported freedom fighters in Asia, Africa, and Latin America willing to fight and die for a democratic future." Echoing many of the arguments made in the 1980s to support the anti-Sandinista insurgency, Lott insisted that in the post–Cold War period, America—with no rival capable of challenging its military supremacy anywhere on the horizon—needed to move "beyond containment to a policy of rollback."

If one champions anti-Communist "democratic revolutionaries" with as much brio as did the United States in Nicaragua in the 1980s, it is easy to believe that one actually is a revolutionary. Reagan, though, despite his lofty rhetoric, adopted a more unassuming role. Like his predecessor, he was hamstrung by the antimilitarism generated by America's disaster in Southeast Asia. Public opinion polls consistently showed that voters did not favor an invasion of Nicaragua, while bumper stickers reminded the electorate that "El Salvador is Spanish for Vietnam." High-level military officers repeatedly advised the president against direct military involvement. So when hawks called for the United States to lead a "war of national liberation" in Cuba, Reagan gave them Grenada, with a population of ninety thousand, instead.

Yet despite Reagan's general caution in the realm of diplomacy everywhere but in Central America and Grenada, there is a slippery slope between his brand of realism and Bush's preemptive idealism. As Reagan himself liked to point out, "ideas do have consequences, rhetoric is policy, words are action."[5] In hearings held recently by the House Armed Services Committee to address the fallout of the occupation of Iraq, the committee's Republican chairman, Duncan Hunter, intent on legitimating the invasion and occupation, pressed retired army general Wesley Clark to concede that Bush's policies were similar to those of Reagan in Eastern Europe. "Reagan," Clark felt it necessary to remind his interrogator, "never invaded Eastern Europe."[6] When the legend becomes fact, print the legend.

But such confusion is understandable, for Reagan did, rhetorically in general and actually in Central America, put the United States on the offensive. At the annual Conservative Political Action Conference just following Bush's reelection, Karl Rove, Bush's chief of staff for policy, hailed Reagan's belief that the "power of liberty" would enable Americans to "transcend" Soviet Communism rather than merely contain it. Bush, he believed, had taken the next step, pushing conservatism beyond "reactionary" to "forward-looking." "The president made a powerful case in the inaugural speech and before for spreading human liberty and preserving human dignity," insisted Rove, whose portfolio following the election was broadened to include foreign policy. "This was once the preserve of liberalism, but a fellow named Ronald Reagan changed all that." Conservatives today, he said, are "seizing the mantle of idealism."[7]

Andrew Bacevich points out that in "neoconservative lore, 1980 stands out not only as a year of crisis but as the year when the nation decisively turned things around."[8] And nowhere was that turn-around more dramatic and more attributable to American resolve than in Central America. As part of a nationalist backlash bent on reversing what many insisted was a dangerous decline of U.S. power and authority, yet occurring nearly simultaneously with U.S. victory in the Cold War, Reagan's Central American policy became the crucible in which the Hobbesian and Kantian impulses of U.S. foreign policy came together: it rehabilitated overt violence as a legitimate instrument of state, pushed the Republican Party to embrace democratization and nation building as diplomatic objectives, and gave neoconservative intellectuals an opportunity to rehearse the exaggerated rhetorical style for which they have become famous.

Today, the fusion of Hobbes and Kant achieves its highest and most articulate expression in the worldview of a group of policy intellectuals for whom the embrace of violence on behalf of a pure ideal has taken on near-metaphysical meaning. "Military conquest," insists Joshua Muravchik, "has often proved to be an effective means of implanting democracy." "The best democracy program ever invented," says Michael Ledeen, "is the U.S. Army."[9] In the name of extending the "empire of liberty," the young Max Boot has made a career of advising the military to resurrect murderous—and, until recently, discredited—counterinsurgent tactics deployed in the Philippines, Central America, and Vietnam, including the notorious Phoenix program.[10] For her part, *Wall Street Journal* columnist Peggy Noonan, one of George H. W. Bush's speechwriters, conjures the road to war as Christ's Calvary, with America as a crucified nation bearing its pain so others may be free. At the start of the conflict, she wished for a high number of U.S. fatalities for, she writes, a hard war would remind "the world" that "America still knows how to suffer."[11]

Noonan's prayer suggests that the current drive toward global hegemony, spurred as it is by economic and geopolitical imperatives, is as much a domestic as a foreign affair, reflecting the long conservative crusade to return to Americans, after the crises of the 1960s and 1970s, their sense of themselves as citizens of a righteous and providential nation. The crusade has been broad and all-encompassing, reaching into every nook of American politics and culture. Yet its first significant advance took place through the work of the Office of Public Diplomacy, which taught militarists how to execute an aggressive foreign policy in Central America even in the face of overwhelming public disapproval.

The Office of Public Diplomacy was disbanded in the late 1980s after it came out that it was using public funds and CIA and Pentagon operatives to manipulate public opinion. Yet the tactics it perfected—namely, the fusion of PR media manipulation and "grassroots" activism in a centrally coordinated, generously financed campaign—are now established components of American foreign policy. In the 1991 Gulf War, the White House worked closely with the Committee for a Free Kuwait, which had contracted the services of Hill and Knowlton, a PR firm with close ties to the Republican Party, to rally mass support. Taking a page straight out of Otto Reich's playbook, the war lobbyists produced a series of staged photographs (of mannequins!) purportedly showing Iraqi atrocities, created videos of Kuwaiti "resistance fighters," convinced thirteen governors to declare a "Free Kuwait Day," distributed T-shirts with the same message, organized churches to hold a day of prayer for Kuwait, organized focus groups to test the administration's message, distributed media kits, and flooded talk shows with experts testifying on the need for war. They even marched fifteen-year-old "Nayirah" to Capitol Hill, where she claimed to be a "volunteer" at a Kuwaiti hospital in which she witnessed Iraqi soldiers pulling babies out of incubators, leaving them "on the cold floor to die," so as to take the machines back to Iraq. "Nayirah," it turns out, was the daughter of Kuwait's ambassador to the United States and the story was a complete fabrication.[12]

In the twelve years between the first and second Gulf Wars, "perception management" came to assume an even greater role in both intelligence gathering and in building support for war. Well before the Clinton administration made "regime change" in Iraq official U.S. policy, first the CIA and then the Pentagon paid hundreds of millions of dollars to the Rendon Group, a public relations company led by John Rendon, to lay the groundwork for the removal of Saddam Hussein. Rendon virtually created from whole cloth the Iraqi National Congress, that would-be liberation movement championed by the neocons, placing the now discredited Ahmed Chalabi at its head. After 9/11, the White House set up an Office of Global Communication. Where the Office of Public Diplomacy worked hard to keep the U.S. in the Central American wars, this new enterprise, which coordinated the work of PR cadres like Rendon, committed itself to starting a war in Iraq. The office produced a daily set of talking points and vetted all communication issued by the president and his advisers. Benador Associates, another Republican-linked PR firm, advised "terrorism experts" to fine-tune their opinions, suggesting that they "downplay their enthusiasm for invading nations *other* than Iraq." Rendon and other government-contracted public relations firms coached Iraqi dissidents on how to sound good on TV and synchronized the message of conservative think tanks and analysts with that of the White House. The campaign was so centralized that "no one—not even Vice President Dick Cheney—freelances on Iraq," reported *Newsweek*.[13]

The propaganda campaign that led the U.S. to war in Iraq was different from the Office of Public Diplomacy only in that it operated on a global scale rather than primarily, as did Reich's outfit, a domestic one. According to investigative journalist James Bamford, the Pentagon paid Rendon to operate an "Information War Room" to monitor news from all over the world and respond instantly with a barrage of "counterpropaganda."[14] As did Public Diplomacy, Rendon's organization flooded media sources with disinformation, often supplied by supposedly independent journalists who were in fact on Rendon's—and by extension the Pentagon's—payroll. "We functioned twenty-four hours a day," said Rendon. "We maintained situational awareness, in military terms, on all things related to terrorism. We were doing 195 newspapers and 43 countries in fourteen or fifteen languages. If you do this correctly, I can tell you what's on the evening news tonight in a country before it happens."

Consider this chain of influence: the Pentagon funded the Rendon Group, which organized the Iraqi National Congress and trained its members in the arts of propaganda. The INC, in turn, put Iraqi defectors in contact with CIA operatives. When one such defector, Adnan Ihsan Saeed al-Haideri, who claimed to have first-hand knowledge of Iraqi Weapons of Mass Destruction, failed a CIA lie detector test, Chalabi, never one to miss a main chance, put al-Haideri, in contact with *New York Times* reporter Judith Miller. Miller based her then influential but now infamous December 2001 front page "Iraqi Tells of Renovations at Sites for Chemical and Nuclear Arms" story on this one source. That story was then seized on by the Bush administration as justification for war and recycled by papers and TV news stations around the world. Needless to say, al-Haideri's account was a complete fabrication.

It was in Central America that the public relations people who advised the Reagan administration first made an important rhetorical shift when they polled the public and found that the word *terrorism*, intangible as it is, generated more negative connotations than did *Communism* to describe America's enemy. After 9/11, *terrorism* gave way to the even more gossamer *evil*, a word that, whatever role it plays in the specific cosmology of the president and his New Christian Right base, resonates broadly with America's sense of itself as a purpose-driven nation. Bush's ability to stay incuriously on message, like Reagan's communicative skills, is undoubtedly high on the list of PR "exploitable assets." The combination of big-money power, Madison Avenue expertise, and grassroots energy with which to intimidate political opponents into supporting a hard line in Central America is replicated in any number of campaigns, including the Swift Boat Veterans for Truth broadsides against John Kerry, which were as much about imperial policy as they were about a domestic presidential election.

The military's success at establishing cordial and respectful relations with journalists covering Central America, while at the same time cultivating their loyalties through promises of privileged access, paved the way for the tight control the Pentagon exercised over the media in Iraq.[15] Likewise, the appointment of Negroponte, associated as he is with Reagan's Contra war, as director of national intelligence is a reminder that many of the post-9/11 intelligence "reforms" were first proposed in the 1980s to monitor the Latin American solidarity movement. Oliver North's plan to place dissenting Americans in detention centers in the event of a U.S. invasion of Nicaragua, along with the FBI investigation and harassment of CISPES activists, is today ratified by the Patriot Act and other successful efforts to restrict constitutional guarantees and human rights in the name of national security, such as the practice of "extraordinary rendition."[16] Rendition allows suspects in the war on terror to be swept off the street in whatever country they find themselves and whisked, without record of their capture, to a third country, where they can be held and interrogated indefinitely in secret prisons—a globalization of the system of disappearances that reigned in Latin America during the Cold War.[17]

In fact, all of George W. Bush's abuses of power—the manipulation of intelligence and the media, the building of an interagency war party that operated autonomously from Washington's foreign policy establishment, the illegal wiretaps, and the surveillance of antiwar activists—have their most immediate antecedents in Reagan's Central American policy, which in retrospect has to be understood as the first battle in the New Right's crusade to roll back restrictions placed on the imperial presidency in the wake of Vietnam, Watergate, COINTELPRO, and other scandals of the 1970s.

But the most consequential initiative taken by the Reagan administration to cure America of the Vietnam syndrome was the building of populist nationalist and Christian support for an aggressive foreign policy meant to counter what seemed to many the permanently entrenched dissent that emerged from the antiwar protests of the 1960s and 1970s. Jeane Kirkpatrick's argument that the Sandinista revolution could only sustain itself by continually mobilizing its base through an expansive foreign policy turns out to be an accurate description of the New Right, as we have seen. The Reagan revolution pulled into its gravitational field a diverse constellation of economic elites, militarists, religionists, realists, and idealists, helping these groups to cohere through a renewed engagement with the world. An expansionist foreign policy likewise produced a coherent ideological response to the malaise of the 1970s, linking a renewal of America's moral and political culture to both the dismantling of the welfare state at home and the export of free-market capitalism abroad.

In particular, Reagan's wars in Central America created an affinity between neoconservatives and Christian evangelicals: both came to share a crisis-ridden view of the world and a sense that America was in decline. But they also shared a belief that decline could be reversed through a restoration of moral clarity and authority and a recognition that evil existed in the world. Along with militarists and conservative intellectuals, the religious right has long nurtured a suspicion of America's ruling elites and the multilateral institutions that trespass on national sovereignty. Yet their experience in the 1980s has drawn them nearer to the strange optimism of the neocons regarding the capacity of American power to mend the world. For some the lodestar may be Winston Churchill, for others Jesus Christ, but today a broad consensus prevails among the most passionate constituents of the conservative movement as to the righteousness of American power and its place in the unfolding of history. Thus, when Pat Robertson suggested in the summer of 2005 that Washington preemptively assassinate Hugo Chávez before U.S. relations with Venezuela worsened, he was merely taking to a logical conclusion the principles elaborated in Bush's 2002 National Security Strategy.

The worldview that unites the secular and religious branches of the conservative movement regarding foreign policy manifests itself today in the carefully crafted cadences of Bush's oratory, which cribs from scripture to replace Jesus with America: "America stands as a beacon of light to the world," he said in his Ellis Island address on the first anniversary of 9/11, "and the light shines in the darkness, and the darkness has not overcome it."[16] It is captured in Bush's oft-repeated insistence that "freedom is not America's gift to the world, it's God's gift to mankind." The idea of "freedom" serves as the coalition's universal signifier uniting secular nationalists, political liberals, corporate or ideological free-market dogmatists, and evangelicals. The concordance is confirmed in a shared appreciation of the threat facing America: the war on terror, says Norman Podhoretz, is more accurately understood as a war against radical Islam and should be identified as such.[17] Jerry Falwell, Pat Robertson, and Franklin Graham, son of Billy, agree, believing Mohammed to be a terrorist and Islam evil and wicked.[18] Even the "moderate" Institute for Religion and Democracy (which, though it still monitors Protestant denominations for any residual sympathy they may harbor for liberation theology, is now more concerned with combating liberal religious tolerance of Islam) has condemned the World Council of Churches for refusing to confront the "deep physical, social and spiritual deficits within the Islamic world."[19] The alliance also finds bureaucratic expression in places like the Pentagon, which brings together secular realists like Rumsfeld, neoconservative ideologues like Undersecretary of Defense for Intelligence Stephen Cambone, who served as a key link in the chain of command that oversaw the interrogations at Abu Ghraib, and Christian soldiers like Lieutenant General William Boykin. After revealing that he had inside information that the United States would win the war on terror because Christ is "bigger" than Allah and warning that "Satan" plans to "destroy" America "as a Christian army," Boykin was promoted to the number-two slot in charge of intelligence in the Pentagon.

An expansive foreign policy remains as critical today for the conservative coalition as it did during the 1980s—even more so considering the heightened sense of expectation and entitlement conservative activists have now that they control the executive and legislative branches and are driving the agenda in the judiciary. As columnist David Brooks has recently observed, the conservative movement is "split into feuding factions that squabble incessantly, . . . neocons arguing with theocons, the old right with the new right, internationalists versus isolationists, supply siders versus fiscal conservatives." Yet they agree on foreign policy: "Now most Republicans," Brooks says, citing a *New York Times* poll, "believe the U.S. should try to change dictatorships into democracies."[21] Likewise, America's privileged position within the world's global financial system—dependent as it is on the maintenance of political primacy in order to continue to prop up a deeply indebted economy—demands an aggressive foreign policy. On this fact, neither major political party disagrees. But the need for the New Right to maintain a constant level of mobilization to hold its coalition together—especially since the domestic goals of many of its constituencies are unattainable—could push this aggression to an even more dangerous extreme.

The component elements of the new revolutionary imperialism reinforce each other, creating ever more crises that call for ever more intervention. America's imposition of free-trade absolutism produces throughout the world perpetual instability—thus justifying the need for an imperial power to impose order. "Hard Wilsonianism"—that odd mix of unapologetic violence and blinding idealism that motivates neocons—finds its expression in frontline repression, in Abu Ghraib's and Gitmo's interrogation rooms, in the leveling of Fallujah, and in the scores of unexplained deaths of prisoners in United States custody. It is manifested in the actions of members of the Eighty-second Airborne Division, who for seventeen months, even after the abuses at Abu Ghraib were exposed, beat their Iraqi prisoners with metal baseball bats, perhaps believing that broken bones would make Muslims more receptive to Western values.[22] Such violence will generate more anger, more "extremism," which, sooner or later, will need to be met with more repression. At home, the refusal of either major political party to develop an alternative to unbridled free trade, along with the success of the Republican Party in redistributing wealth upward through tax cuts and the gutting of social entitlements, propels economic insecurity, leading to domestic discontent that can only be contained through constant mobilization against a shapeless, and thus perpetual, enemy. Dick Cheney at least has predicted that the war on terror could be over in half a century, but Bush has warned that it may never end.

❧

Jeane Kirkpatrick once wrote that "thought set free from experience is unlimited by the constraints of experience or of probability. If history is not relevant then the future is free from the past. Theories cut loose from experience are usually blindingly optimistic. They begin not from how things are but how they ought to be, and regularly underestimate the complexities and difficulties concerning how you get there from here." Drawing on such a respect for history and experience, the history of the United States in Latin America should help us imagine what to expect if American power remains unchallenged.

Like any empire before it, the United States will not tilt too far in favor of democracy at the expense of stability. That such a tilt never occurred in Latin America—a place where American leaders had long believed themselves to be agents of progressive revolutionary change—is a fairly good indication that it will not happen now on a global level. The precarious misery generated by free-market absolutism will predictably lead to challenges to America's interests and authority—and, just as predictably, they will have to be dealt with, as they were in Latin America, with an increasingly heavy hand. Talk of the "Salvador option," in other words, is not an indication of the failure of Washington's imperial policy but an admission of its essence.

There are, of course, important differences between Latin America and the Middle East, not least of which is the nature of Washington's opponents in both places. In Guatemala, Nicaragua,

and El Salvador, the United States fought against democratic movements. In the Middle East, this is clearly not the case. This difference, in fact, points to another lesson. Reagan's revolutionary claims
notwithstanding, his interventions in Central America were designed
either to defend or to restore the region's old regimes. Indeed,
nowhere in Latin America during the Cold War did Washington
ever try to set up a government from scratch. It was the burden of
the hemisphere's genuinely revolutionary regimes—in Cuba,
Nicaragua, Chile, and, before that, in Guatemala—and its revolutionary movements, in El Salvador and elsewhere—to attempt this
difficult task, and we know the outcomes of those efforts. But creating a new regime is precisely what the Bush administration believed
it could do in the Middle East and elsewhere.

The Contra war provides an illustrative example of the difficulties of establishing a new political order, with the United States
finding itself in the untenable position of the Sandinistas. Seeking
to demonstrate to a frightened rural population that the Sandinistas could not establish effective sovereignty, the Contras destroyed cooperatives, schools, clinics, and power stations and
executed civilians, including foreigners who were helping to rebuild Nicaragua. The Contras, and their U.S. patrons, felt no need
to establish ideological legitimacy. All they had to do was wear
down a fledgling regime through unpredictable acts of persistent
terror. With the Sandinistas unable to deliver security, much less a
better life, popular support tipped to their enemies, who started
out, we should not forget, as a rump of discredited old regime
repressors—"dead enders," to apply Rumsfeld's description of the
Baathist remnants who reportedly organized the initial resistance
to the U.S. occupation of Iraq.

The first insurgent generation of civilian militarists had only to
tear down a tottering power—and a U.S. foreign policy already discredited from failure in Vietnam. They were able to play out their
fantasy of revolution in an inconsequential "sweet waist" of a land—

Pablo Neruda's description of tragedy-drenched Central America—where the wreckage of their actions could be easily ignored. Yet Iraq is not Arabic for Central America: the stakes are higher and the task of establishing a governing consensus much greater than anything the United States has faced in its own hemisphere. Whatever the ultimate outcome of Bush's invasion of Iraq, a small group of rebels has managed to tie down the most technologically powerful military in world history for years in a deadly, financially draining, and morally discrediting insurgency. In normal times, such a result would suggest the importance of recognizing limits. But we are not living in normal times. "We're an empire now," boasted a Bush staffer after the invasion of Iraq, "and when we act, we create our own reality."[23]

Today's new imperial revolutionaries, however, continue to ignore perhaps the most obvious question raised by the United States's imperial track record: If Washington was unable to bring prosperity, stability, and meaningful democracy to Latin America, a region that falls squarely within its own sphere of influence and whose population shares many of its values, then what are the chances that it will do so for the world?

Notes

∨

INTRODUCTION: The Camel Not in the Koran

1. James Mann, *The Rise of the Vulcans: The History of Bush's War Cabinet*, New York: Viking, p. 16.
2. October 20, 1971, Conversation 597–3, cassette 1293, President Nixon phone conversation with H. R. Haldeman, 9:28 a.m.–12:20 p.m., http://www.gwu.edu/~nsarchiv/NSAEBB/NSAEBB95/mex18.pdf; accessed on May 9, 2004.
3. Joseph S. Nye, "The Misleading Metaphor of Decline," *Atlantic*, March 1990.
4. Geir Lundestad, "Empire by Invitation? The United States and Western Europe, 1945–1952," *Journal of Peace Research* 23 (September 1986): 263–77.
5. David Corn, "Beltway Bandits," *Nation*, April 17, 1989.
6. Anatol Lieven, *America Right or Wrong: An Anatomy of American Nationalism*, New York: Oxford University Press, 2004; Thomas Frank, *What's the Matter with Kansas?: How Conservatives Won the Heart of America*, New York: Metropolitan Books, 2004.

CHAPTER ONE: How Latin America Saved
the United States from Itself

1. Fordlandia is discussed in Warren Dean, *Brazil and the Struggle for Rubber: A Study in Environmental History*, Cambridge: Cambridge University

Press, 1987; Elizabeth D. Esch, "Fordtown: Managing Race and Nation in the American Empire, 1925–1945," dissertation, New York University, 2003; Susanna Hecht and Alexander Cockburn, *The Fate of the Forest: Developers, Destroyers, and Defenders of the Amazon*, New York: Verso, 1989; and Marianne Schmink, "Big Business in the Amazon," *People of the Tropical Rain Forest*, ed. Julie Sloan Denslow and Christine Padoch, Berkeley: University of California Press, 1988.

2. Thomas F. O'Brien, *The Revolutionary Mission: American Enterprise in Latin America, 1900–1945*, Cambridge: Cambridge University Press, 1996, p. 1.

3. Esch, "Fordtown," p. 97.

4. Ibid., p. 113.

5. A. J. Langguth, *Hidden Terrors*, New York: Pantheon, 1978, pp. 104, 123. The Business Group for Latin America evolved into the Council of the Americas and eventually was composed of more than 200 firms responsible for more than 80 percent of U.S. investment in Latin America. See Gerard Colby with Charlotte Dennett, *Thy Will Be Done: The Conquest of the Amazon: Nelson Rockefeller and Evangelism in the Age of Oil*, New York: Harper-Collins, 1995, p. 474.

6. Seymour Hersh, *The Price of Power: Kissinger in the Nixon White House*, New York: Summit Books, 1983, p. 259; Greg Palast, "A Marxist Threat to Cola Sales? Pepsi Demands a US Coup: Goodbye Allende, Hello Pinochet," *Guardian*, November 8, 1998; Peter Frawley, "Former Ambassador Alleges Cover-Up of Illegal American Activities in Chile," *Harvard Crimson*, February 17, 1977.

7. Clair Cooper, "Suit Accuses DaimlerChrysler in Killings of Argentine Workers," *Sacramento Bee*, January 15, 2004; David Kravets, "Argentine War Victims Sue Mercedes-Benz," Associated Press, January 15, 2004; and Deborah Levenson-Estrada, *Trade Unionists against Terror, Guatemala City, 1954–1984*, Chapel Hill: University of North Carolina Press, 1994.

8. "Ford Motor Is Linked to Argentina's 'Dirty War,'" *New York Times*, November 27, 2002; Arquidiocese de São Paulo, *Brazil: Nunca mais*, Rio de Janeiro: Petrópolis Vozes, 1985, p. 73. Cf. Langguth, *Hidden Terrors*, New York: Pantheon, 1978, pp. 104, 123.

9. Harry Bernstein, "Some Inter-American Aspects of the Enlightenment," *Latin America and the Enlightenment*, ed. Arthur Whitaker, Ithaca: Cornell University Press, 1961, pp. 53–55.

10. Samuel Eliot Morison, *Maritime History of Massachusetts, 1783–1860*, Boston and New York: Houghton Mifflin, 1921; Arthur P. Whitaker, *The United States and the Independence of Latin America, 1800–1830*, New York: Norton, 1964.

11. Gerard Colby, *Thy Will Be Done*, p. 75.

12. Mira Wilkins, *The Emergence of Multinational Enterprise: American Business Abroad from the Colonial Era to 1914*, Cambridge: Harvard University

Press, 1970; Mark Gilderhus, *Diplomacy and Revolution: U.S.-Mexican Relations under Wilson and Carranza*, Tucson: University of Arizona Press, 1977, p. 1.

13. Ralph Arnold, *The First Big Oil Hunt: Venezuela, 1911–1916*, New York: Vantage Press, 1960.

14. Josiah Strong, *Our Country: Its Possible Future and Its Present Crisis*, rev. ed., New York: Baker and Taylor Company, 1891, p. 28.

15. Colby, *Thy Will Be Done*, p. 45.

16. O'Brien, *Revolutionary Mission*, pp. 293, 315.

17. Lester Langley and Thomas Schoonover, *The Banana Men: American Mercenaries and Entrepreneurs in Central America, 1880–1930*, Lexington: University of Kentucky Press, 1995.

18. From a report commissioned by the U.S. Navy titled "An Indicator of Informal Empire: Patterns of U.S. Navy Cruising on Overseas Stations, 1869–97," cited in William Appleman Williams, *Empire as a Way of Life*, New York: Oxford University Press, 1980, p. 122.

19. Ovidio Diaz Espino, *How Wall Street Created a Nation: J. P. Morgan, Teddy Roosevelt, and the Panama Canal*, New York: Four Walls Eight Windows, 2001.

20. Chalmers Johnson, *The Sorrows of Empire: Militarism, Secrecy, and the End of the Republic*, New York: Metropolitan Books, 2004, p. 45; David Healy, *Drive to Hegemony*, Madison: University of Wisconsin Press, 1988.

21. See Robert Kaplan, "Indian Country," *Wall Street Journal*, September 25, 2004.

22. Max Boot, *The Savage Wars of Peace: Small Wars and the Rise of American Power*, New York: Basic Books, 2002, p. 108.

23. Faustin Wirkus and Taney Dudley, *The White King of La Gonave*, Garden City: Garden City Publishers, 1931, pp. 66–68, cited in Mary Renda, *Taking Haiti: Military Occupation and the Culture of U.S. Imperialism, 1915–1940*, Chapel Hill: University of North Carolina Press, 2001, pp. 155–56.

24. Michael J. Schroeder, "The Sandino Rebellion Revisited: Civil War, Imperialism, Popular Nationalism, and State Formation Muddied Up Together in the Segovias of Nicaragua, 1926–1934," *Close Encounters of Empire: Writing the Cultural History of U.S.–Latin American Relations*, ed. Gilbert M. Joseph et al., Durham: Duke University Press, 1998, p. 222.

25. Renda, *Taking Haiti*, p. 154.

26. Peter Maass, "The Way of the Commandos," *New York Times Magazine*, May 1, 2005.

27. Harold Denny, "Marines Push Drive in Nicaragua Wilds," *New York Times*, January 21, 1928.

28. Schroeder, "Sandino Rebellion Revisited," p. 222.

29. Captain Kenneth Jennings, "Sandino against the Marines: The Development of Air Power for Conducting Counterinsurgency Operations in Central America," *Air University Review*, July–August 1986.

30. William Appleman Williams, *The Tragedy of American Diplomacy*, New York: Dell Publishing Company, 1972, p. 15; see also Walter LaFeber, *The New Empire: An Interpretation of American Expansion, 1860–1898*, Ithaca: Cornell University Press, 1998.

31. Williams, *Tragedy of American Diplomacy*, p. 46.

32. Eric Love, *Race over Empire: Racism and U.S. Imperialism, 1865–1990*, Chapel Hill: University of North Carolina Press, 2004, p. 197. For Roosevelt's and Wilson's turn against imperialism, see John Judis, "What Woodrow Wilson Can Teach Today's Imperialists," *New Republic*, June 9, 2003.

33. Rudyard Kipling's "White Man's Burden," in Love, *Race over Empire*, p. 200.

34. For the story of the SDIC, see Cyrus Veeser, *A World Safe for Capitalism: Dollar Diplomacy and America's Rise to Global Power*, New York: Columbia University Press, 2002.

35. David Green, *Containment of Latin America: A History of the Myths and Realities of the Good Neighbor Policy*, Chicago: Quadrangle, 1971, p. 144.

36. *The Year of Crisis, 1933*, vol. 2 of *The Public Papers and Addresses of Franklin D. Roosevelt*, New York: Random House, 1938.

37. Fredrick B. Pike, *FDR's Good Neighbor Policy: Sixty Years of Generally Gentle Chaos*, Austin: University of Texas Press, 1995, pp. 129–32.

38. John Mason Hart, *Empire and Revolution: The Americans in Mexico since the Civil War*, Berkeley: University of California Press, 2002.

39. Wilkins, *Emergence of Multinational Enterprise*; Gilderhus, *Diplomacy and Revolution*, p. 1.

40. I thank Matthew Vitz for providing me with these citations from his research on political conflict on the Mexican border.

41. Colby, *Thy Will Be Done*, p. 82.

42. "Marine Fliers Slain Fighting to the End," *New York Times*, November 9, 1927, sect. 1, p. 14.

43. Richard V. Salisbury, *Anti-Imperialism and International Competition in Central America, 1920–1929*, Wilmington: Scholarly Resources Books, 1989, p. 115.

44. John Edwin Fagg, *Pan Americanism*, Malabar: Krieger Publishing, 1982, pp. 161–62.

45. For policy intellectuals' criticism of U.S. actions in Latin America in the second half of the Hoover administration, see the essays under the heading "Our Future Relations with Latin America," *Annals of the American Academy of Political and Social Science* 156 (July 1931): 110–36.

46. Cited in Thomas J. McCormick, "Walking the Tightrope: Adolf A. Berle and America's Journey from Social to Global Capitalism, 1933–1945," *Behind the Throne: Servants of Power to Imperial Presidents, 1898–1968*, ed. McCormick and Walter LaFeber, Madison: University of Wisconsin Press, 1993, p. 138.

47. Pike, *FDR's Good Neighbor Policy*, p. 220; Frederick Marks, *Wind over Sand: The Diplomacy of Franklin Roosevelt*, Athens: University of Georgia Press, 1988, p. 218.

48. Marks, *Wind over Sand*, p. 217.
49. Frank Niess, *A Hemisphere to Itself: A History of U.S.–Latin American Relations*, London: Zed Books, *1990*, pp. 115–23.
50. Colby, *Thy Will Be Done*, p. 95.
51. Thomas Ferguson and Joel Rogers, *Right Turn: The Decline of the Democrats and the Future of American Politics*, New York: Hill and Wang, 1986, pp. 52–53.
52. "Overseas Sales of United States Drug Products," *Digest of International Developments, Drugs and Toiletries*, vol. 7, part 3, no. 19, January 1949. Many thanks to Suzanna Reiss for this citation.
53. Philip Jessup, "The Saavedra Lamas Anti-War Draft Treaty," *American Journal of International Law* 27, no. 1 (January 1933): 109–14. The treaty is found in vol. 28, no. 3, Supplement: Official Documents (July 1934): 79–84.
54. See Jorge Americano, *The New Foundation of International Law*, New York: Macmillan, 1947; Pedro Batista Martins, *Da unidade do direito e da supremacia do direito internacional*, Rio de Janeiro: Imprensa Nacional, 1942; Levi Carneiro, *O Direito internacional e a democracia*, Rio de Janiero: A Coelho Branco, 1945; José Maria Velasco Ibarra, *Derecho internacional del futuro*, Buenos Aires: Editorial Americalee, 1943.
55. Latin America's role in building the postwar order, especially the Universal Declaration, is discussed in Paulo G. Carozza, "From Conquest to Constitutions: Retrieving a Latin American Tradition of the Idea of Human Rights," *Human Rights Quarterly* 25 (2003): 281–313, and Hernán Santa Cruz, *Cooperar o perecer: El dilema de la comunidad mundial*, 2 vols., Buenos Aires: Grupo Editor Latinoamericano, 1984.
56. Santa Cruz, *Cooperar o perecer*, vol. 1, p. 42.
57. *F.D.R.: His Personal Letters, 1928–1945*, ed. Elliott Roosevelt, New York: Duell, Sloan and Pearce, 1950, pp. 1445–47.
58. Peter Gowan, *The Global Gamble: Washington's Faustian Bid for World Dominance*, London: Verso, 1999.
59. Green, *Containment of Latin America*.
60. Leslie Bethell and Ian Roxborough, eds., *Latin America between the Second World War and the Cold War, 1944–1948*, Cambridge: Cambridge University Press, 1992.
61. David Schmitz, *Thank God They're on Our Side: The United States and Right-Wing Dictatorships, 1921–1965*, Chapel Hill: University of North Carolina Press, 1999, pp. 140–57.
62. Ibid., p. 145.
63. Walter LaFeber, "Thomas C. Mann and the Devolution of Latin American Policy: From the Good Neighbor to Military Intervention," *Behind the Throne*, ed. McCormick and LaFeber, p. 174.
64. Kermit Roosevelt, *Countercoup: The Struggle for Control of Iran*, New York: McGraw-Hill, 1979; Nick Cullather, *Secret History: The CIA's Classified Account of Its Operations in Guatemala, 1952–1954*, Stanford: Stanford Uni-

versity Press, 1999; Stephen Schlesinger and Stephen Kinzer, *Bitter Fruit: The Story of the American Coup in Guatemala*, Cambridge: Harvard University Press, 1999; Piero Gleijeses, *Shattered Hope: The Guatemalan Revolution and the United States, 1944–1954*, Princeton: Princeton University Press, 1991; and Office of the Historian, Department of State, *Foreign Relations of the United States, 1952–1954: Guatemala*, Washington: Government Printing Office, 2003.

65. For Bernays's role, see his *Biography of an Idea* (New York: Simon and Schuster, 1965) and the BBC documentary *Century of the Self*, episode 2, "The Engineering of Consent," 2002.

66. Cullather, *Secret History*, p. 66.

67. Ibid., p. 83.

68. "Memorandum from William Robertson of Operation PBSUCCESS to the Chief of the Project," available at www.state.gov/r/pa/ho/frus/ike/guat/20181.htm.

69. See the discussion of this manual in Greg Grandin, *The Last Colonial Massacre: Latin America in the Cold War*, Chicago: University of Chicago Press, 2004, p. 238.

70. Cullather, *Secret History*.

71. *The United Nations; The Western Hemisphere*, vol. 2 of *Foreign Relations of the United States, 1951*, Washington: Government Printing Office, 1979, p. 1440.

72. Available at: http://www.fas.org/irp/offdocs/nsc-hst/nsc-68.htm; accessed on May 2, 2004.

73. John F. Kennedy, "Preliminary Formulations of the Alliance for Progress," Presidential Address for Latin American Diplomats and Members of Congress, March 13, 1961.

74. Colby, *Thy Will Be Done*, p. 392.

75. John Newhouse, *Imperial America: The Bush Assault on the World Order*, New York: Knopf, 2003, and Peter Gowan, "US : UN," *New Left Review*, November–December 2003.

76. Niall Ferguson, *Colossus: The Price of America's Empire*, New York: Penguin, 2004, p. 58.

77. Boot, *Savage Wars of Peace*, p. 181.

CHAPTER TWO: THE MOST IMPORTANT PLACE IN THE WORLD: TOWARD A NEW IMPERIALISM

1. "Remarks by the President at 2002 Graduation Exercises of the United States Military Academy, West Point, New York," at www.whitehouse.gov/news/releases/2002/06/20020601-3.html.

2. Max Boot, "What the Heck Is a 'Neocon'?" *Wall Street Journal*, December 30, 2002.

3. Charles Krauthammer, "A Unipolar World," American Enterprise Institute annual dinner, February 10, 2004 (Washington, D.C.), broadcast on

C-Span, February 16, 2004; Paul D. Wolfowitz, New School University, September 21, 2003. See also the Democratic Party's pre-9/11 version of "democratic realism," in Will Marshall, "Democratic Realism: The Third Way," *Blueprint Magazine*, January 1, 2000.

4. Russ Olson, "You Can't Spit on a Foreign Policy," Society for Historians of American Foreign Relations Newsletter, September 2000.

5. Ibid.

6. Lt. Gen. James D. Hughes, Remarks at Patricia Nixon's Funeral, June 26, 1993, available at http://www.nixonfoundation.org/Research_Center/ Nixons/PatNixonFuneral.html.

7. Alan McPherson, *Yankee No! Anti-Americanism in U.S.–Latin American Relations*, Cambridge: Harvard University Press, 2003, p. 34.

8. Jeremy Suri, *Power and Protest: Global Revolution and the Rise of Détente*, Cambridge: Harvard University Press, 2003, p. 256.

9. James Mann, *The Rise of the Vulcans: The History of Bush's War Cabinet*, New York: Viking, 2004, p. 76.

10. Mahmood Mamdani, *Good Muslim, Bad Muslim: America, the Cold War, and the Roots of Terror*, New York: Pantheon, 2004, p. 79.

11. Memorandum of Conversation, "NSC meeting—Chile," November 6, 1970. Available at http://www.gwu.edu/~nsarchiv/news/20001113/701106 .pdf; accessed on May 22, 2004.

12. "Conversation between Richard Nixon and Daniel Patrick Moynihan on the Ability of Blacks to Lead Nations," October 7, 1971, Conversation 10–116, cassettes 1049 and 1050, 10:32–10:58 a.m., http://www.gwu.edu/ ~nsarchiv/NSAEBB/NSAEBB95/mex16.pdf; accessed on May 4, 2004.

13. Walter LaFeber, *Inevitable Revolutions: The United States in Central America*, New York: Norton, 1993, p. 203.

14. See the National Security Archive Electronic Briefing Book, no. 133, edited by Carlos Osorio and Kathleen Costar, posted August 27, 2004, at www .gwu.edu/~nsarchiv/NSAEBB/NSAEBB133/index.htm. The National Security Archive Web page links to other declassified documents detailing U.S. involvement in Uruguay, Chile, El Salvador, Guatemala, and Brazil.

15. "Korry Seeks to Testify at Sorenson Hearing," *Washington Post*, January 10, 1977. Cf. Thomas Powers, *The Man Who Kept the Secrets: Richard Helms and the CIA*, New York: Knopf, 1979, p. 230.

16. Seymour Hersh, *The Price of Power: Kissinger in the Nixon White House*, New York: Summit Books, 1983, p. 270.

17. Seymour Hersh, "Hearings Urged on CIA's Role in Chile," *New York Times*, September 9, 1974; Seymour Hersh, "House Unit Meets on Chilean Leaks," *New York Times*, September 26, 1974.

18. Seymour Hersh, "Helms Said Nixon Sought Chilean Coup," *New York Times*, February 10, 1975.

19. All fourteen volumes can be accessed at http://www.aarclibrary.org/ publib/church/reports/.

20. For the FBI's surveillance and harassment of political activists, see David Cunningham, *There's Something Happening Here: The New Left, the Klan, and FBI Counterintelligence*, Berkeley: University of California Press, 2004.
21. Cynthia J. Arnson, *Crossroads: Congress, the Reagan Administration, and Central America*, New York: Pantheon, 1989.
22. Arnson, *Crossroads*, pp. 13–14, 27–30.
23. John Dinges, *The Condor Years: How Pinochet and His Allies Brought Terrorism to Three Continents*, New York: New Press, 2004.
24. Chalmers Johnson, *The Sorrows of Empire: Militarism, Secrecy, and the End of the Republic*, New York: Metropolitan Books, 2004, pp. 60–61.
25. Jeane J. Kirkpatrick, *Dictatorships and Double Standards: Rationalism and Reason in Politics*, New York: Simon and Schuster, 1982, p. 29.
26. Michael Klare, "Have R.D.F. Will Travel," *Nation*, March 8, 1980.
27. Robert M. Gates, *From the Shadows: The Ultimate Insider's Story of Five Presidents and How They Won the Cold War*, New York: Simon and Schuster, 1996. Cf. Steve Coll, *Ghost Wars: The Secret History of the CIA, Afghanistan, and Bin Laden, from the Soviet Invasion to September 10, 2001*, New York: Penguin, 2004.
28. *Le Nouvel Observateur*, January 15–21, 1998.
29. Mann, *Rise of the Vulcans*, pp. 112–13.
30. Ibid., p. 45.
31. Johnson, *Sorrows of Empire*, p. 63. For "strategic class," see Kurt M. Campbell, "China Watchers Fighting a Turf War of Their Own," *New York Times*, May 20, 2000.
32. Quoted in William M. LeoGrande, *Our Own Backyard: The United States in Central America, 1977–1992*, Chapel Hill: University of North Carolina Press, 1998, p. 82.
33. Peter Kornbluh and Martha Honey, "The Case of Ollie's Airstrip," *Nation*, February 22, 1993.
34. LaFeber, *Inevitable Revolutions*, p. 271.
35. Lars Schoultz, *National Security and United States Policy toward Latin America*, Princeton: Princeton University Press, 1987, pp. 273–74.
36. Robert Tucker, "The Purposes of American Power," *Foreign Affairs*, Winter 1980–81, p. 272. In this early essay, Tucker parses, without necessarily endorsing, the logic that propelled increasing U.S. involvement in Central America throughout the 1980s: "In Central America there are no vital raw materials or minerals whose loss might provide the basis for legitimate security concerns. Yet Central America bears geographical proximity to the United States, and historically it has long been regarded as falling within our sphere of influence. We have regularly played a determining role in making and in unmaking governments. In Central America our pride is engaged as it cannot possibly be engaged in Africa or in Southeast Asia. If we do not apply a policy of a resurgent America to prevent the coming to power of radical regimes in Central America, we have even less reason to

do so in other areas where conventional security interests are not apparent. Reasons of pride and historic tradition apart, it is here, if anywhere, that we enjoy clear military superiority and may expect to retain such superiority in the future. In Central America, then, one risk of an ambitious containment policy would be absent. . . . If our claims ought not to extend to the internal order of states here, there is still less reason for extending them elsewhere in the Third World."

37. LaFeber, *Inevitable Revolutions*, p. 275.

38. Roy Gutman, *Banana Diplomacy: The Making of American Policy in Nicaragua, 1981–1987*, New York: Simon and Schuster, 1988, and LeoGrande, *Our Own Backyard*, are the two best accounts of the bureaucratic shaping of Reagan's Central American policy.

39. The Heritage Foundation, "Jeane J. Kirkpatrick," www.heritage.org/About/kirkpatrick.cfm.

40. Theodore H. White, "The Action Intellectuals," *Life*, June 23, 1967.

41. For example, see Kalman Silvert, *The Americas in a Changing World: A Report of the Commission on United States–Latin American Relations*, New York: Quadrangle/New York Times Book Co., 1975.

42. Zbigniew Brzezinski, *Between Two Ages: America's Rule in the Technetronic Era*, New York: Viking, 1970, p. 289.

43. Unless otherwise cited, quotations from Kirkpatrick come from the introduction to *Dictatorships and Double Standards*, as well as from the essays "Dictatorships and Double Standards" and "U.S. Security & Latin America," first published in *Commentary* and reprinted in this volume.

44. Y [Louis Halle], "On a Certain Impatience with Latin America," *Foreign Affairs*, July 1950, pp. 565–79.

45. Published a year later as "The Hobbes Problem" in the American Enterprise Institute's *Public Policy Papers* (Washington, D.C., 1981); reprinted in *The Central American Crisis Reader*, ed. Robert S. Leiken and Barry Rubin, New York: Summit Books, 1987.

46. Christopher Hitchens, "Minority Report: Rebel Movements, Nicaraguan Contras," *Nation*, July 19, 1986; Holly Sklar, *Reagan, Trilateralism, and the Neoliberals: Containment and Intervention in the 1980s*, Boston: South End Press, 1986.

47. Walter LaFeber, "Thomas C. Mann and the Devolution of Latin American Policy." Thomas J. McCormick and Walter LeFeber, eds., *Behind the Throne: Servants of Power to Imperial Presidents, 1898–1968*, Madison: University of Wisconsin Press, 1993.

48. Gutman, *Banana Diplomacy*, p. 97.

49. "Excerpts from State Department Memo on Human Rights," *New York Times*, November 5, 1981. For Abrams's authorship of the memo, see Aryeh Neier, *Taking Liberties: Four Decades in the Struggle for Human Rights*, New York: Public Affairs, 2003, pp. 185–86.

50. Gutman, *Banana Diplomacy*, p. 27.

51. Benjamin Schwarz, "Dirty Hands: The Success of U.S. Policy in El Salvador—Preventing a Guerrilla Victory—Was Based on 40,000 Political Murders," *Atlantic Monthly*, December 1998.

52. Commonwealth Club, San Francisco, California, February 22, 1985, U.S. Department of State, Bureau of Public Affairs, Current Policy no. 659.

53. Gutman, *Banana Diplomacy*, pp. 139–40.

54. Ibid., p. 271.

55. Robert Kagan, *A Twilight Struggle: American Power and Nicaragua, 1977–1990*, New York: Free Press, 1996, p. xvi.

56. William Shawcross, *Sideshow*, New York: Simon and Schuster, 1979, p. 268.

57. Gutman, *Banana Diplomacy*, p. 71.

58. "Conversation between Richard Nixon and Daniel Patrick Moynihan on the Ability of Blacks to Lead Nations," October 7, 1971, Conversation 10–116, cassettes 1049 and 1050, 10:32–10:58 a.m., http://www.gwu.edu/~nsarchiv/NSAEBB/NSAEBB95/mex16.pdf; accessed on May 4, 2004.

59. Jeane Kirkpatrick, *Idealism, Realism, and the Myth of Appeasement*, London: Alliance Publishers, 1984, p. 18.

CHAPTER THREE: GOING PRIMITIVE:
THE VIOLENCE OF THE NEW IMPERIALISM

1. Perhaps cribbing from the same set of talking points, New York Times columnist David Brooks made an identical argument a week earlier ("The Insurgency Buster," *New York Times*, September 28, 2004).

2. Michael Hirsh and John Barry, "The Salvador Option," *Newsweek*, January 8, 2005.

3. For Steele, Peter Maass, "Way of the Commandos," *New York Times Magazine*, May 1, 2005; Jon Lee Anderson, "The Uprising," *New Yorker*, May 3, 2004. For Steele's involvement in the Iran-Contra scandal, see David Corn, "From Iran-Contra to Iraq," *Nation*, May 7, 2005, and Lawrence Walsh, *Firewall: The Iran-Contra Conspiracy and Cover-up*, New York: Norton, 1997.

4. "UK Aid Funds Iraqi Torture Units," *Guardian*, July 3, 2005.

5. Seymour Hersh, "The Coming Wars: What the Pentagon Can Now Do in Secret," *New Yorker*, January 24, 2005.

6. Benjamin Schwarz, "Dirty Hands: The Success of U.S. Policy in El Salvador—Preventing a Guerrilla Victory—Was Based on 40,000 Political Murders," *Atlantic Monthly*, December 1998.

7. John Waghelstein, "Counterinsurgency Doctrine and Low-Intensity Conflict in the Post-Vietnam Era," *The American War in Vietnam: Lessons, Legacies, and Implications for Future Conflicts*, ed. Lawrence Grinter and Peter Dunn, New York: Greenwood Press, 1987.

8. For El Mozote, see Mark Danner, *The Massacre at El Mozote: A Parable of the Cold War*, New York: Vintage, 1994, and *From Madness to Hope*, the U.N. truth commission report, available online at www.usip.org/library/tc/doc/

reports. Waghelstein praises the Atlacatl Battalion in *El Salvador at War: An Oral History of Conflict from the 1979 Insurrection to the Present*, ed. Max Manwaring and Court Prisk, Washington: National Defense University Press, 1988, p. 235.

9. Comisión para el Esclarecimiento Histórico, *Memoria del silencio*, Caso Ilustrativo 50, "Masacre del Río Pixcaya."

10. This recomposition of the military is discussed in chapter 2 of Andrew Bacevich, *The New American Militarism: How Americans Are Seduced by War*, New York: Oxford University Press, 2005.

11. Theodore Shackley, *The Third Option: An American View of Counterinsurgency*, New York: McGraw-Hill, 1981, p. 20.

12. Mann, *Rise of the Vulcans*, pp. 120–22.

13. Michael McClintock, *Instruments of Statecraft: U.S. Guerrilla Warfare, Counterinsurgency, and Counterterrorism, 1940–1990*, New York: Pantheon, 1992; Michael T. Klare and Peter Kornbluh, eds., *Low-Intensity Warfare: Counterinsurgency, Proinsurgency, and Antiterrorism in the Eighties*, New York: Pantheon, 1988.

14. Benjamin Schwarz, *American Counterinsurgency Doctrine: The Frustrations of Reform and the Illusions of Nation Building*, Santa Monica: RAND, 1991, p. 71.

15. Michael McClintock, *The American Connection: State Terror and Popular Resistance in El Salvador*, London: Zed Books, 1985.

16. A detailed account of this operation is given in Grandin, *Last Colonial Massacre*, pp. 73–104.

17. McClintock, *Instruments of Statecraft*, p. 222. For a further description of Yarborough's activities in Colombia, see also Gerard Colby with Charlotte Dennett, *Thy Will Be Done: The Conquest of the Amazon: Nelson Rockefeller and Evangelism in the Age of Oil*, New York: HarperCollins, 1955, pp. 391–95.

18. Senate Select Committee to Study Governmental Operations with Respect to Intelligence Activities, Final Report, Book 2, *Intelligence Activities and Rights of Americans*, Washington: Government Printing Office, 1976; Senate Subcommittee on Constitutional Rights, *Federal Data Banks, Computers, and the Bill of Rights: Hearings before the Senate Subcommittee on Constitutional Rights*, Washington: Government Printing Office, 1971.

19. Department of the Army, *Human Factors Considerations of Undergrounds in Insurgencies*, p. 184; Malcolm Browne, *The New Face of War*, Indianapolis: Bobbs-Merrill, 1965, pp. 119–20. The use of the "Eye of God" by death squads can be traced to the pioneering counterinsurgency work of legendary CIA agent Edward Lansdale in the Philippines in the late 1940s, who used the tactic to terrorize rebel sympathizers. See McClintock, *Instruments of Statecraft*, ch. ten.

20. David Galula, *Counterinsurgency Warfare: Theory and Practice*, London: Pall Mall Press, 1964, p. 124.

21. Department of State, "Guatemala: Vigilantism Poses Threat to Stability," May 12, 1967, available at the National Security Archive.

22. Colby, *Thy Will Be Done*, p. 472.
23. McClintock, *Instruments of Statecraft*, pp. 230–42.
24. See, e.g., Douglas Pike, *The Viet Cong Strategy of Terror*, Saigon: U.S. Information Agency, 1970; Nathan Leites and Charles Wolf, *Rebellion and Authority: An Analytic Essay on Insurgent Conflicts*, Chicago: Markham Publishing Company, 1970; Albert Fisher, "To Beat the Guerrillas at Their Own Game," *Military Review*, December 1963.
25. Ron Robin, *The Making of the Cold War Enemy: Culture and Politics in the Military-Intellectual Complex*, Princeton: Princeton University Press, 2001, pp. 189–99.
26. Leites and Wolf, *Rebellion and Authority*, p. 155.
27. In McClintock, *Instruments of Statecraft*, p. 237.
28. Leites and Wolf, *Rebellion and Authority*, pp. 96, 99.
29. U.S. Department of the Army, *U.S. Army Handbook of Counterinsurgency Guidelines for Area Commanders: An Analysis of Criteria*, Washington: Department of the Army, 1966, p. 225.
30. Andrew Bacevich, James D. Hallums, Richard H. White, and Thomas F. Young, *American Military Policy in Small Wars: The Case of El Salvador*, Washington: Pergamon-Brassey's, 1988, pp. 1, 14.
31. Steven Metz, "Counterinsurgency: Strategy and the Phoenix of American Capability," Carlisle Barracks: Strategic Studies Institute, U.S. Army War College, 1995.
32. Victor Rosello, "Lessons from El Salvador," *Parameters* (Journal of the U.S. Army War College), Winter 1993–94, p. 100.
33. Manwaring and Prisk, *El Salvador at War*, p. 407.
34. John Waghelstein, *El Salvador: Observations and Experiences in Counterinsurgency*, An Individual Study Project, Senior Officers Oral History Program, Charles Carlton interviewer, Carlisle Barracks: U.S. Army Military History Institute, 1985.
35. Clifford Kraus and Tim Carrington, "U.S. Effort to Win 'Hearts and Minds' Gains in El Salvador," *Wall Street Journal*, September 8, 1986.
36. Kenneth Freed, "Rebels Target U.S.-Aided Programs in Rural El Salvador," *Los Angeles Times*, January 13, 1989; Freed "Weekend Warriors Aid Salvador Rebels' Strategy," *Los Angeles Times*, November 2, 1989.
37. Robert S. Leiken and Barry Rubin, eds., *The Central American Crisis Reader*, New York: Summit Books, 1987, p. 563.
38. Schwarz, *American Counterinsurgency Doctrine*, pp. vi–vii.
39. Sigifredo Ochoa Perez, "A Voice of Dissent from the Salvadoran Military," *Wall Street Journal*, July 17, 1987.
40. Chris Hedges, "Salvadoran Land Reform Plowed Under by Rightists," *Christian Science Monitor*, October 18, 1983.
41. Frank Smyth, "Quagmire in the Making," *Progressive*, June 1988.
42. For "frail government institutions," see Thomas Enders, "El Salvador: The Search for Peace," *Department of State Bulletin*, September 1981, p. 71. For "thugs," see Schwarz, *American Counterinsurgency Doctrine*, p. 72.

43. Schwarz, *American Counterinsurgency Doctrine*, p. 79.

44. Ibid., p. 80.

45. Ibid.; Kraus and Carrington, "U.S. Effort to Win 'Hearts and Minds' Gains in El Salvador."

46. Benjamin Schwarz, "Dirty Hands: The Success of U.S. Policy in El Salvador—Preventing a Guerrilla Victory—Was Based on 40,000 Political Murders," *Atlantic Monthly*, December 1998.

47. In Leiken and Rubin, *Central American Crisis Reader*, pp. 506–9.

48. *New York Times*, February 25, 1981.

49. Steven Strasser, "Teaching the ABC's of War," *Newsweek*, March 28, 1983. See also Richard Halloran, "Salvador Gets Rights Lesson from the U.S.," *New York Times*, April 18, 1982.

50. "Salvador Gets Rights Lesson from the U.S.," *New York Times*, April 15, 1982.

51. Waghelstein, *El Salvador*, p. 25.

52. For the "torture" manuals, see the Department of Defense's response: "Fact Sheet Concerning Training Manuals Containing Materials Inconsistent with U.S. Policy," available at www.gwu.edu/~nsarchiv/nsa/. See also "Church-Protected Refugee Says He Raped, Tortured," *Minneapolis Star and Tribune*, July 8, 1984; Allan Nairn, "Behind the Death Squads," *Progressive*, May 1984; Nairn, "Confessions of a Death Squad Officer," *Progressive*, March 1986; Raymond Bonner, "U.S. Advisors Saw 'Torture Class,' Salvadoran Says," *New York Times*, January 11, 1982; Dennis Volman, "Salvador Death Squads, a CIA Connection?" *Christian Science Monitor*, May 8, 1984; and "Salvadoran Killings Cited; Deserter Links U.S. Advisers to Army Unit," *Washington Post*, October 27, 1989.

53. Walter Pincus, "CIA Manual Discussed 'Coercive' Measures," *Washington Post*, January 28, 1997.

54. Clifford Krauss, "U.S., Aware of Killings, Kept Ties to Salvadoran Rightist, Papers Suggest," *New York Times*, November 9, 1993; "Salvadoran Deserters Disclose Green Beret Torture Role," *Covert Action Quarterly*, March 1982, p. 17; Colman McCarthy, "Confessions of an Assassin," *Washington Post*, November 19, 1989; "U.S. Officials Deny Complicity in Death Squad Killings," *Houston Chronicle*, October 28, 1989; "Salvadoran Deserter Tells of Death Squad Assignments," *San Francisco Chronicle*, October 14, 1989.

55. The account of Caballero is in James LeMoyne, "Testifying to Torture," *New York Times Magazine*, June 5, 1988.

56. James Hodge and Linda Cooper, "Roots of Abu Ghraib in CIA Techniques," *National Catholic Report*, November 5, 2004; Walter Pincus, "Iraq Tactics Have Long History with U.S. Interrogators," *Washington Post*, June 13, 2004. For the memos, see Mark Danner, *Torture and Truth: America, Abu Ghraib, and the War on Terror*, New York: New York Review of Books, 2004.

57. Pincus, "CIA Manual Discussed 'Coercive' Measures."

58. Ibid.
59. Casualty figures are from Mitchell A. Seligson and Vincent McElhinny, "Low-Intensity Warfare, High-Intensity Death: The Demographic Impact of the Wars in El Salvador and Nicaragua," *Demographic Diversity and Change in the Central American Isthmus*, ed. Anne Pebley and Luis Rosero-Bixby, Santa Monica: RAND, 1997, p. 66.
60. Holly Sklar, *Washington's War on Nicaragua*, Boston: South End Press, 1988, p. 83.
61. For the continuation of U.S. aid despite Carter's restrictions, see McClintock, *American Connection*, p. 216; Tanya Broder and Bernard D. Lambek, "Military Aid to Guatemala: The Failure of U.S. Human Rights Legislation," *Yale Journal of International Law* 13, no. 1 (1988); "U.S. Military Aid for Guatemala Continuing Despite Official Curbs," *New York Times*, December 19, 1982; and U.S. General Accounting Office, National Security and International Affairs Division, *Military Sales: The United States Continuing Munition Supply Relationship with Guatemala, Report to the Chairman, Subcommittee on Western Hemisphere Affairs*, Washington, General Accounting Office, 1986.
62. For the quotations, see the CIA memo, untitled and dated February 1982, and the Department of State memo "US-Guatemalan Relations: Arms Sales," November 26, 1982, reproduced in my *Denegado en su totalidad: Documentos Estadounidense liberados*, Guatemala City: Asociación para el Avance de las Ciencias Sociales en Guatemala, 2001.
63. "Reagan Denounces Threats to Peace in Latin America," *New York Times*, December 5, 1982. Daniel Wilkinson juxtaposes the meeting with the massacre in *Silence on the Mountain: Stories of Terror, Betrayal, and Forgetting in Guatemala*, New York: Houghton Mifflin, 2002, pp. 327–28.
64. James Burnham, *The Struggle for the World*, New York: John Day, 1947; Burnham, *The Coming Defeat of Communism*, New York: John Day, 1950; Burnham, *Containment or Liberation?*, New York: John Day, 1952.
65. Peter Grose, *Operation Rollback: America's Secret War behind the Iron Curtain*, Boston: Houghton Mifflin, 2000.
66. John Foster Dulles, "A Policy of Boldness," *Life*, May 19, 1952, pp. 146–60.
67. Thomas Bodenheimer and Robert Gould, *Rollback: Right-Wing Power in U.S. Foreign Policy*, Boston: South End Press, 1989; Scott Anderson and Jon Lee Anderson, *Inside the League: The Shocking Expose of How Terrorists, Nazis, and Latin American Death Squads Have Infiltrated the World Anti-Communist League*, New York: Dodd, Mead, 1986.
68. Sam Sarkesian, "Political Soldiers: Perspectives on Professionalism in the U.S. Military," *Midwest Journal of Political Science* 16, no. 2 (May 1972), p. 244. For the phrase, see Arthur Moeller van den Bruck, *Germany's Third Empire*, New York: H. Fertig, 1971.
69. Roy Gutman, *Banana Diplomacy: The Making of American Policy in Nicaragua, 1981–1987*, New York: Simon and Schuster, 1988. p. 51.

70. Ibid., p. 45.
71. Ibid., p. 314.
72. Bodenheimer and Gould, *Rollback*, p. 55.
73. The literature on the Iran-Contra scandal is vast. See Lawrence Walsh, *Iran-Contra: The Final Report*, New York: Times Books, 1994; *Taking the Stand: The Testimony of Lieutenant Colonel Oliver L. North*, New York: Pocket Books, 1987; *The Iran-Contra Scandal: The Declassified History*, ed. Peter Kornbluh and Malcolm Byrne, New York: New Press, 1993.
74. For the connection between the Contras and drug running, see "Hearings before the Subcommittee on Terrorism, Narcotics, and International Communications and International Economic Policy, Trade, Oceans and Environment of the Committee on Foreign Relations," U.S. Senate, 100th Congress, 1st session, May 27, July 15, and October 30, 1987; the National Security Archive Electronic Briefing Book no. 2, *The Contras, Cocaine, and Covert Operations*, available at www.gwu.edu/~nsarchiv/NSAEBB/NSAEBB2/nsaebb2.htm.
75. Gutman, *Banana Diplomacy*, p. 266.
76. Edgar Chamorro, cited in a speech given by John Kerry, *Congressional Record* 132 (August 11, 1986): S 11175. Also in *Miami Herald*, September 12, 1985. See also the Human Rights Watch report available at www.hrw.org/reports/1989/WR89/Nicaragu.htm#TopOfPage.
77. Robert Parry, *Lost History: Contras, Cocaine, and Other Crimes*, Arlington: Media Consortium, 1997, p. 89.
78. William M. LeoGrande, *Our Own Backyard: The United States in Central America, 1977–1992*, Chapel Hill: University of North Carolina Press, 1998, p. 413.
79. Ibid., p. 415.
80. Kornbluh, "Nicaragua: U.S. Proinsurgency Warfare against the Sandinistas," *Low-Intensity Warfare*, ed. Klare and Kornbluh, p. 140.
81. Americas Watch, "Human Rights in Nicaragua: Reagan, Rhetoric and Reality," July 1985, p. 16, cited in Kornbluh, "Nicaragua," p. 140; CIA quotation in LeoGrande, *Our Own Backyard*, p. 413.
82. Seligson and McElhinny, "Low-Intensity Warfare, High-Intensity Death," p. 71.
83. *Psychological Operations in Guerrilla Warfare*, New York: Vintage, 1995, p. 51.
84. Kornbluh, "Nicaragua," p. 138.
85. Gutman, *Banana Diplomacy*, pp. 271–72.
86. Ibid., pp. 269–70; Robert Pear, with James Brooke, "Rightists in U.S. Aid Mozambique Rebels," *New York Times*, May 22, 1988; Alan Cowell, "Four Rebel Units Sign Anti-Soviet Pact," *New York Times*, June 6, 1985.
87. Mahmood Mamdani, *Good Muslim, Bad Muslim: America, the Cold War, and the Roots of Terror*, New York: Pantheon, 2004, p. 100.
88. Eric Posner, "All Justice, Too, Is Local," *New York Times*, p. A23, December 30, 2004; John Bolton, "Courting Danger," *National Interest*, Winter 1998–99.

89. Gutman, *Banana Diplomacy*, p. 196.
90. George Crile, *Charlie Wilson's War: The Extraordinary Story of the Largest Covert Operation in History*, New York: Atlantic Monthly Press, 2003. Cf. Mamdani, *Good Muslim, Bad Muslim*.
91. William O'Brien, "Special Operations in the 1980s: American Moral, Legal, Political, and Cultural Constraints," *Special Operations in U.S. Strategy*, ed. Frank R. Barnett, B. Hugh Tovar, and Richard H. Shultz, Washington: National Defense University Press, 1984, pp. 77–78, available at www.ndu.edu/inss/press/nduphp.html.

CHAPTER FOUR: BRINGING IT ALL BACK HOME:
THE POLITICS OF THE NEW IMPERIALISM

1. Norman Podhoretz, "Syria Yes, Israel No?" *Weekly Standard*, November 12, 2001, in Andrew Bacevich, *New American Militarism: How Americans Are Seduced by War*, New York: Oxford, 2005, pp. 95–96.
2. For Boot, see "Reality Check—This Is War," *Los Angeles Times*, May 27, 2004; Peter Beinart, "An Argument for a New Liberalism: A Fighting Faith," *New Republic*, December 13, 2004; for Krauthammer, see "America, Battle-Tested," *Washington Post*, January 18, 2002.
3. Peter Steinfels, *The Neoconservatives: The Men Who Are Changing America's Politics*, New York: Simon and Schuster, 1979.
4. Alfonso Chardy, "NSC Supervised Office to Influence Opinion," *Miami Herald*, July 19, 1987.
5. "Management of Public Diplomacy Relative to National Security," National Security Decision Directive, NSDD 77, January 14, 1983. Unless otherwise cited, all declassified U.S. documents pertaining to the Office of Public Diplomacy or the Iran-Contra scandal are from the National Security Archive's "Iran-Contra Affair" collection and can be accessed by title at http://nsarchive.chadwyck.com.
6. "Meritorious Honor Award," Office of Public Diplomacy for Latin America and the Caribbean, June 1986.
7. "Central American Public Diplomacy" [status report on public diplomacy efforts on Central America], Office of the President, August 13, 1986; "Request to DOD for Two-Year Detail of Four Psy-Op Personnel to the Office of Public Diplomacy—NSC Directives on Public Diplomacy Attached," Office of Public Diplomacy for Latin America and the Caribbean, September 18, 1985; Peter Kornbluh and Robert Parry, "Iran-Contra's Untold Story," *Foreign Policy*, Fall 1988.
8. "Central American Public Diplomacy," National Security Council, May 18, 1983; Robert Parry, *Lost History: Contras, Cocaine, the Press & "Project Truth,"* Arlington: Media Consortium, 1999, p. 76. The phrase *public diplomacy* first appeared in the national security section of the 1976 Republican Party platform, drafted by Richard Allen; William Safire, "Public Diplomacy," *New York Times*, April 21, 1985.

9. Parry, *Lost History*, pp. 61–76; House Committee on Foreign Affairs, *Preliminary Review of Department of State Contracts with International Business Communications, Inc.*, 100th Congress, 1987; Holly Sklar, *Washington's War on Nicarugua*, Boston: South End Press, 1988, p. 244.

10. Committee on Foreign Affairs, U.S. House of Representatives, *State Department and Intelligence Community Involvement in Domestic Activities Related to the Iran/Contra Affair*, Washington: Government Printing Office, 1992, p. 25.

11. "Update of Time-Line for Sixty-Day Public Diplomacy Plan," Office of Public Diplomacy for Latin America and the Caribbean, March 3, 1986.

12. "Public Diplomacy Action Plan: Support for the White House Educational Campaign," Office of Public Diplomacy for Latin America and the Caribbean, March 12, 1985.

13. "Ninety-Day Plan," Office of Public Diplomacy for Latin America and the Caribbean, December 17, 1985; Ronald Reagan, "Central America and U.S. Security," *Vital Interests: The Soviet Issue in U.S. Central American Policy*, Boulder: L. Reinner Publishers, 1998, p. 118.

14. "Ninety-Day Plan," December 17, 1985.

15. "Public Diplomacy Plan Explaining U.S. Central American Policy to the U.S. Religious Community," Office of Public Diplomacy for Latin America and the Caribbean, September 18, 1986, p. 4.

16. Sklar, *Washington's War*, p. 244.

17. "Chronological Event Checklist," National Security Council, March 20, 1985.

18. Marc Edelman, "Soviet-Cuban Involvement in Central America: A Critique of Recent Writings, *Vital Interests*, provides a clear and concise dissection of early administration claims prior to the establishment of the Office for Public Diplomacy. For an example of the office's rapid response to rebel allegations that the Salvadoran military had committed atrocities, see "Example of Distribution of S/LPD Work, the Battle of Suchitoto: An Example of Guerrilla Deception Attached," Office of Public Diplomacy for Latin America and the Caribbean, January 15, 1985.

19. "Ninety-Day Plan," December 17, 1985; Parry, *Lost History*, p. 63; Sklar, *Washington's War*, p. 243.

20. "Ninety-Day Plan," December 17, 1985.

21. Ibid.

22. Parry, *Lost History*, p. 71.

23. "White Propaganda Operations," Office of Public Diplomacy for Latin America and the Caribbean, March 13, 1985. For an example, see John Guilmartin, "Nicaragua Is Armed for Trouble," *Wall Street Journal*, March 13, 1985. See also Guilmartin's feeble defense in response to Theodore Draper, in *New York Review of Books*, March 31, 1988.

24. "Public Diplomacy Action Plan," Office of Public Diplomacy for Latin America and the Caribbean, March 12, 1985.

25. See Peter Kornbluh, "The Anti-Nicaragua Drive," *New York Times*, March 1, 1985, for a rebuttal of many of the charges leveled against the Sandinistas. For example, despite charges of supporting international terrorism and exporting revolution, the United States interdicted not one single major arms cache coming out of Nicaragua.

26. "Reagan Stepping Up Diplomatic Initiative on Central America," AP Wire, March 7, 1986.

27. Department of Defense, *Proceedings of the Low-Intensity Warfare Conference 14–15 January 1986*, Washington: Department of Defense, 1986, p. 145.

28. For an example, see Mark Danner's account of Washington's response to allegations that a Salvadoran military battalion committed a large-scale massacre in the village of El Mozote, *The Massacre at El Mozote: A Parable of the Cold War*, New York: Vintage, 1994.

29. Jefferson Morley and Tina Rosenberg, "The Real Heroes of Contra-gate," *Rolling Stone*, September 10, 1987, pp. 42–50.

30. *Newsweek*, April 29, 1985.

31. William M. LeoGrande, *Our Own Backyard: The United States in Central America, 1977–1992*, Chapel Hill: University of North Carolina Press, 1998, p. 416.

32. "Organization of the State Department's Office of Public Diplomacy and the Caribbean," Office of Public Diplomacy for Latin America and the Caribbean, February 8, 1985.

33. "News Coverage of Central America," Office of Public Diplomacy for Latin America and the Caribbean, November 8, 1984.

34. William Finnegan, "Castro's Shadow," *New Yorker*, October 13, 2002; Joel Bleifuss, "Yikes! It's Otto Reich," *In These Times*, April 16, 2001; Fairness and Accuracy in Reporting, "The Return of Otto Reich: Will Government Propagandist Join Bush Administration?," June 8, 2001.

35. Sklar, *Washington's War*, p. 246.

36. Jason Vest, "Our Man in Little Havana: The Secret Cold War History of Otto Juan Reich," *American Prospect*, May 25, 2001, http://www.prospect.org/authors/vest-j.html.

37. Parry, *Lost History*, p. 88.

38. Cynthia Arnson, *Crossroads: Congress, the Reagan Administration, and Central America*, New York: Pantheon, 1989, p. 177.

39. "Action Plan for the Congressional District Program," drawn up by the Edelman Public Relations firm for Spitz Channell's National Endowment for the Preservation of Liberty, lays out a detailed twenty-five-page strategy to challenge Democratic Majority Leader James Wright in his Fort Worth, Texas, district on his opposition to Contra funding.

40. Arnson, *Crossroads*, p. 179.

41. "Krishna Littledale Notes on Creating the American Anti-Terrorism Committee to Conduct Political Operations against Congressman Michael Barnes," Personal Notes, April 30, 1986.

42. LeoGrande, *Our Own Backyard*, p. 420.

43. Parry, *Lost History*, 139.
44. "Meritorious Honor Award," Office of Public Diplomacy for Latin America and the Caribbean, June 1986.
45. Mark Hertsgaard, *On Bended Knee: The Press and the Reagan Presidency*, New York: Farrar, Straus and Giroux, 1988, p. 101.
46. John Waghelstein, "El Salvador and the Press," September 1985, Occasional Papers Series, Latin American and Caribbean Center, Florida International University.
47. Fred Barnes, "Contra for a Day," *New Republic*, April 7, 1986, pp. 13–16.
48. Parry, *Lost History*, p. 46.
49. LeoGrande, *Our Own Backyard*, pp. 260–82.
50. Christian Smith, *Resisting Reagan: The U.S. Central America Peace Movement*, Chicago: University of Chicago Press, 1996, p. 231.
51. See Frank John Smist, *Congress Oversees the U.S. Intelligence Community, 1947–1989*, Knoxville: University of Tennessee Press, 1994; Loch Johnson, *A Season of Inquiry: The Senate Intelligence Investigation*, Lexington: University Press of Kentucky, 1985; Athan Theoharis, *Spying on Americans: Political Surveillance from Hoover to the Huston Plan*, Philadelphia: Temple University Press, 1978.
52. Jeff Stein, "Reagan's Plans for Intelligence," *Nation*, July 12, 1980.
53. *Mandate for Leadership: Policy Management in a Conservative Administration*, ed. Charles L. Heatherly, Washington: Heritage Foundation, 1981, p. 927. Cf. Joanne Omang, "The Heritage Report: Getting the Government Right with Reagan," *Washington Post*, November 16, 1980.
54. Kevin Johnson, "CIA Role inside the USA Greater," *USA Today*, November 8, 2004.
55. *Mandate for Leadership*, p. 927.
56. Senate Select Committee on Intelligence, *The FBI and CISPES*, 101st Congress, 1st session, 1989, p. 20.
57. Mary Battiata, "Congressman's Foundation Targets Communist 'Threat,'" *Washington Post*, August 22, 1981.
58. Gary M. Stern, *The FBI's Misguided Probe of CISPES*, Washington: Center for National Security Studies, 1988, p. 2.
59. Senate Select Committee on Intelligence, *The FBI and CISPES*, 101st Congress, 1st Session, 1989, p. 20; Ross Gelbspan, *Break-Ins, Death Treats, and the FBI*, Boston: South End Press, 1991; Alfonso Chardy, "Reagan Aides and the 'Secret' Government," *Miami Herald*, July 5, 1987.
60. Ross Gelbspan, "Opponents of U.S. Latin Policy Charge FBI Harassment," *Boston Globe*, March 26, 1985.
61. Ross Gelbspan, "More Probes Found of Latin Policy Foes; FBI Surveillance Called Pervasive," *Boston Globe*, June 18, 1988.
62. For the break-ins, see Gelbspan, *Break-Ins*; House Subcommittee on Civil and Constitutional Rights, Committee of the Judiciary, *Break-Ins at Sanctuary Churches and Organizations Opposed to Administration Policy in Central America: Hearings before the Subcommittee on Civil and Constitutional Rights,*

100th Congress, 1st Session, February 19–20, 1987; John Ward Anderson and Bill McAllister, "No Links Seen in Break-Ins, FBI Says," *Washington Post*, December 5, 1986; and "Burglars Ransack SE Office of Group Battling Contra Aid," *Washington Post*, December 5, 1986.

63. Daniel Shaw, "Salvadoran Calls Assault Political," *Washington Post*, July 11, 1987; Ross Gelbspan, "Tentacles of Salvador Death Squads Feared Stretching to United States," *Boston Globe*, November 7, 1987; Cristina Garcia, "Death Squads Invade California," *Time*, August 3, 1987.

64. "Nicaraguan Active Measures Directed against Lieutenant Colonel Oliver North/National Security Council," Federal Bureau of Investigations, June 11, 1986; "Report on Investigation of Jack Terrell and Request for Investigations of Others," National Security Council, July 23, 1986; "Terrorist Threat: [Jack] Terrell," National Security Council, July 28, 1986.

65. Robert Pear, "President Pardons 2 Ex-F.B.I. Officials in 1970s Break-In," *New York Times*, April 16 1981; David Wise, "The F.B.I. Pardoned," *New York Times*, April 28, 1981. One of the pardoned FBI agents was Mark Felt, who in 2005 was revealed to be Deep Throat of Watergate fame. Richard Nixon, unaware of the role Felt played in ending his presidency, not only testified at Felt's 1980 trial but contributed to his defense fund.

66. Sara Diamond, *Spiritual Warfare: The Politics of the Christian Right*, Boston: South End Press, 1989, p. 171.

67. William A. Rusher, "A New Party: Eventually, Why Not Now?" *National Review*, May 23, 1975, p. 55.

68. Fred Hiatt, "Private Groups Press 'Contra' Aid," *Washington Post*, December 10, 1984; Peter Stone, "Private Groups Step Up Aid to Contras," *Washington Post*, May 3, 1985.

69. Paul Valentine, "The Fascist Specter behind the World Anti-Red League," *Washington Post*, May 28, 1978; Anderson and Anderson, *Inside the League*, p. vii.

70. Russ Bellant, *The Coors Connection: How Coors Family Philanthropy Undermines Democratic Pluralism*, Boston: South End Press, 1991, p. 76.

71. Diamond, *Spiritual Warfare*, pp. 181–83.

72. Gerard Colby with Charlotte Dennett, *Thy Will Be Done: The Conquest of the Amazon: Nelson Rockefeller and Evangelism in the Age of Oil*, New York: HarperCollins, 1995.

73. John Saloma, *Ominous Politics: The New Conservative Labyrinth*, New York: Hill and Wang, 1984, p. 61.

74. Smith, *Resisting Reagan*, pp. 59–60.

75. Rousas John Rushdoony, *Roots of Inflation*, Vallecito: Ross House Books, 1982, pp. 22, 23.

76. See Diamond, *Spiritual Warfare*, pp. 148–53; "Outreach Working Group on Central America Meeting with Hispanic Evangelical Leaders," September 14, 1986, Office of the President, available in National Security Archive, Iran-Contra Collection.

77. "Meeting Re Central America Freedom Program" [internal NEPL minutes of Contra lobbying strategy meeting], National Security Council, February 13, 1986.

78. Joseph Peschek, *Policy-Planning Organizations: Elite Agendas and America's Rightward Turn*, Philadelphia: Temple University Press, 1987, p. 224. See also the April 1978 issue of *Commentary*, which printed the proceedings of twenty-six scholars, many affiliated with the American Enterprise Institute, in a symposium titled "Capitalism, Socialism, and Democracy."

79. Joseph Peschek, *Policy-Planning Organizations*, p. 225.

80. Michael Novak, *Will It Liberate? Questions about Liberation Theology*, New York: Paulist Press, 1986; Peter Berger and Michael Novak, *Speaking to the Third World: Essays on Democracy and Development*, Washington: American Enterprise Institute, 1985; Michael Novak and Michael P. Jackson, eds., *Latin America: Dependency or Interdependence?*, Washington: American Enterprise Institute, 1985; and Richard John Neuhaus, "Liberation Theology and the Cultural Captivity of the Gospel," *Liberation Theology*, ed. Ronald Nash, Milford: Mott Media, 1984.

81. Michael Novak, *Toward a Theology of the Corporation*, Washington: American Enterprise Institute, 1981, p. 1.

82. Michael Novak, *The Spirit of Democratic Capitalism*, New York: Simon and Schuster, 1982, p. 278.

83. Rus Walton, *Biblical Solutions to Contemporary Problems*, Brentwood: Wolgemuth and Hyatt, 1988, p. 177. See also David Chilton, *Productive Christians in an Age of Guilt-Manipulators*, Tyler: Institute for Christian Economics, 1981; and John Eidsmoe, *God and Caesar: Biblical Faith and Political Action*, Westchester: Crossway Books, 1984.

84. In Michael Lienesch, *Redeeming America: Piety and Politics in the New Christian Right*, Chapel Hill: University of North Carolina Press, 1993.

85. In Lienesch, *Redeeming America*, p. 135.

86. Chilton, *Productive Christians*, p. 92.

87. Diamond, *Spiritual Warfare*, p. 151; Cynthia Brown, "The Right's Religious Red Alert," *Nation*, March 12, 1983.

88. "Symposium on Christianity and the American Revolution," *Journal of Christian Reconstruction* 3 (Summer 1976).

89. Chilton, *Productive Christians*, p. 453.

90. Francis Schaeffer, "The Secular Humanist World View versus the Christian World View and Biblical Perspectives on Military Preparedness," *Who Is for Peace?*, ed. Francis Schaeffer, Vladimir Bukovsky, and James Hitchcock, Nashville: Thomas Nelson, 1983, pp. 30–31; Eidsmoe, *God and Caesar*, p. 223.

91. Sara Diamond, *Roads to Dominion: Right-Wing Movements and Political Power in the United States*, New York: Guilford Press, 1995, p. 218.

92. Sklar, *Washington's War*, p. 325.

93. Diamond, *Spiritual Warfare*, p. 172.

94. Angelyn Dries, *The Missionary Movement in American Catholic History*, New York: Orbis, 1998, pp. 230ff.

95. Diamond, *Roads to Dominion*, p. 206.

96. Brodenheimer and Gould, *Rollback*, p. 207.

97. Jack Wheeler, "Fighting the Soviet Imperialists: The New Liberation Movements," *Reason*, June–July 1985, pp. 36–44; James T. Hackett, ed., "The State Department v. Ronald Reagan: Four Ambassadors Speak Out," Heritage Lecture 44, Heritage Foundation, 1985; Benjamin Hart, "Rhetoric vs. Reality: How the State Department Betrays the Reagan Vision," Backgrounder 484, Heritage Foundation, 1986; David Ottawa, "Rebels' Backers on Hill Press Aid Issue; Administration Accused of Ambiguity in Military Efforts," *Washington Post*, January 16, 1986; Howard Phillips, "'Made in Moscow' State Dept. Policy for Angola Must Be Overturned," Conservative Caucus Member's Report 9, no. 3 (December 1985).

98. "A Little Help from Friends," *Newsweek*, September 7, 1984; Alfonso Chardy, "Groups Won't Cut Contra Aid," *Dallas Morning News*, June 16, 1985; Robert Greenberger, "Right-Wing Groups Join in Capitol Hill Crusade to Help Savimbi's Anti-Communists in Angola," *Wall Street Journal*, November 25, 1985; Robert Pear, with James Brooke, "Rightists in U.S. Aid Mozambique Rebels," *New York Times*, May 22, 1988.

99. Alan Cowell, "Four Rebel Units Sign Anti-Soviet Pact," *New York Times*, June 6, 1985; Michael Sullivan, "Rebels Opposing Marxist Regimes in 4 Nations Unite," *Washington Times*, June 6, 1985; Walter Shapiro and Peter Younghusband, "Lehrman's Contra Conclave," *Newsweek*, June 17, 1986.

100. Rus Walton, *Biblical Solutions to Contemporary Problems: A Handbook*, Brentwood: Wolgemuth & Hyatt, 1988, p. 165.

101. Sara Diamond, "Right Wing's Televangelists Manipulate U.S. on Contra Aid and Apartheid," *Sequoia*, September–October 1986; Joanne Omang, "D'Aubuisson Honored by Conservatives at Capitol Hill Dinner," *Washington Post*, December 5, 1984.

102. *Covert Action Quarterly* 27 (Spring 1987): 26.

103. *Covert Action Quarterly* 18 (Winter 1983): 19.

104. Diamond, *Spiritual Warfare*, p. 177.

105. Eidsmoe, *God and Caesar*, p. 214.

106. In Lienesch, *Redeeming America*, p. 228.

107. Michael D'Antonio, "The Christian Right Abroad," *Salt & Light*, Fall 1987.

108. Pat Robertson, *The New World Order*, Nashville: Thomas Nelson, 1991, p. 13.

109. Joshua Green, "God's Foreign Policy," *Washington Monthly*, November 2001.

110. Bob Woodward, "Cheney Upholds Power of Presidency," *Washington Post*, January 20, 2005.

111. That these first two dimensions—reestablishing a moral foundation and rehabilitating unconventional warfare tactics—are to some degree con-

tradictory is more than evident in the disaster that now prevails in Iraq: you can't both go on the global offensive in the name of democratic revolution and rely on murderous thugs to enforce your authority.

CHAPTER FIVE: THE THIRD CONQUEST OF LATIN AMERICA: THE ECONOMICS OF THE NEW IMPERIALISM

1. Gordon Lafer, "Neoliberalism by Other Means: The 'War on Terror' at Home and Abroad," *New Political Science* 26 (September 2004): 328; Coalition Provisional Authority Briefing, June 26, 2004, available at www.defenselink.mil/transcripts/2004/tr20040626-0950.html.

2. The U.S. government socializes investment risk in Iraq, providing below-market-priced insurance to corporations through its Overseas Private Investment Corporation. See Naomi Klein, "Risky Business," *Nation*, January 5, 2004.

3. Richard Stevenson, "Bush Says Patience Is Needed as Nations Build a Democracy," *New York Times*, May 19, 2005.

4. Jeff Madrick, "Economic Scene," *Wall Street Journal*, October 2, 2003. Cf. Duncan Kennedy, "Shock and Awe Meets Market Shock," *Boston Review*, October 2003.

5. Naomi Klein, "Baghdad Year Zero: Pillaging Iraq in Pursuit of a Neocon Utopia," *Harper's*, September 2004.

6. W. W. Rostow, *The Stages of Economic Growth: A Non-Communist Manifesto*, Cambridge: Cambridge University Press, 1960, pp. 11, 166–67.

7. William Greider, "Rolling Back the 20th Century," *Nation*, May 12, 2003.

8. See the documentation in the appendix to Milton Friedman and Rose Friedman, *Two Lucky People: Memoirs*, Chicago: University of Chicago Press, 1998, pp. 591–602.

9. Friedman and Friedman, *Two Lucky People*, pp. 402, 452.

10. Kimberly Phillips-Fein, "Top-Down Revolution: Businessmen, Intellectuals, and Politicians against the New Deal, 1945–1964," Ph.D. dissertation, Columbia University, 2005, ch. 2.

11. Friedman and Friedman, *Two Lucky People*, p. 400.

12. Juan Gabriel Valdés, *Pinochet's Economists: The Chicago School in Chile*, Cambridge: Cambridge University Press, 1995, p. 94; cf. Paul Strassman, "Development Economics from a Chicago Perspective," *The Chicago School of Political Economy*, ed. Warren Samuels, East Lansing: Michigan State University Press, 1976, pp. 277–96.

13. William Benton, *The Voice of Latin America*, New York: Harper, 1961, p. 169, n. 3.

14. Valdés, *Pinochet's Economists*, p. 159.

15. U.S. Senate, *Covert Action in Chile, 1963–1973: Staff Report of the Select Committee to Study Governmental Operations with Respect to Intelligence Activities*, Washington: Government Printing Office, 1975, available at http://foia.state.gov/Reports/ChurchReport.asp. See also the subsequently

released information detailing U.S. government and corporate involvement in Allende's downfall, available at www.gwu.edu/~nsarchiv/.

16. *Newsweek*, January 21, 1974.
17. Sidney Blumenthal, *The Rise of the Counter-Establishment: From Conservative Ideology to Political Power*, New York: Times Books, 1986, p. 111.
18. The *Barrons* quotation is in Valdés, *Pinochet's Economists*, p. 37; "A Draconian Cure for Chile's Economic Ills?" *Business Week*, January 12, 1976.
19. Statistics on the growth and collapse of the economy during the reign of the Chicago Boys come from Valdés, *Pinochet's Economists*, pp. 16–39; Patricio Silva, "Technocrats and Politics in Chile: From the Chicago Boys to the CIEPLAN Monks," *Journal of Latin American Studies* 23 (May 1991): 385–410; and Pamela Constable and Arturo Valenzuela, *A Nation of Enemies: Chile under Pinochet*, New York: Norton, 1991, pp. 172–96.
20. Letter to Ambassador John Davis Lodge, March 15, 1978, William A. Rusher Collection, Library of Congress.
21. Hayek Collection, box 101, folder 26, Hoover Institution Archives, Palo Alto, Calif.
22. *El Mercurio*, April 12, 1981.
23. *London Times*, August 3, 1978.
24. Constable and Valenzuela, *Nation of Enemies*, p. 187.
25. Valdés, *Pinochet's Economists*, p. 29.
26. Constable and Valenzuela, *Nation of Enemies*, p. 186.
27. Ibid., p. 187.
28. Valdés, *Pinochet's Economists*, p. 30.
29. Constable and Valenzuela, *Nation of Enemies*, p. 171.
30. *El Mercurio*, August 8, 1981.
31. *Washington Post*, August 13, 1981; *Boston Globe*, August 30, 1981; *El Mercurio*, August 9, 1981.
32. Cristián Larroulet, ed., *Public Solutions to Public Problems: The Chilean Experience*, Santiago: Fundación Libertad y Desarrollo, 1993, p. 7.
33. Richard Stevenson, "For Bush, a Long Embrace of Social Security Plan," *New York Times*, February 27, 2005. During his 2000 run for the presidency, Bush explicitly credited the Chicago Boys for his plan to privatize Social Security: "Back in 1980, Chile faced problems with its retirement system. They decided to convert the pay-as-you-go system into a system of personal retirement accounts—in which contributions are invested in a safe portfolio of bonds and shares . . . to empower the common man. . . . The Chilean economists who originally designed these reforms studied here in the United States—at Harvard and the University of Chicago. They learned here and now it is time for us to learn from them" ("George W. Bush's Speech on Latin America," August 27, 2000, *NewsMax.com*; www.newsmax.com/articles/?a=2000/8/26/195405). Bush didn't mention that the cost of the conversion to private accounts was one of the precipitating factors in Chile's 1982 collapse.

34. Constable and Valenzuela, *Nation of Enemies*, p. 190.
35. The flyer is reproduced in Holly Sklar, *Reagan, Trilateralism, and the Neo-liberals: Containment and Intervention in the 1980s*, Boston: South End Press, 1986, p. 17.
36. Peter Stone, "Private Groups Step Up Aid," *Washington Post*, May 3, 1985; *Texas Observer*, March 7, 1986; Michael Isikoff, "U.S. Ex-Officials Lead 'Contra' Fund Drive," *Washington Post*, May 9, 1985; Anderson and Anderson, *Inside the League*, p. 120.
37. William Martin, "The Christian Right and American Foreign Policy," *Foreign Policy*, Spring 1999.
38. Joanne Omang, "D'Aubuisson Honored by Conservatives at Capitol Hill Dinner," *Washington Post*, December 5, 1984.
39. Thomas Ferguson and Joel Rogers, *Right Turn: The Decline of the Democrats and the Future of American Politics*, New York: Hill and Wang, 1986, p. 78.
40. David Vogel, "The Power of Business in America: A Re-appraisal," *British Journal of Political Science* 13, no. 1 (1983): 33.
41. John S. Saloma, *Ominous Politics: The New Conservative Labyrinth*, New York: Hill and Wang, 1984, pp. 65–66.
42. The conservative assault on liberal internationalism was relentless. For examples, see the essays by Edward Luttwack, Ken Adelman, Fred Iklé, Paul Nitze, and Albert Wohlstetter in W. Scott Thompson, ed., *National Security in the 1980s: From Weakness to Strength*, San Francisco: Institute for Contemporary Studies, 1980. For how defense intellectuals exaggerated the Soviet threat, see State Department and CIA official Arthur Macy Cox, "The CIA's Tragic Error," *New York Review of Books*, November 6, 1980, and CIA analyst Melvin Goodman, "The Politics of Getting It Wrong," *Harper's*, November 2000. For corporate funding of New Right defense advocacy groups, see Ferguson and Rogers, *Right Turn*, p. 88; Thomas Byrne Edsall, *The New Politics of Inequality*, New York: Norton, ch. 3; Vogel, "Power of Business in America," 19–43; Jerry Sanders, *Peddlers of Crisis: The Committee on the Present Danger*, Boston: South End Press, 1983; Joseph Peschek, *Policy-Planning Organizations: Elite Agendas and America's Rightward Turn*, Philadelphia: Temple University Press, 1987, p. 35.
43. The three quotations are from Klare, "Have R.D.F. Will Travel," *Nation*, March 8, 1980.
44. Henry Nau, "Where Reaganomics Works," *Foreign Policy*, Winter 1984–85, pp. 21–22.
45. "The Reagan Victory: Corporate Coalitions in the 1980 Campaign," ed. Thomas Ferguson and Joel Rogers, *The Hidden Election: Politics and Economics in the 1980 Presidential Campaign*, New York: Pantheon Books, 1981, pp. 17–18.
46. Peschek, *Policy-Planning Organizations*, pp. 28–29, 32, 34–35.
47. "Latins Welcome Word on Reagan by Rockefeller," *New York Times*, November 11, 1980.

48. William Greider, *The Education of David Stockman and Other Americans*, New York: Dutton, 1982, p. 58.
49. Ferguson and Rogers, *Right Turn*, pp. 118–19, 250.
50. David Harvey, "Neo-Liberalism and the Restoration of Class Power," available at http://people-link5.inch.com/pipermail/portside/Week-of-Mon-20040802/006320.html.
51. Nau, "Where Reaganomics Works," p. 27.
52. Peschek, *Policy-Planning Organizations*, pp. 71–72.
53. Ferguson and Rogers, *Right Turn*, p. 94.
54. Robert Kuttner, *The End of Laissez-Faire: National Purpose and the Global Economy after the Cold War*, New York: Knopf, 1991, pp. 79–80.
55. Vincent Ferraro and Melissa Rosser, "Global Debt and Third World Development," *World Security: Challenges for a New Century*, ed. Michael Klare and Daniel Thomas, New York: St. Martin's Press, 1994, p. 335.
56. William Ryrie, "Latin America: A Changing Region," *IFC Investment Review*, Spring 1992. Cited in Doug Henwood, "Clinton's Trade Policy," *Free Trade and Economic Restructuring in Latin Amrerica*, ed. Fred Rosen and Deidre McFadyen, New York: Monthly Review Press, 1995, p. 30.
57. "New Proposals for the Debt Crisis," *Current Legal Issues Affecting Central Banks*, ed. Robert Effros, Washington: International Monetary Fund, 1992, p. 94. Cited in Henwood, "Clinton's Trade Policy," p. 29.
58. Nau, "Where Reaganomics Works," pp. 14–37; Ferguson and Rogers, *Right Turn*, pp. 116–17.
59. For Reagan in Cancún, see the series of articles in the *Boston Globe* on October 22 and October 25, 1981, as well as Reagan's "Statement at the First Plenary Session of the International Meeting on Cooperation and Development in Cancún, Mexico," October 22, 1981, at www.reagan.utexas.edu/resources/speeches/1981/102181c.htm.
60. Steven Topik and Allen Wells, eds., *The Second Conquest of Latin America: Coffee, Henequen, and Oil during the Export Boom, 1850–1930*, Austin: University of Texas Press, 1998.
61. Constable and Valenzuela, *Nation of Enemies*, p. 191.
62. Donald Huddle, "Post-1982 Effects of Neoliberalism on Latin American Development and Poverty: Two Conflicting Views," *Economic Development and Cultural Change* 45 (July 1997): 883.
63. Mark Alan Healey and Ernesto Semán, "The Costs of Orthodoxy," *American Prospect*, January 1–12, 2002.
64. Eric Dash, "Pinochet Held 125 Accounts in U.S. Banks, Report Says," *New York Times*, March 16, 2005.
65. Constable and Valenzuela, *Nation of Enemies*, p. 191.
66. Jim Shultz, "Bolivia: The Water War Widens," *NACLA Report on the Americas*, January–February 2003, p. 34.
67. William Canak, "Debt, Austerity, and Latin America in the New International Division of Labor," *Lost Promises: Debt, Austerity, and Development in Latin America*, Boulder: Westview, 1989.

68. For one such alternative, see Samuel Bowles, David Gordon, and Thomas Weisskopf, *Beyond the Waste Land: A Democratic Alternative to Economic Decline*, New York: Doubleday, 1983.

69. James Mann, *The Rise of the Vulcans: The History of Bush's War Cabinet*, New York: Viking, p. 180.

70. Friedman and Friedman, *Two Lucky People*, p. 408.

71. Henwood, "Clinton's Trade Policy," p. 29.

72. Andrew Bacevich, *New American Militarism: How Americans Are Seduced by War*, New York: Oxford University Press, 2005, p. 24. For other examples of the hawkishness of Clinton's chief foreign policy advisers, see Clinton's NSC analyst Philip Bobbit, *The Shield of Achilles: War, Peace, and the Course of History*, New York: Knopf, 2002, and Warren Christopher, *In the Stream of History: Shaping Foreign Policy for a New Era*, Stanford: Stanford University Press, 1998.

73. Andrew Bacevich, *American Empire: The Realities and Consequences of U.S. Diplomacy*, Cambridge: Harvard University Press, 2002, pp. 98–99.

74. Paul Wolfowitz, "Remembering the Future," *National Interest*, Spring 2000.

CHAPTER SIX: GLOBALIZATION'S SHOWPIECE:
THE FAILURE OF THE NEW IMPERIALISM

1. Anatol Lieven, *America Right or Wrong: An Anatomy of American Nationalism*, New York: Oxford, 2004, p. 222.

2. "Wave of vengeance": Elisabeth Bumiller, "Filmmaker Leans Right, Oval Office Swings Open," *New York Times*, September 8, 2005; "rid the world of evil": Andrew Bacevich, *The New American Militarism: How Americans Are Seduced by War*, New York: Oxford, 2005, p. 2; "free and open societies": "Remarks by the President at 2002 Graduation Exercises of the United States Military Academy, West Point, New York," at www.whitehouse.gov/news/releases/2002/06/20020601-3.html.

3. Barry R. McCaffrey, Testimony before the House National Security Committee, March 8, 1995, in U.S. Department of Defense, *Defense Issues*, vol. 10, no. 50.

4. William S. Cohen, Speech to the Western Hemisphere Symposium, April 15, 1997, published in U.S. Department of Defense, *Defense Issues*, vol. 12, no. 24.

5. William Easterly, "The Lost Decades: Developing Countries' Stagnation in Spite of Policy Reform, 1980–1998," World Bank, February 2001, available at www.worldbank.org/research/growth/pdfiles.

6. Donald L. Huddle, "Post-1982 Effects of Neoliberalism on Latin American Development and Poverty: Two Conflicting Views," *Economoic Development and Cultural Change*, 1997, vol. 45, issue 4, pp. 881–97.

7. Juan Forero, "Free Trade Proposal Splits Bolivian City," *New York Times*, March 9, 2005.

8. In Bolivia, prior to restructuring, 69 percent of revenues came from income and profits. Today, 77 percent comes from taxes on consumption

(Carlos Arze and Tom Kruse, "The Consequences of Neoliberal Reform," *NACLA Report on the Americas*, November–December 2004).

9. Mark Alan Healey and Ernesto Semán, "The Costs of Orthodoxy," *American Prospect*, January 1–14, 2002.

10. Doug Henwood, "Clinton's Trade Policy," *Free Trade and Economic Restructuring in Latin America*, ed. Fred Rosen and Deidre McFadyen, New York: Monthly Review Press, 1995, p. 35.

11. Healey and Semán, "Costs of Orthodoxy."

12. Andrew Wheat, "The Fall of the Peso and the Mexican 'Miracle,'" *Multinational Monitor*, available at http://multinationalmonitor.org.

13. William Finnegan, "The Economics of Empire: Notes on the Washington Consensus," *Harper's*, May 2003.

14. "Venezuela: From Showcase to Basket Case," Cato Institute Policy Analysis 251, March 25, 1996.

15. Duncan Green, *Silent Revolution: The Rise of Market Economies in Latin America*, London: Latin American Bureau, 1995, p. 230.

16. Green, *Silent Revolution*.

17. Carlos Arze and Tom Kruse, "The Consequences of Neoliberal Reform," *NACLA Report on the Americas*, November–December 2004.

18. Data on Chile come from Paul Drake and Iván Jáksic, eds., *El modelo chileno: Democracia y desarrollo en los noventa*, Santiago: LOM, 1999; Paul Drake, "Forward," and Peter Winn, "Introduction," both in *Victims of the Chilean Miracle: Workers and Neoliberalism in the Pinochet Era, 1973–2002*, ed. Winn, Durham: Duke University Press, 2004; and Manuel Barrera, "Macroeconomic Adjustment in Chile and the Politics of the Popular Sectors," *What Kind of Democracy? What Kind of Market? Latin America in the Age of Neoliberalism*, ed. Philip Oxhorn and Graciela Ducatenzeiler, University Park: Pennsylvania State University Press, 1998.

19. *IT Jungle Newsletter*, January 12, 2004, at http://www.itjungle.com/tfh/tfh011204-story04.html, citing UBS Warburg's "World Prices and Earnings Survey."

20. Larry Rohter, "Chile's Retirees Find Shortfall in Private Plan," *New York Times*, January 27, 2005.

21. Green, *Silent Revolution*, p. 234.

22. Mary Jordan, "Social Breakdown Turns Deadly in Guatemala: Drugs, Broken Justice System and Resurgent Militarism Are Blamed for Growing Lawlessness," *Washington Post*, October 26, 2003; Ana Arana, "The New Battle for Central America," *Foreign Affairs*, November–December 2001.

23. Social and economic figures come mostly from the CIA's World Factbook, found online at http://www.cia.gov/cia/publications/factbook/ geos/gt.html.

24. David Gonzalez, "Central America's Cities Grow Bigger, and Poorer," *New York Times*, March 17, 2002.

25. David Gonzalez, "Malnourished to Get Help in Guatemala," *New York Times*, March 20, 2002.

26. Lisa Sandberg, "Panama: Democracy and Disgrace. Invasion Toppled a Dictator, but Corruption Now Rules," *San Antonio Express-News*, November 23, 2003.
27. "2 Get Citizenship Posthumously; U.S. Marines Were Natives of Mexico and Guatemala," *San Diego Union-Tribune*, April 2, 2003.
28. "Return of Death Squads?" *Toronto Sun*, March 7, 2005.
29. Ken Steir, "Feral Cities," *New York Times Magazine*, December 12, 2004; Mike Davis, "Planet of Slums," *New Left Review*, March–April 2004; Suketu Mehta, *Maximum City: Bombay Lost and Found*, New York: Knopf, 2004; Nancy Schepre-Hughes, *Death without Weeping: The Violence of Everyday Life in Brazil*, Berkeley: University of California Press, 1992.
30. The Jubilee Debt Campaign estimates that, spread over a twenty-year period, it would cost each inhabitant of the industrialized world just four dollars to cancel the market-value debt of fifty-one of the poorest countries.
31. John Walton and David Seddon, *Free Markets and Food Riots: The Politics of Global Adjustment*, Cambridge: Blackwell Publishers, 1994; George Caffentzis and Silvia Federici, "A Brief History of Resistance to Structural Adjustment," *Democratizing the Global Economy: The Battle against the IMF and World Bank*, ed. Kevin Danaher, San Francisco: Global Exchange and Common Courage Press, 2001.
32. In Spain, the election of Socialist José Luis Rodríguez Zapatero following the March 2004 terrorist bombing set back the Washington Consensus, as Spain and its powerful banking houses have in the past worked in concert with the IMF–Treasury Department–Wall Street regime to open up Latin America to finance capital. Not only has Rodríguez Zapatero gently nudged Spain away from the United States and Britain and toward the German- and French-dominated Eurozone, but he has bucked Washington's objections to its sale of aircraft and coast guard boats to Venezuela.
33. Naomi Klein, "The Daily War," *Guardian*, March 17, 2003.
34. Tina Rosenberg, "The Free-Trade Fix," *New York Times Magazine*, August 18, 2002.
35. Joseph Contreras and Michael Isikoff, "Hugo's Close Call," *Newsweek*, international ed., April 29, 2002; "Venezuela Coup Linked to Bush Team," *Observer*, April 21, 2002.
36. Paul Krugman, "Let Them Hate as Long as They Fear," *New York Times*, March 6, 2003.
37. Eric Nurse, "Leaders' Comments Upset Reich," Miami Herald.com, April 4, 2003.
38. Pablo Bachelet, "4 Nations That Won't Sign Deal with U.S. Risk Aid Loss," *Miami Herald*, December 18, 2004; Luis Bredow and Jim Shultz, "U.S. Threatens Bolivia in Effort to Secure Criminal Court Immunity," *Pacific News Service*, March 3, 2005.
39. Larry Rohter, "A Leftist Takes Over in Brazil and Pledges a 'New Path,' " *New York Times*, January 2, 2003.

40. Moisés Naim, "Five Wars of Globalization," *Foreign Policy*, January–February 2003.
41. U.S. Department of Defense, "Remarks by Secretary of State Rumsfeld," November 17, 2004, available at www.defenselink.mil/transcripts/2004.
42. Statement of Major General Gary D. Speer, United States Army Acting Commander in Chief, United States Southern Command, to the Senate Western Hemisphere Subcommittee, April 24, 2002.
43. Jack Epstein, "General Seeks Boost for Latin American Armies," *San Francisco Chronicle*, April 30, 2004.
44. Washington Office on Latin America, "Blurring the Lines: Trends in U.S. Military Programs with Latin America," September 2004; Epstein, "General Seeks Boost for Latin American Armies."
45. "Grupos de Presión preocupan a George W. Bush," *Prensa Libre*, May 13, 2005. See also David Cloud, "Like Old Times: U.S. Warns Latin Americans against Leftists," *New York Times*, August 19, 2005.
46. "Latin America 2020: Discussing Long-Term Scenarios," Summary of Conclusions of the Workshop on Latin American Trends, Santiago, Chile, June 7–8, 2004.
47. Bruce Finley, "U.S. Casts a Wary Eye South," *Denver Post*, November 12, 2004.
48. Washington Office on Latin America, "Blurring the Lines," p. 3.
49. Ibid.
50. Bruce Finley, "S. America Balking at Terror War," *Denver Post*, November 18, 2004.
51. Linda Farthing and Kathryn Ledebur, "The Beat Goes On: The U.S. War on Coca," *NACLA Report on the Americas*, November–December 2004.
52. Christian Parenti, "Bolivia's Battle of Wills," *Nation*, July 4, 2005.
53. Jim Shultz, "When the War on Drugs Becomes the War on the Poor: Your Tax Dollars at Work," *Sacramento Bee*, August 1, 1999.
54. For a discussion of alternatives to neoliberal absolutism that some Bolivians are trying out at the grassroots level, see Kevin Healy, "Toward an Andean Rural Development Paradigm?" *NACLA Report on the Americas*, November–December 2004.
55. Farthing and Ledebur, "The Beat Goes On."
56. Adam Isacson, "Washington's 'New War' in Colombia: The War on Drugs Meets the War on Terror," *NACLA Report on the Americas*, March–April 2003; Winifred Tate, "Into the Andean Quagmire: Bush II Keeps Up March to Militarization," *NACLA Report on the Americas*, November–December 2001.
57. Thomas Ginsberg, "United States Merges Antiterror Fight, War on Drugs in Colombia," *Philadelphia Inquirer*, December 1, 2002.
58. *Andes 2020: A New Strategy for the Challenges of Colombia and the Region*, Washington: Council on Foreign Relations, 2004.
59. Human Rights Watch, "The 'Sixth Division': Military-Paramilitary Ties and U.S. Policy in Colombia," New York: Human Rights Watch, 2001.

60. Frank Smyth, "U.S. Arms for Terrorists?" *Nation*, June 13, 2005.

61. Juan Forero, "Colombia Yields 2 Accused Soldiers to U.S.," *New York Times*, May 6, 2005; "Colombian Officials Ask U.S. Response Following Arrest of U.S. Soldiers," *USA Today*, May 11, 2005.

62. Nicholas Moss, "Ecuador Base Lets US Spy Planes Watch Drugs Trade," *Financial Times*, March 24, 2003.

63. Just as the end of the Vietnam War produced thousands of veterans who of-fered their services as anti-Communist mercenaries, the end of the Cold War resulted in, by some estimates, a worldwide decommission of six mil-lion soldiers, many of whom found employment in the proliferation of secu-rity firms like DynCorp and Military Professional Resources Inc. See Peter Warren Singer, *Corporate Warriors: The Rise of the Privatized Military Industry*, Ithaca: Cornell University Press, 2003; see also the two-part series on cor-porate mercenaries by Victoria Burnett, Thomas Caton, Joshua Chaffin, Stephen Filder, and Andy Web-Vidal, *Financial Times*, August 11, 2003.

64. For DynCorp, see the Center for International Policy's Colombia Project at www.ciponline.org/colombia/dyncorp.htm.

65. Juan Tamayo, "Private Firms Take on Jobs, Risks for U.S. Military in An-des Drug War," *Miami Herald*, May 22, 2001.

66. Danielle Knight, "Ecuadorians File U.S. Suit over Plan Colombia," Inter Press Service, September 24, 2001.

CONCLUSION: IRAQ IS NOT ARABIC FOR LATIN AMERICA

1. Kristol's comments were made on C-Span's *Washington Journal*, March 28, 2003. For Negroponte's role in covering up Honduran human rights abuses, see the *Baltimore Sun* series by Gary Cohn and Ginger Thompson starting June 11, 1995. Jack Binns, Negroponte's predecessor in Honduras, believes that Negroponte was "complicit in abuses" and that he "tried to put a lid on reporting abuses"; see Scott Shane, "Poker-Faced Diplomat, Negro-ponte Is Poised for Role as Spy Chief," *New York Times*, March 29, 2005.

2. Rich Lowry, "Smearing Negroponte," *National Review*, February 22, 2005.

3. Robert Kaplan, "Supremacy by Stealth," *Atlantic Monthly*, July–August 2003, p. 78.

4. Michael Hirsh and John Barry, "Salvador Option," *Newsweek*, January 8, 2005. Cf. Maass, "Way of the Commandos." Dexter Filkins, "Sunnis Ac-cuse Iraqi Military of Abuses," *New York Times*, November 29, 2005. "Abuse Worse than under Saddam, says Iraqi Leader," *The Observer*, No-vember 27, 2005.

5. "Remarks by the President during the Heritage Foundation Dinner," April 22, 1986, in James Allen Smith, *The Idea Brokers*, New York: Free Press, 1991, p. 20.

6. Dana Milbank, "Same Committee, Same Combatants, Different Tune," *Washington Post*, April 7, 2005.

7. David Kirkpatrick, "Bush Moved Conservatism Past Reactionary, Rove Says," *New York Times*, February 18, 2005.

8. Andrew Bacevich, *The New American Militarism: How Americans Are Seduced by War*, New York: Oxford, 2005, p. 78.
9. Ibid., p. 85.
10. Max Boot, "The Lessons of a Quagmire," *New York Times*, November 16, 2003.
11. Peggy Noonan, "We Can Take It," *Wall Street Journal*, March 31, 2003, available at http://peggynoonan.com.
12. John R. MacArthur, *Second Front: Censorship and Propaganda in the Gulf War*, New York: Hill and Wang, 1992.
13. See Sheldon Rampton and John Stauber, *Weapons of Mass Deception: The Uses of Propaganda in Bush's War on Iraq*, New York: Penguin, 2003; "U.S. Pays PR Guru to Make Its Points," *Chicago Tribune*, May 12, 2002; and Martha Brant, "Ladies and Gentlemen . . . the Band: Selling the War in Iraq," *Newsweek*, September 2002.
14. James Bamford, "The Man Who Sold the War," *Rolling Stone*, November 2005.
15. In Panama, the Pentagon corralled reporters into "media pools," confining them to a military base from which they were unable to witness the bombing of El Chorrillo and other poor neighborhoods; see MacArthur, *Second Front*, p. 58.
16. David Cole and James X. Dempsey, *Terrorism and the Constitution: Sacrificing Civil Liberties in the Name of National Security*, New York: New Press, 2002.
17. Dana Priest, "Foreign Network at Front of CIA's Terror Fight; Joint Facilities in Two Dozen Countries Account for Bulk of Agency's Post 9/11 Successes," *Washington Post*, November 18, 2005.
18. Jim Wallis, "Dangerous Religion: Bush's Theology of Empire," *Sojourners*, December 19, 2003, available at http://progressivetrail.org/articles/031218Wallis.shtml.
19. Norman Podhoretz, "World War IV: How It Started, What It Means, and Why We Have to Win," *Commentary*, September 2004.
20. Muqtedar Khan, "Preachers of Bigotry," *Al-Ahram Weekly Online*, June 5, 2003, available at www.brookings.edu/views/op-ed/fellows.
21. Diane Knippers, "The Evangelical Case for Dialogue with Muslims: Oversimplification Undermines Honest Dialogue, Accurate Education, and Genuine Christian Mission," available at http://www.beliefnet.com/story/127/story_12714_1.html.
22. David Brooks, "A House Divided, and Strong," *New York Times*, April 5, 2005.
23. Human Rights Watch, "Leadership Failure: Firsthand Accounts of Torture of Iraqi Detainees by the U.S. Army's 82nd Airborne Division," available at http://hrw.org/reports/2005/us0905/.
24. Ron Suskind, "Without a Doubt," *New York Times Magazine*, October 17, 2004.

Acknowledgments

First I'd like to thank Molly Nolan and Marilyn Young, who in spring 2003, on the eve of the U.S. invasion of Iraq, organized a teach-in where the basic argument of this book first took shape. Molly was strict in keeping the long list of speakers to five minutes, cutting me off before I finished: hence this book. Steve Fraser and Sara Bershtel have been dream editors, patient, precise, wise, and clear-eyed. Metropolitan's Kate Levin was also a delight to work with. Adam Gaffney tenaciously uncovered much of the buried history of New Right involvment in Central America, particularly as it related to the Office of Public Diplomacy and Iran-Contra. He not only helped me with important research and fact-checking but our conversations made this a much better book. Among the many friends and colleagues who pointed me to relevant sources or helped me think through arguments, I'd especially like to thank Gordon Lafer (show me the tungsten!), Corey Robin, Daniel Wilkinson, Kim Phillips-Fein, Frank Goldman, Bethany Moreton, Mark

Healey, Marilyn Young, Charlie Bright, who directed me to the importance of Reagan in Cancun, Robert Perkinson, Suzanna Reiss, and Matthew Vitz. Matt, who along with Joaquín Chávez, Aldo Marchesi, Katie Benwood, John Patrick Leary, Ramón Suárez, Paul Kershaw, Aaron Love, and Benyair Orellana, was in a seminar with me on the "new imperialism," where many of the ideas presented here first developed. My appreciation also goes to Kate Doyle, whose work with the National Security Archive is largely responsible for what we know about the workings of empire in Latin America. Other friends I'd like to thank for help along the way are Deborah Levenson, Carlota McAllister, Elizabeth Oglesby, Maureen Linker, Bob Wheeler, Harry Harootunian, Kristin Ross, Jeff Gould, Emilia Viotti da Costa, Allen Hunter, Jack Wilson, Andrew Ross, Sarah Hill, Peter Brown, Gil Joseph, Matt Hausmann, Patricia Pessar, Jolie Olcott, Peter Herman, Ada Ferrer, Sinclair Thomson, Diane Nelson, Nick Cullather, Dave Sanders, Joe Nevins, John French, and Arno Mayer. Also thanks to Manu Goswami for the camel not in the Koran, and for so much more. During the course of thinking and writing about this book, I received support from NYU's International Center for Advanced Studies, the American Council of Learned Societies Charles Ryskamp Fellowship Program, and the John Simon Guggenheim Memorial Foundation.

Index

About the Author

GREG GRANDIN, teaches Latin American history at New York University and is the author of two previous books, *The Last Colonial Massacre* and the award-winning *The Blood of Guatemala*. The recipient of a 2004 Guggenheim fellowship, Grandin has served on the United Nations Truth Commission investigating the Guatemalan civil war and has written for *Harper's*, the *Nation*, and the *New York Times*. He lives in Brooklyn, New York.

The American Empire Project

⌣

In an era of unprecedented military strength, leaders of the United States, the global hyperpower, have increasingly embraced imperial ambitions. How did this significant shift in purpose and policy come about? And what lies down the road?

The American Empire Project is a response to the changes that have occurred in America's strategic thinking as well as in its military and economic posture. Empire, long considered an offense against America's democratic heritage, now threatens to define the relationship between our country and the rest of the world. The American Empire Project publishes books that question this development, examine the origins of U.S. imperial aspirations, analyze their ramifications at home and abroad, and discuss alternatives to this dangerous trend.

The project was conceived by Tom Engelhardt and Steve Fraser, editors who are themselves historians and writers. Published by Metropolitan Books, an imprint of Henry Holt and Company, its titles include *Hegemony or Survival* by Noam Chomsky, *The Sorrows of Empire* by Chalmers Johnson, *Crusade* by James Carroll, *How to Succeed at Globalization* by El Fisgón, *Blood and Oil* by Michael Klare, *Dilemmas of Domination* by Walden Bello, *War Powers* by Peter Irons, *Devil's Game* by Robert Dreyfuss, *Imperial Ambitions* by Noam Chomsky, *In the Name of Democracy*, edited by Jeremy Brecher, Jill Cutler, and Brendan Smith, *A Question of Torture* by Alfred McCoy, and *Failed States* by Noam Chomsky.

For more information about the American Empire Project and for a list of forthcoming titles, please visit www.americanempire project.com.